D1223213

THE CLASSIC CUISINE OF THE ITALIAN JEWS

II

Pitigliano: Panorama
Drawing by Samuele (Lello) Servi

THE CLASSIC CUISINE OF THE ITALIAN JEWS II

More Menus, Recollections and Recipes

by

EDDA SERVI MACHLIN

Food Illustrations by Janina Rubinowicz

Croton-on-Hudson GIRO PRESS Publishers

First Printing 1992

Published by:
GIRO PRESS
P.O. Box 203
Croton-on-Hudson, N.Y. 10520

ISBN 1-878857-03-7

Printed in the United States of America
First Edition

To Gene

CONTENTS

ACKNOWLEDGMENTS

My sincere gratitude to the many readers and users of my first volume who have relentlessly encouraged me to undertake the task of writing this second one.

Thanks to friends and family who have been helpful in locating for me kosher Italian recipes. Among these, I want to mention with particular gratitude and affection my brother Gino Servi and his wife Metella of Florence, my sister Marcella Servi Siegel of Jerusalem, my brother Mario Servi of Parma, and my cousin Eugenia Servi of Leghorn.

For their contribution of unusual recipes, my thanks go also to Wanda Nahum Caro of Florence, to Giovanna Franci Zignani of the Università di Bologna, to Carmelita Mazzoli, baker in Pitigliano, and to Sig.ra Paola Gardi of Florence for her *Cassata Siciliana.*

The drawings of Pitigliano, with the exception of the panorama that was made by my late brother Samuele (Lello) Servi, have been kindly provided by my former sixth-grade drawing teacher Giuseppe Romani of Pitigliano, whose friendship with my family goes back at least three quarters of a century. My dear friend and neighbor Bernice Myers has selected among Romani's drawings the one that appears on the cover and has added color to it.

Lawrence L. Groobert has diligently edited the manuscript, and my two daughters, Rona and Gia, have provided much wise counsel regarding the text.

Finally I must say in all frankness that without the patience, the understanding, the moral support as well as the concrete help of my husband, Gene, this work would have never seen the light.

PREFACE

IN THE WAKE OF THE WAVE OF INTEREST caused by the first volume of *The Classic Cuisine of the Italian Jews,* I was flooded with letters and telephone calls suggesting that I write a second book, a sequel to my first one. Not only were my readers and critics intrigued by the new food ideas, but they were also fascinated with the historical references and with the anecdotes that often accompanied the recipes. Not many people in America were familiar with, or even aware of, the life and deeds of the Italian Jews, and I had brought to the attention of a large number of Americans something that needed amplification. But my first effort had left me exhausted and for a while I went back to another love of mine: teaching Italian.

Lately, with the awakened curiosity in the history of Italian Jewry which has swept through Italy and has spilled over to other countries as well, my readers and friends have made a fresh attempt at persuading me to give the world more of what I know.

It has taken me a long time, but I have finally come full circle to the point I had reached when I embarked on my first project: I write partly to comply with my readers' requests, but also and above all because I *must*, because I have knowledge that seeks to come out and it is imperative that I allow it. I say it as it springs forth from my memory and my willingness to share with my readers not only more of the Italian Jewish recipes everyone seems to appreciate so much, but also fragments of my heritage, my first-hand familiarity with one aspect of recent world history, and some of my personal experiences as an Italian Jew, both in Italy and in America.

As for the recipes in this volume, most are authentic originals of what the Italian Jews have prepared throughout the centuries for their holidays and everyday meals. However, I have introduced some variations and, whenever possible, simplifications of the ways in which these recipes can be prepared. There are myriad things we can do with our time and if we can save some time in the kitchen while still preparing delectable meals, why not try. One good example is Tuscan bread, which was made during my childhood and for centuries on end before then, using a very primitive sourdough starter, dried and hard so that it could be kept without refrigeration and easily transported if necessary. But bread making, when I was growing up in Pitigliano, was a lengthy and unnerving process, and nearly always a traumatic experience for the bread maker. Since timing is crucial, and yeast baking quite unpredictable, a number of things could — and often did — go wrong. Here I have described not only another way of making Tuscan bread with a moister and much easier sourdough starter, but also how to make it with commercial yeast. The latter method, if not authentic, is much simpler to follow and the result is quite acceptable.

I have also included the kosher recipes that either I or members of my family or friends have created during our long experience as intransigent cooks and connoisseurs of good food. And in tribute to the many farmers who gave us shelter during the World War II inferno, I have also added those peasants' dishes which happen to be kosher.

Like the Jews, the peasants of Pitigliano and surrounding areas have dwindled in number (due to postwar progress rather than wartime extermination) and their world, as I have known it in my youth, and especially during my peregrinations as an escapee from the Nazi-fascists, is equally vanished. One small example of the changes that have taken place can be illustrated by the following anecdote. When my husband and I went to Pitigliano during our honeymoon, every morning before dawn we were awakened by the collective braying of the donkeys carrying the peasants to their fields. A few years later, we took our children to

Pitigliano where, based on my bedtime stories, they expected to hear the asinine morning concert. By then, however, motor scooters had substituted the donkeys and all we heard was the sputtered roar of the "motorized asses".

But I remember that society and culture prior to modernization and mass urbanization. It was a world with a rich and precise etiquette that taught me a great deal about human behavior and interrelations. Among the many invaluable things I have learned from those farmers I especially remember and appreciate their way of eating. I am recording here some of their dishes that might otherwise be lost as well.

I hope my readers, Jews and non-Jews, old and new alike, will enjoy learning about a slice of history, about some of my personal experiences, and above all using my new collection of recipes.

Edda Servi Machlin
Croton-on-Hudson, NY
August, 1992

Pitigliano - Farmer and his donkey.

La Figlia del Ghetto
CHILD OF THE GHETTO

Ghetto of Pitigliano: Gate to the Temple

WHEN I BEGAN TO LECTURE after my first book was published, I was amazed at the number of questions asked of me by my audiences, both those who had read my book and were familiar with my stories, and those who knew very little or nothing at all about the very existence of the Italian Jews. Italian, for them, was synonymous with Catholic.

The questions that were most frequently asked by the latter were: "What and who is an Italian Jew? An Italian who has married a Jew? The offspring of such an intermarriage? And what is Italian Jewish cuisine? A combination of 'Italian' and 'Jewish' cooking?".

My readers, on the other hand, were more likely to ask, "What was it like for you to grow up in Fascist Italy? How did you survive? And what happened then? When did you come to America and why?"

In order to obtain an answer to the first group of questions, one has to become familiar with at least a smattering of the history of the Jews of Italy.

Without laying claim to be able to condense in a few paragraphs what has taken scholars of the subject years of research and voluminous tomes to describe, I will make an attempt to give my readers a superficial knowledge of who and what an Italian Jew is.

Let me start right off by saying that the core of what we call Italian Jewry today consists of the direct descendants of the Jews who came from the land of Israel and settled in Italy long before the advent of Christianity, and of the Jews who came from different countries at different times, starting from those distant days down to our own.

It is believed that Jews have lived in the Italian peninsula since the time of King Solomon, when they traveled the Mediterranean Sea with the Phoenician traders and the region where Rome was to rise was still under Etruscan rule. But even sticking just to recorded history, there is evidence that when Simon Maccabeus sent an embassy from Jerusalem to Rome to establish diplomatic relations with the Roman Senate, in 139 B.C.E., there was already in that city a well-established Jewish community which gave the ambassadors a warm reception. After the destruction of the second Temple in 70 C.E., the leadership and the strongest and best-looking youths were brought to Rome in chains as slaves by Titus.*

In the twenty-odd centuries that intervened since these two historical events, Jews have contributed conspicuously and constantly to the life and progress of Italy — including its renowned cuisine.

This long, uninterrupted residence of Jews on the Italian soil makes them as Italian as those we are accustomed to call "Italians." At the same time these ancient residents of Italy are also undeniably Jewish having maintained for two millennia their identity, holding on to the perennial ethical and human values of their religion, against tremendous odds. Not only were they able to keep their sanity and high level of literacy while compelled to live in dire poverty and in unsanitary conditions in crowded, restricted areas, but to maintain their ancient dietary laws as well.

Over the centuries, in order to make life more pleasant for themselves, the Italian Jews ably exploited their local resources, and used their imagination and their religious symbolisms to prepare meals that were varied and appetizing, and in doing so they elevated the task of cooking to a veritable art.

I might add here parenthetically that although the Jews of Europe were stereotyped as being moneylenders — e.g. Shylock — only a tiny percentage of them practised this occupation. In Italy the majority of Jews were artisans: men were shoemakers, tailors, tanners, saddlers, cabinet makers, printers, scribes, bookbinders, etc.; but there were also actors, musicians, poets, and small shopkeepers; some were in the professions: physicians, lawyers, architects, school teachers, and university professors; and a few were generals and statesmen. Among the women there were a few actresses, singers, and even fortune-tellers; but the majority of them were school teachers, weavers, embroiderers, dressmakers, and, at least all the women I have known, outstanding cooks.

Matters, even in periods of relative freedom and integration, did not

* According to the British historian Cecil Roth, whom I met in New York shortly after my arrival from Italy, the Servi branch of my family descends from these slaves. Arguably the name Servi could be either the literal translation of the word servants or slaves, or of the name Levi — the Levis being the servants or assistants to the Cohens, the high priests of the Temple.

always run smoothly for the Jews of Italy: intermittently they were subject, according to the whims of the ruling popes and secular rulers, to mass conversions, expulsions, false accusations, and all sorts of persecution and physical abuse including death. Fortunately for them, the political tapestry of Italy was so fragmented that at all times at least some could move from one hostile rejecting region to a friendly welcoming one.

In the most recent history, the one I am familiar with first hand, the war against the Jews that swept through Europe prior to and during World War II claimed a heavy toll also in the country which prides itself in having the oldest community of Jews outside of Israel. The Italians, as a people who have lived side by side and married Jews for millennia, have shown on the whole more compassion and humanity than people in most of the other European countries. Nevertheless, the courage and humaneness of many cannot obfuscate the tragic reality that the number of Italian citizens of Jewish faith who perished either in Italy or in the Nazi death factories during the years 1943-45 equals 8,000[1] (which does not include the several thousands of Jews who lived in Italy in that period without being Italian citizens, nor those who gave their lives fighting the Nazi-fascists while in the resistance), and perhaps as many were lost to Catholicism. My beautiful grandmother was among the first deportees from Rome dragged out of their beds by the Germans in the early morning of October 16th, 1943; her three Roman grandchildren, my first cousins ages five to nine, were among those Jews who were saved by friends in the Vatican. However, they were all made Catholics, and the youngest one now teaches Catechism in a Sunday school.

By the time I was born, 1926, the Jewish community of Italy had been emancipated, lively and vibrant for almost a century, had disproportionately contributed with valor and blood to the unity of Italy and to the outcome of World War I, and had been totally integrated in every aspect of Italian life. (In order to hasten this process of integration, our Jewish secular school — which was the first school Pitigliano ever had — had been closed down and the Jewish children walked to public school with all the other children.)

A few years hence fascism and human madness brought again destruction and martyrdom.

The signs that something was changing for the Jews must have been in the air for a long time, but they did not become evident to most Jews until the first half of the 1930s.

At first it was a subtle anti-Semitic campaign spread by means of spo-

1. Liliana Picciotto Fargion - *Il Libro della Memoria* - Murcia, Milano, 1991.

radic articles that appeared in one or two fascist newspapers with the connivance and even the collaboration — albeit anonymously — of the fascist dictator Benito Mussolini himself. By the beginning of the second half of the 1930s, the campaign — now evolved into ferocious propaganda — was picked up by most of the national media which managed to poison the ears and the hearts of much of the public with caricatures, stereotypes, and myths.

2

I RECALL THAT PERIOD very vividly because of one incident, perhaps not as grave as many others I was later to experience, but devastating nonetheless, because in spite of the fact that I had been subject to anti-Semitic remarks by Christian peers my entire life, this was the first time in which an adult was involved.

I was about eleven years old when the possibility of taking piano lessons came my way. Partly because I had always known that I had a knack for music, but mainly to counteract somewhat the cloud of dejection that enveloped me, I jumped at the opportunity. When I told Mamma, she replied that besides not owning a piano, we most certainly didn't have money for such frivolous aspirations. I knew that, and proceeded to explain to Mamma that a friend was willing to give me lessons for free and to let me stay at her home after each lesson to practice for a few hours.

Mamma was puzzled. Who would give me lessons for nothing in these times of penury? Who was this friend!?

I told her about Luana. "She is older than I, but she likes me, and often, when I walk home from school, she walks with me to talk about music."

I was lying a little. Luana, a very pretty girl of sixteen, was madly in love with my fifteen-year-old brother and took every opportunity to talk with me about him. In order to be less conspicuous we would climb to the courtyard of the Bishopric and sit next to the well and talk.

Mamma was silent for a long while. Luana was a stranger, her family had moved only recently from another city, and therefore we couldn't trust them as we did the majority of Pitiglianesi. Besides, she was a Christian and our relationships with Christians in 1937 had already become quite strained.

Finally, reluctantly, she assented, undoubtedly taking into consideration the fact that, while taking piano lessons, I would be spared the aura of despair that had come to characterize every bit of conversation carried on among the adults in our Jewish community.

I became so close to Luana and her family that I was almost part of

Pitigliano - The well in the Bishopric courtyard.

the family myself. I was making stupendous progress and Luana derived genuine pleasure in teaching me.

One day, in the middle of our lesson, Luana's mother stormed into the house furiously. Heedless of my presence, she began to scatter things all around as she related to her daughter the heated discussion she had had with the principal of the middle school regarding problems with her younger son.

I kept to myself, not knowing where to cast my eyes, waiting for the storm to pass, and trying very hard not to listen. But in spite of my efforts, I heard every word that was yelled and one sentence particularly struck me. "He had no right to treat me like that," sputtered the woman while beating her chest. "I am a respectable person, I am not a child of the ghetto!"

A rush of blood rose to my head. I was born and lived in the ghetto. *I was* the child which that "respectable person" was so proud not to be. I sneaked out of that house in tears and ran home, fully aware of the implications of that woman's words, and, of course, also aware that this painful episode would mark the end of my cherished piano lessons.

The poisonous propaganda had began to yield results. More and more people gained courage from it to surface their own atavic Church-inspired anti-Semitic sentiments.

A year later, at the time I celebrated my Bat Mitzvà, the tension had mounted to the point that episodes such as the one which had occurred during my last piano lesson had become frequent, almost the norm.

At the end of the summer of 1938, the first of the anti-Jewish laws (the *Leggi Razziali*, as they were called then), aimed at banishing Jewish children from public schools was promulgated and enforced.

Then, gradually but inexorably, all the civil and human rights were taken one by one from these exceptionally peace-loving, ethical, hardworking people as a group. Forced labor was instituted, detention areas and concentration camps sprang up throughout the country, and even a death camp was established on Italian soil in the Risiera di San Sabba, near Trieste.[2]

Many Italians, even among those who until then had been anti-Semitic and, strange as it might seem, staunch Fascists, could not bear to comply with such an iniquity and enormous injustice, and helped the way they could. Mamma could not get over the fact that when two guards of the neofascist Republic of Salò (established after the armistice between the Allies and the Badoglio government was signed on September 8, 1943) were sent to our home to arrest her, my father and my nine-year-old

2. Giuseppe Mayda -*Ebrei Sotto Salò* - Feltrinelli Editore, Milano, 1978.

Pitigliano - Gate whence we fled the night of November 27, 1943, after having been warned that a round-up of the Jews would take place the next day

brother (the other four of us ranging from thirteen to twenty-one years of age had already escaped to the woods after a tip from a compassionate, knowledgeable neighbor had alerted us to the impending round-up of Jews), one of the guards, while holding his rifle in readiness, kept on repeating, "Why didn't you go into hiding, why did you wait for us?" And they both looked the other way while Mamma was smuggling our most precious books and valuables into the apartment of another trustworthy neighbor who would give our possessions back to us if we ever came back alive.

The farmers who lived on their farms outside of Pitigliano, by giving shelter and food to partisans, escaped prisoners of war, and Jewish refugees, played a prominent role in the effort of saving human lives, often at risk of their own. Towards the end of the conflict in our region, however, food became so scarce that the majority of the farmers had barely enough for themselves, and began to refuse to open their doors to us. But there were always some among them willing to stretch the little they had to share it with us.

Some Jews, especially those who had means, found refuge in Switzerland, or went to England, or made the leap to America. But the majority of those who survived in Italy, including my family, owed their lives to their own wits, to a good measure of luck, and above all to the generosity and good will of those courageous fellow humans among the Christians.

3

BECAUSE OF THE relatively small number of Jews left in Italy today, many think that their cuisine is limited and that it appeals only to them. Not so. The Italian Jewish cuisine is far from being limited, having its roots in as many cultures as there are places from which the Jews have flocked to Italy at different times. Moreover, it appeals to all who appreciate truly good food.

From North Africa and the Middle East there has been a continuous emigration toward Italy throughout the centuries. Names such as Nahum and Habib are typical of these Jews, and *Cuscussú, Concia di Melanzane* and *Rosette di Purim* are but few examples of the dishes they brought from their countries of origin.

The year 1492 brought the discovery of the New World which opened for all the oppressed people of Europe opportunities never imagined before. Marranos — those Spanish Jews who had been converted to Catholicism forcibly, but secretly continued to practice the religion of their forefathers — are said to have been included in Colombus's first and second expeditions.

But 1492 was also the year that saw the culmination of the long and tragic period of the Holy Inquisition with the expulsion of all the Jews from Spain.

It is estimated that about 50% of the Spanish Jews sought refuge in nearby Portugal — only to be expelled from there, too, a few years later. Others found friendly shelter in the Netherlands, in North Africa, in the Levant, and in Sicily (from where in good time they were expelled as well since Sicily was under Castilian-Aragonese rule.) The majority of the refugees perished during their voyages and never regained their freedom. However, tens of thousands of them were able to settle in mainland Italy, first in the south, and eventually, when expelled also from there, in the center and north, thus shifting the Jewish demography of the country forever.

When the Sephardim, or Spanish Jews, made their entry into Italy, they found that Jews had lived there for over fifteen centuries and called themselves Italkim, or Italian Jews. These had their own liturgy, their own rites, their own Judaico-Italian dialect, and their own ways of preparing food. However, in time, the sophisticated Sephardim, by their sheer number, had an impact on the life and customs of their Italian brethren. Many Spanish words and inflexions could still be heard in the speech of the Jewish elders in Pitigliano when I was growing up. Moreover, the surnames of some of my relatives were undoubtedly of Spanish origin: Bueno, Cardoso, Colon, Roccas, Spagnoletto, and others.

The Spanish Jews (from mainland Spain and from Sicily alike) were given three months' notice to leave their country, during which they tried to sell all their property in the belief that they could take the proceeds with them. When the moment to leave arrived, however, they were not allowed to take any valuables, nor their personal effects (only one old dress, one old pair of shoes, one old mattress, one old set of sheets, one old blanket and a little food and money for the trip were permitted), nor the tools of their trades with them. All of their possessions were confiscated by the Catholic crown. However, no one could prevent them from taking their unshakeable faith, their language, and their memories — the Iberian Jews of their cultural as well as material splendor of the years that preceded the Inquisition, and the Sicilian Jews of the peaceful cohabitation they had enjoyed with their neighbors and the scenes of regret and sincere sorrow on the part of the latter when they were compelled to leave their homes behind — and the know-how of their traditional foods. *Pan di Spagna, Carciofi Ripieni* , and the world famous flan, which the expelled Sephardim subsequently forced from Portugal brought to Italy under the name of *Latte alla Portoghese*, Portuguese-style milk, come first to mind.

Jews came to Italy also from France (Gallichi, Lattes), and from Central and Eastern European countries (Polacco, Russi, Tedesco) and they contributed to the enrichment of the Italian Jewish cuisine (*Vellutina di Spinaci, Polpettine di Carne e Patate*).

These are only a few examples intended to illustrate the fact that the Italian Jewish cuisine is varied and rich. Proof of this is that since my first book was published, there has been a rush among better Italian restaurants throughout America to feature festivals and lectures on Italian Jewish cuisine, and many have become very successful by offering in their menus a selection of recipes from it.

4

WHEN I FIRST CAME TO NEW YORK some thirty-odd years ago, the tastes of the natives were nowhere near what they are today. I recall that friends and relatives thought they were being nice to me by taking me out for dinner in Italian restaurants. I would not hurt their feelings by refusing, but their good intentions were indeed paving the road to my culinary hell! "Italian" food was, even in some of the better restaurants, mediocre, to put it mildly. I have eaten the most unpalatable ossobuchi and eggplant parmigiana in some of those restaurants. In inexpensive restaurants the keynote was spaghetti with meat balls, a dish I had never tasted or even heard of in all my life in Italy.

There is nothing wrong with inventing a new dish, especially if one had recently emigrated to the country of plenty where the cost of ground meat was next to nothing and one could convert the few crumbs of red meat which one could afford to put in a sauce in the old country into spheres the size of ping-pong balls!

Nothing wrong indeed. What was wrong was the way this dish was prepared and served. The meat was overly abundant and overseasoned; the tomato sauce overcooked and smothering; the spaghetti cooked until the texture resembled that of a thick glue.

Eventually I learned to decline the invitations and invited people to dine at my apartment instead. Since it is well known that a way to a man's heart is through his palate, my cooking might have swayed quite a few inveterate bachelors toward considering marriage.

But more of this later.

So, what made me come to America in the first place?

5

MY FAMILY, THE SEVEN OF US, had survived the ordeal — four in hiding with the partisans, and three in the Italian concentration camp of Roccatederighi, near Siena. Out of eighty-four inmates, my family were among the fortunate fourteen left behind by the retreating Germans. The other seventy were crammed in alphabetical order into two small buses and driven to the cattle-car trains that took them to the death factories. None of them survived. Because their surnames started with the last few letters of the alphabet, those fourteen, including my parents and ten-year-old brother, were left to their fascist guards who, as a result of the rapid Allied advance, abandoned them to their own wits. By the time the Germans came back for them (and they *did* come back!), the fourteen emaciated and scared Jews, holding their breath inside one small bathroom, heard the trampling of the frantic soldiers who were searching in every corner of the building. The soldiers then tried to open the bathroom door with their rifle butts, but — incredibly — finally gave up and left for good.

It took another month and lots of changes of luck (my older brother and I walked seven days and nights between the two fronts to try to reach our parents and younger brother, while the other brother and sister stayed with the partisans to liberate our village) before the seven of us, after having been liberated — two near Pitigliano by the French, and five

Pitigliano - Jewish cemetary and bridge after reconstruction.

near the concentration camp by the Americans — were finally reunited.

After a few difficult years of readjustment to a "normal" life in Pitigliano, where the Jewish community had dwindled down to a handful of souls and the Temple was largely destroyed as a consequence of the bombing of the nearby bridge, we left the village for Florence where we had more opportunity to make a life for ourselves.

In more ways than one, the move turned out to be very positive. However, we did not fare well in our need for a vibrant Jewish life as we had known as children in Pitigliano. The Jewish community of Florence had also been decimated, and the survivors were still mourning their losses. Jewish young people were looking for companionship, and intermarriages were becoming the rule rather than the exception. More and more often among our new female friends we heard the refrain, "I'd rather marry a Christian than end up a spinster."

For us — my younger sister and myself, that is — the alternative was either to marry within our faith someone who shared our heritage and experience, or remain single. There was a history in our family of mixed marriages which had ended in disasters, and there was a history of single people who had lived productive and dignified lives. In our view there was nothing shameful about remaining single, and marrying just for the sake of getting married was never even considered.

While we waited for the right Jewish man to come our way, we took advantage of the opportunities that the city offered and got ourselves the education that had been denied to us during our school-age years when all Jewish children had been banished from public schools. Nothing formal, of course, but we didn't let one day go by without our auditing a lecture at the university, visiting a museum or gallery, studying a foreign language, or taking an educational trip.

It was upon our return from one of these trips that we received a call from a Jewish young man just arrived from New York. A friend of a friend had given him our telephone number. He and my sister first met under the statue of David in Piazza Signoria. After a few months of correspondence, my sister followed her future husband to New York, got married within ten days of her arrival, and nine months later their son David was born.

By the time my sister was an expectant mother again, it had become apparent to me that my ideal man was nowhere in sight. I had to go and fetch him! Not without apprehension, I boarded a ship (the *Cristoforo Colombo* — what else?) and off I went to the land of opportunity.

I arrived in New York one chilly March morning when the Statue of Liberty was enveloped in a thick morning mist and the Hudson river was covered with floating slabs of ice. By the time the cab drove me to my sister's apartment on the Upper West Side, the sun had broken through the fog, I was dazzled and elated, and my love affair with America had begun.

A month after my arrival, twins Debora and Danny were born to my younger sister, when her first child was barely eighteen months old. So, my first impressions of the New World were — besides the luminous spaciousness of Riverside Park and the Palisades — an army of formula bottles and mountains of diapers — diapers and formulas, formulas and diapers. Who wanted to get married?

I did!

It took another two years for the magic to happen.

6

DURING THE TWO YEARS I spent in New York as a single female Jew from Italy, I was besieged by Jewish bachelors who wanted to befriend me, date me, marry me. Even admitting to my attractiveness, this was certainly extraordinary behavior on the part of those young men. I was intrigued by this incredible popularity, and finally summoned enough courage to ask someone.

The young man, a medical student, gave me a very curious answer. "You see," he began, "you embody the most desirable attributes a Jewish man could possibly want in his wife."

"How so?"

"You are Italian, very much Italian, and this satisfies the American Jew's need to marry a *Shiksa*. However you are also Jewish, and this satisfies the Jewish mother's dream to see her son happily married to a nice Jewish girl."

He left me dumb struck. Was that a fact? I had never thought of myself as "Italian" in the sense that the Jewish young man meant. But of course, I was born and raised in Italy, so my manners and behavior must have been similar to those of my Catholic compatriots.

It was at that time, as I mentioned above, that after eating in many Italian restaurants, I began to cook more and more at home, using my memory of what my mother and father and aunts and friends prepared in Italy. People began to ask for doggy bags, and names of recipes. Whereas I was flattered by their asking for leftovers and happily complied, I was embarrassed to confess that my recipes had no names. Mamma was such a great cook that not only festive meals, but every meal she prepared for the family twice a day every day, was a gourmet delight. Yet, when we children asked her, "What's this?," her reply would invariably be, "It's eatable stuff!"

The idea occurred to me to record and name my recipes. The insistence of my friends that I share with them my secret recipes inspired me to conduct a large scale research which led to a considerable collection. Eventually, what I thought of as a legacy to my children and a few intimate friends caught the attention of a publisher and my "secret" recipes became public domain.

Do I regret it?

Yes, somewhat. I am a rather private individual and being in the public eye can be a disturbing intrusion at times. On the other hand, I am happy to see my prophecy fulfilled. When my first book saw the light, the cultural attache of the Italian Consulate gave an elegant and delightful reception in my honor. To the question, "What do you predict the life of the book will be," I answered unhesitatingly, "It will be a great success, and from now on — America will eat better."

Everybody laughed.

7

SINCE THEN AMERICANS, and especially New Yorkers, have indeed made tremendous strides in the matter of food taste. The diverse people that form our society have taught us to enjoy a large variety of cuisines. The world has become smaller, more and more people have traveled to all corners of the earth and have learned first hand about, and indeed tasted, the specialties that various countries offer. The food industry has caught on quickly and has responded by importing all sorts of delicacies. Wonderfully exotic foods, once inaccessible to most people, are no longer reserved for the very privileged few. They have become known by and within reach of an increasingly larger number of people.

There is now a new breed of Americans who would raise a brow to an overcooked, overseasoned dish of spaghetti and meat balls. The new breed not only knows about sauces other than tomato, such as pesto sauce, but also the difference between a mediocre and a superb one. These new Americans have developed a taste for olive oil, and not just *any* olive oil, but the best tasting among the extra virgin olive oils, truffle-flavored olive oil, etc. The children of those Americans who used *any* vinegar, now know and use balsamic vinegar and herb vinegar; and people who once only knew steamed frozen Lima beans, have now learned to appreciate all varieties of beans and prepare them in many different ways. The list goes on and on.

It is my challenge and privilege to present my new collection of recipes to these new, most sophisticated Americans and to all those who can appreciate the legacy of this *child of the ghetto.*

Il Segreto della Buona Cucina

THE SECRET OF GOOD CUISINE

THE SECRET OF GOOD CUISINE, according to my mother, is no secret at all. She had a persuasive saying, *"Metti buono e cava buono,"* which implies that if you use good ingredients you will end up with a good dish. This is true, but only to a point. It is true that the first rule of thumb for the attainment of a superb dish is to use ingredients that are the freshest and of the finest quality. On the other hand, this precaution in itself is no guaranty of a perfect result.

First, there is the question of quantities, of proportions. In olden times, when written recipes were a rarity, the cooks who would end up with a fabulous dish by putting in "a little bit of this and a little bit of that" were practically doing little else with their lives than cook, and had developed such dexterity and experience that seldom did they make a mistake. Today our lives and minds are cluttered with all kinds of responsibilities and demands, and cooking is only one of the many tasks we are called on to perform as if we were trained professionals in all of them. Sometimes even with the written recipe in front of us and the perfect ingredients ready to be measured we do make mistakes, as happened to me once, when I really wanted to make a good impression. I was baking my favorite cake, and since it preserves beautifully in the freezer, I decided to make two at the same time so I would have one ready for my next dinner. I diligently doubled every ingredient except — my mind must have wandered — the sugar. The result was a bland-tasting cake when it should have been an outstanding one. What's worse, I didn't realize it until I used it on my guests. They insisted that it was "delicious," but I knew Americans to be the most generous of peoples, and I knew that my favorite cake, my *pièce de résistance*, was a pitiful failure! What else would

I have forgotten if I had to rely on my memory alone?!

Then there is also the important question of the techniques and methods used in the preparation of certain foods. My mother, the advocate of "use good ingredients and the result will be good," was by instinct such a great cook that she had no notion of how much she knew. She took for granted that what she did know — with the exception of her ability to clean artichokes in her Roman Jewish way, which her Pitiglianesi sisters-in-law were ignorant of until she taught them — was common knowledge to all. With all the respect and admiration I have for my mother, I disagree also on the point that given the good ingredients and the right amounts anyone would know what to do with them. She might have not known it, but even though no one had ever taught her how to do certain things, she had no doubt learned them by observation or even by osmosis from her elders, the way I learned from her, and my children from me. I have never given my children a lesson or a demonstration, and yet they are excellent cooks in their own right.

The point I am trying to make is clear. Not everyone has the good fortune to come from a household of skillful cooks; but even if this were the case, there are still ways of preparing foods which not everyone knows about, and it is to fill this gap that I am including a few pointers in the section called "*Metodi e Tecniche*".

TODAY THE EMPHASIS on good eating is not so much in how good is what we eat as in how much we eat of a given food. The key word is moderation. There is nothing wrong with "moderation" as opposed to "excess." It would be nice if we were able to avoid all excesses. However, my emphasis is not in "how much" but precisely in "how good," how satisfying is what we eat. In fact I have a theory that if what we eat is of the finest quality, if it satisfies our sense of smell and our taste buds, the likelihood is we won't eat it in excess. If the food is truly tasty, we want it to linger in our mouth so we can savor it longer. While we are enjoying the taste, our brains receive the message that we are satisfied and our voraciousness quiets down before we have a chance to ingest large quantities. Once in a while — i.e. in observance of a tradition — we do eat more than usual or eat "bad" foods without feeling guilty or getting sick. For example, seldom, if ever, do we eat French fries or any other fried foods, except on the last night of Chanukà when we make a whole meal, from hors d'oeuvres to dessert, out of fried foods. We don't get sick when indulging on occasion, because I take the precautions of, say, interspersing the meal with cooked leafy vegetables, lots of salads and fresh fruits, skinning the chicken totally before I fry it, and substituting the used oil with fresh oil for each new batch of fried food I make.

SPEAKING OF OIL, I have a comment to make. Whenever I prepare a dish that requires oil, I use exclusively Italian olive oil. That should not be a surprise. I am Italian and I am used to certain tastes. But not all Italian oils satisfy me. I am picky about my oil and I favor only a few brands among the many I can choose from. Today there are so many olive oils on the market, one doesn't know which to use. These oils are imported not only from Italy, but from other countries as well, and many are produced right here in America. To find the olive oil that best satisfies your palate, you might have to try a few. Start with one small bottle at a time. When you first open the bottle, sniff it. Not only does the smell tell you whether an oil is fresh or rancid, but also if you think you might like it or not. Then pour a few drops of it onto the palm of your clean hand and taste it. Let it stay in your mouth for a few seconds before swallowing it. In addition to the flavor, this will give you the aftertaste and the degree of acidity. If you have doubts, repeat this tasting a few times until you are able to tell for sure whether this particular oil suits you.

Please note that I make a distinction between olive oil and extra virgin olive oil. The former has been refined and lends itself better for cooking, not imposing a strong flavor on your dish; the latter is best for salads and other dishes for which raw oil constitutes one of the distinct flavors and an enhancement to the overall taste of a dish. More on oils on page 36.

TO SUM IT UP, the secret of good cuisine *does* consist first and foremost in the use of the finest and freshest ingredients. However, it also consists in the skillful mastering of certain ways of preparing them, and in the wisdom of enhancing the quality of a dish with little touches, such as adding a tablespoon of just-chopped herbs and a generous sprinkle of fresh oil to a finished sauce, or rubbing garlic over the blade of the knife with which you slice tomatoes for a salad.

It is not necessary to read through the various techniques that follow right now (even though it never hurts to read helpful material before tackling any new recipe), because you will find a reference in each recipe that requires a particular or unusual technique.

To facilitate the task of finding them, the techniques are listed in alphabetic order using the names of the ingredients and sometimes also those of the techniques themselves.

METODI E TECNICHE
Methods and Techniques

AL DENTE. When directions call for pasta or rice cooked *al dente,* this means that they should not be overcooked but should instead remain slightly underdone and chewy. Not only do pasta and rice cooked al dente taste better, but they are also more digestible. Starchy foods are mainly digested in the mouth, and if they are overcooked they are likely to be swallowed before the first and very important stage of digestion is accomplished.

ALMONDS AND OTHER NUTS. The flavor of most nuts is enhanced by toasting them. Very oily nuts such as walnuts and pinoli, however, taste better if left alone. When a recipe calls for toasted nuts, place them on a baking sheet in single layer and place the sheet under the broiler for 4 to 5 minutes, shaking the sheet a couple of times. Or toast them in the microwave oven, using the same timing. Allow to cool at least 10 minutes before chopping in a blender or processor. Mixed with dried fruits such as dates, unsulphured figs and apricots, apples, raisins, and currants, nuts make a healthful and delightful snack, appetizer, or dessert.

AROMATIC OLIVE OIL. To make your own aromatic olive oil, place 1 teaspoon, or one small branch, or a few pieces of your favorite spice or herb into a small pan with 4 tablespoons of oil and a sprinkle of salt. Sauté for one minute. Cool to room temperature, then add to 1 pint of oil in a glass jar and tightly close the lid. Leave at room temperature and use after not less than three weeks. After the first use, refrigerate. The oil will coagulate since it freezes at higher temperature than water. Leave the jar at room temperature until the oil resumes its liquid state before measuring and using, then refrigerate again. The herbs and flavors I generally use to make aromatic oil are: black peppercorns; red hot peppers; garlic; porcini mushrooms; truffles; rosemary branches; sage leaves; and fennel branches or seeds.

AROMATIC VINEGAR. Kosher aromatic vinegar can be purchased in America.

ARTICHOKES. For most dishes that use artichokes in this book, you need to buy small to medium ones, and to prepare them in such a way that when you eat you don't have to discard anything. The Roman Jews, who made great use of artichokes in their famous cuisine, devised an ingenious method for ridding the artichokes of their inedible parts. Here is how it works.

Keep the artichokes immersed in cold water for at least one hour before starting to trim them, so they are nice and crisp. Have at hand a bowl containing cold water, the juice of one lemon and the two squeezed halves. Take one artichoke at a time from its bath and pull and discard the smallest outer leaves. Hold the artichoke by the bottom in your left hand, and a small sharp knife firmly in your right hand, the sharp side of its blade facing you. Insert the tip of the blade behind one leaf where the tender part — the whitest — meets the tough, darker-green part, and cut toward you, letting the latter fall off. With your left hand rotate the artichoke a little in a clockwise motion. After rotating the artichoke, insert the blade in the next leaf and cut the tough part off. Continue to slowly turn and cut at the same time, in an upward spiral until all the inedible sections of the leaves are eliminated and you are left with the edible portion attached to the untrimmed bottom. Peel the green layer off the bottom and the stem; then drop the trimmed artichoke into the acidulated water until you are ready to cook. Preparing artichokes with the method described above requires some practice. You will know that you have mastered this skill when the artichoke thus cleaned looks like the one you started with, only rounder, smaller and lighter in color. Fresh and tender artichokes do not have choke at all. If you find that the ones you bought do have choke, however, remove it before cooking, because you really want to be able to eat everything without actually choking.

These directions are for right-handed people. If you are left-handed, simply reverse the process.

BALSAMIC VINEGAR. See VINEGAR.

BEANS. Fresh beans in their shells or already shelled (*fagioli sgranati*) are a rarity in America. If you find them or grow them yourself, you will have a treat during their brief season. They cook in less time then the dried ones and they are more easily digested. However, since we cannot rely on them all year round, we turn to the dried beans which have greater nutritive value. See DRIED BEANS.

BEATING EGG WHITE. The best method for beating egg white is the good old one of using an unlined copper bowl and a hand whip. An electric beater, however, is a good enough substitute, provided all the white gets beaten. The purpose of beating egg white is to allow it to incorporate as much air as possible so that it makes whatever it is used for lighter.

BLACK PEPPER. See PEPPER

BOILED EGGS. To make the perfect-looking hard-boiled eggs, have the eggs at room temperature; place them in a pot and add cold tap water to cover. Bring the water to a rapid boil, then turn the heat off and let the eggs cook gently as water and eggs return to room temperature. This will prevent the unsightly greenish-gray color and the undesirable hard, chewy texture of overcooked yolks which will, instead, remain friable and of a beautifully rich yellow. For soft-boiled eggs let the eggs cook for one, two, or three minutes according to the degree of softness desired. Then transfer to individual egg holders.

BREAD. Bread can be divided into two main categories: bread made with a baking powder, and yeast bread. We will not concern ourselves with the former. The latter represents probably one of the most ancient known branches of the culinary art. Yet, for all its seniority, yeast-bread baking is also one of the most difficult skills to master. Too many factors go into the baking of yeast bread, and it is rare that all of them are favorable at the same time. Relative humidity, atmospheric temperature, freshness of the yeast, consistency of the dough, leavening time, and oven temperature are only some of the things that can go wrong when one attempts to bake a yeast bread. However, this negative preamble is not intended to discourage anyone from trying, but to let the novices know that if they don't succeed at first, they are in good company. Few foodstuffs are so appetizing as a freshly baked homemade bread. So go ahead and try some of the yeast-bread recipes and the rewards, in spite of some inevitable frustrations, will be plentiful. To avoid some of the drawbacks, make sure that:

1. the place where you do your preparation is draft-free;
2. the ingredients are at room temperature, except for those that are supposed to be warm;
3. the yeast is fresh (for the commercial one, look at the date; for the homemade sourdough starter, see *Lievito Casalingo* at page 223);
4. the dough is stiff rather than soft, unless otherwise specified in the recipe;
5. you do not under- or over-leaven. (In winter use a warm oven (turned off!); in summer watch carefully. If the loaves look fully leavened, place them in a hot oven. If you are ready to bake and the loaves look slightly underleavened, place them in a cold oven and set the thermostat at the temperature required by the recipe. While the oven gets hot

it gives the loaves a chance to leaven some more. For an electric oven, it is a good practice to place a small pan with cold water in the lower rack.)

At any rate, rarely is a home baked bread so damaged that it cannot be eaten.

BREAD PAP. To make the bread pap that is generally used to soften ground-meat patties and loaves, place the stale bread in a saucepan with cold water to cover and let it soak until swollen and soft. Pour out any excess of water and cook the bread, stirring, until quite dry.

BROTH. Broth is a liquid soup made by boiling meats, fish, or vegetables in water. When the broth is made with meats, it ends up having a more or less thick stratum of fat at the surface. To remove this fat while the broth is hot, you may have to use an apposite vessel with a spout that starts low, where there is no fat, thus avoiding the fat at the surface when you transfer the strained broth to another pot. If you don't have such a vessel, place the broth in the refrigerator for several hours until the fat is coagulated, then procede to remove it with a slotted spoon.

BUTTERFLYING MEAT. See TURKEY BREAST.

CHICK PEAS. See DRIED BEANS.

CHOCOLATE SHAVINGS. To make shavings, lightly and quickly pass a chunk of milk chocolate over a sharp slicer. Gather the shavings into a container as you make them and keep refrigerated until you are ready to use, lest they lose their beautiful, curly shape.

CHOCOLATE SYRUP. To make a dense chocolate syrup, milk chocolate is best. Place the pieces of chocolate in a glass or ceramic container and place the container in a 200 °F oven until the pieces begin to melt. Remove from oven, quickly add some boiling water and stir vigorously. If you use the microwave oven, place chocolate and boiling water in the container and microwave for 1 minute, then remove and stir vigorously. The proportions should be 3 tablespoons of boiling water for each 1/2-pound chocolate.

COLD WATER STEAM. The tastiest pot roasts are first browned in abundant olive oil and then cooked with the help of some steam. When the meat is well browned on all sides, cooking of the inside must be done quickly to preserve tenderness. A sprinkle of water over the very hot oil generates the steam that will penetrate the inside of the piece. This is best achieved if you keep a bowl with cold water next to the range; when sprinkling is needed, dip your clenched fist inside the bowl of water, then forcefully open it over the roast. Be careful not to linger over the pot while doing this because steam can burn you as easily as boiling water.

DEFAT. To defat is a culinary term that means "to remove the fat." See BROTH for instructions.

DRIED BEANS. Most people are discouraged from cooking dried beans because they have been misled into believing that dried beans must be soaked for many hours or overnight before cooking them. Even though this preconception is very old and hard to die, nothing could be further from the truth. Beans — whether the soft lentils or the hard chick peas — cook beautifully without any previous soaking. Follow my directions and you will find yourself cooking beans more often than ever.

Remove all stones and debris from beans, then rinse them two or three times in warm water. Place in a large non-ferrous pot with warm water four to six times their volume (i.e., 2 to 3 quarts of water for each pound of beans). Add 1 tablespoon salt and bring to a rapid boil. Immediately reduce the heat to its lowest point and simmer, covered, for 10 to 20 minutes. Add 1 clove of garlic with husk on and 2 sage leaves to the pot and simmer 1/2 to 1 hour longer. Cooking time depends on many factors, such as freshness and size of beans, alkalinity of the water, and altitude at which cooking is performed. Keep in mind that lentils take the shortest time to cook (20 minutes at most), and chick peas the longest (1 to 2 hours). If beans are to be used subsequently in another recipe that requires additional cooking take them from the heat while they are still *al dente.*

EGGS. As a rule I use extra large eggs in my recipes. I make sure (and so should you) to always buy the freshest eggs. Even though eggs (the yolks only) contain cholesterol, they also contain lecithin and are one of the best sources of protein, iron, and some of the B complex vitamins. So, eggs have been and always will be part of my diet.

Make sure to run cold water over the vessel in which you have prepared, cooked and eaten your eggs before cleaning it or putting it into the dishwasher, to prevent a lingering, unpleasant odor subsequent to washing.

For hard-boiled and soft-boiled eggs, see BOILED EGGS.

EGG WHITE. See BEATING EGG WHITE and FOLDING EGG WHITE.

FOLDING EGG WHITE. To incorporate beaten egg white into a mixture without losing much of the frothiness that makes the mixture soft and airy, mix 1/4 of the beaten egg white with the mixture. Then place the remaining egg white on top of the mixture. Holding the bowl with one hand and a plastic or rubber spatula in the other hand, introduce the blade of the spatula perpendicularly into the mixture; with a swift motion of the hand, turn the spatula and pull it out. Turn the bowl slightly, so that each time you dip the spatula, it will be on a different spot. Continue to introduce and pull out the spatula while turning the bowl, until all the white has been incorporated.

HARD BOILED EGGS. See BOILED EGGS.

HOMEMADE PASTA. Fresh egg noodles can now be found in every supermarket. However, for the orthodox among us, homemade pasta, made only with fresh eggs and flour, is the only acceptable one. I used to make enormous sheets of pasta totally by hand with the aid of an especially long and heavy rolling pin. Now I use the hand-operated machine with stainless steel rollers. The electric extrusion type gives an unsatisfactory result. Homemade pasta is easy to make and it is very versatile. Slightly beat the eggs. Add enough flour to make a stiff dough. Knead to smoothness and place in the refrigerator between two dishes for approximately 1 hour. To roll the pasta thin, use the old-fashioned heavy rolling pin, or the machine with rollers that give different thicknesses. Once obtained the desired thickness, the pasta sheet can be cut into capellini, tagliolini, fettuccine, tagliatelle, and pappardelle, that is, from the thinnest to increasingly wider noodles; or left in the sheet form for lasagne, tortelli, tortellini, etc. Egg noodles, unlike other pasta, should be always drained thoroughly after cooking.

KALE. See SPINACH AND OTHER LEAFY VEGETABLES

KASHRUT. In the first volume of *The Classic Cuisine of the Italian Jews*, I tried to explain not only what kashrut laws are, and presumably the reasons for their being, but also the differences of interpretation of such laws by the two major Jewish ritual currents, the Sephardic and the Ashkenazic. Here I want to reiterate that although the Ashkenazim in America eat only the upper part of the animal (from the waist up, as one rabbi jokingly told me) in Israel (and in Italy when I was growing up) people eat all parts, as long as the sciatic nerve has been removed from the animal. A few of my recipes call for the leg or rump. This is not intended as disrespect for the orthodox, but as an encouragement for the

Americans to follow the example of the Israelis.

MUSHROOMS. See PORCINI MUSHROOMS.

OLIVE OIL. See Section on page 36, and also AROMATIC OLIVE OIL.

OMELETTES. There are two types of omelette. French omelettes are light and fluffy and folded over themselves without turning, while the other type is dense and in some cases needs to be turned. To turn the latter, use the help of a dish slightly smaller than the pan. When the bottom is firm, place the dish upside down over the omelette. Hold the handle of the pan in one hand and place the other hand over the dish. Firmly holding both, quickly turn pan and dish so that the latter now rests on your hand and the omelette on the dish. (Do this over the sink to prevent any oil that escapes from dropping on the burner ; also make sure that no oil spills on your hand when you turn the pan and dish.) Add a little fresh oil to the pan, then slide the omelette from the dish to the pan and cook the other side.

PAP. See BREAD PAP.

PASSOVER FLOUR. Passover flour is the finest, purest (no bran, which would cause it to leaven quckly) wheat flour which has been expressly ground and carefully watched by a *mashgiach* for use on Passover. It is not available in supermarkets, but kosher stores on the Lower East Side of Manhattan carry it, and I suppose that it can be found in similar stores in other parts of the country.

PASTA. With the word "pasta" Americans designate all types of noodles that are cooked in salted water, drained and dressed with a sauce. (See also page 107.) How the pasta is drained determines very much the result of a dish. Therefore, the following instructions should be given attention. For store-bought hard pasta drain more or less dry, according to need. The degree of draining depends on the cut of pasta and on the density of the sauce to be used with the pasta. Cut pasta such as ziti and cannelloni is best drained with a pasta colander. For long pasta such as spaghetti and linguine, a two-tine long fork or a multi-pronged scoop are better suited than a colander. If the sauce is a dense one such as pesto or butter, you should drain the pasta very quickly so that it doesn't lose too much of its moisture. If the sauce is somewhat runny, such as a tomato-based sauce, take your time to drain the pasta thoroughly before dressing it. Fresh egg noodles should always be drained thoroughly.

PASTA FATTA IN CASA. See HOMEMADE PASTA.

PEPPER. The two types of pepper we use most are: hot red, which comes either whole, crushed or ground; and black, available in either corns or coarsely and finely ground state. Once in a while white pepper is called for in a fish or dairy recipe. I prefer to buy pepper corns and grind them myself for that fresh and delightful aroma that is released in grinding. I often indicate the use of coarsely ground or crushed black pepper. If you don't own a peppermill that can be regulated to grind from fine powder to coarse particles, place a few pepper corns on your working surface, then place the blade of a large knife on them and with the palm of your hand push forcefully down until corns are crushed. Use immediately and make fresh coarse pepper as you need it.

PEPPERS. By peppers we mean always sweet peppers, unless otherwise specified. Both green peppers, the bell-shaped and the so-called Italian peppers, are fine for most dishes. For colorful and delicious *peperoni sott'olio* red, yellow, and orange peppers are best. I favor, whenever possible, the imported ones which are sweeter and brighter than their domestic counterparts. However the latter are less expensive and quite acceptable.

PORCINI MUSHROOMS. Unless you are able to find fresh porcini on the American market, you must resort to the dehydrated ones. To restore dry porcini mushrooms to their soft state you must soak them in warm water for at least 10 minutes. Since porcini are not washed before being dried, you also have to remove and discard any parts on which dirt is still clinging. The water where you have soaked the porcini is too precious to be thrown away, but you must take great care not to include any dirt when you use it. The best way is to decant the liquid, after the mushrooms have been lifted with a fork, slowly into another container so that the heavier dirt remains at the bottom. You might have to repeat this step several times until no dirt at all remains at the bottom of the container. Even after the dehydrated porcini are restored to softness they don't compare with the fresh ones. When the texture of fresh mushrooms is desired, fresh Shitake mushrooms are, in my opinion, a good enough substitute.

POT ROAST. See COLD WATER STEAM.

RICOTTA. The word *ricotta* in Italian means "cooked twice." This name derives from the fact that ricotta is a by-product of cheese making. After the curdled milk is heated and the casein gathered to make pecorino (from *pecora*, sheep), the remaining liquid is brought to a boil and the white substance that surfaces, the ricotta, is gathered into wicker baskets to drain. The best tasting ricotta, in Italy, is made with sheep's milk. What we call "ricotta" here has nothing to do with what I just described and it does not bind with other ingredients in the same manner. In order to obtain something similar to the real ricotta, we must cook the one we buy again. Place ricotta into a heavy-bottomed sauce pan and bring it to a boil, stirring frequently. Turn the heat down to minimum and simmer, stirring occasionally, for 5 minutes. Allow ricotta to cool before measuring it. To reduce moisture from ricotta without cooking it, place it into a sieve and place the sieve over a bowl. Let it drain in the refrigerator at least overnight, but better for several days, before using it.

SALT. Sodium chloride, the common table salt, has been abused, overused, and forced into the American diet through so-called junk and processed foods for so many years, that now that we have become more conscious of our diet, many of us have gone to the extreme of eliminating salt altogether. Unless we have a medical problem, and are specifically asked by our physician to avoid salt, we shouldn't deprive ourselves of the pleasure that salt provides in making food tastier. I know a young girl who stopped eating peas, a highly nutritious food she likes very much, because she has heard that they contain sodium. When I asked her if she had high blood pressure or any other problem for which sodium is forbidden, she answered that she had absolutely no physical problems, but *"sodium, sodium,"* she kept repeating as if she were talking about arsenic! Besides the fact that people can *die* from lack of sodium, certain foods are so enhanced by adding a little salt to them that we should feel sorry for those who are not allowed it, rather than mocking them by using their diet without having their problems.

SOFT-BOILED EGGS. See BOILED EGGS.

SOUP. See BROTH.

SPINACH AND OTHER LEAFY VEGETABLES. In order to retain most of their valuable nutrients, leafy vegetables should be cooked with no water other than the water they retain in washing. To drain cooked leafy vegetables, don't pour the whole potful into a colander, because no matter how many times you have rinsed them before cooking, there is always a chance that some dirt has been left behind. The best way is to lift the vegetables with a two-tine long fork so that any sand that might still be there remains at the bottom of the pot. When the directions call for thoroughly drained vegetables, wait until these are cool enough to be handled, then gather into balls and squeeze the liquid out with your hands. Or place in a piece of cheesecloth and then wring the liquid out.

SUGAR. Unless otherwise stated, by sugar I always mean the granulated white type. Once in a while you will find directions for vanilla-flavored sugar. In Italy one can buy *zucchero vanigliato*, a finely powdered sugar with a strong vanilla fragrance. Since I don't believe you can readily find it already prepared in the U.S. market, here is the way to make your own. Place 2 cups of confectioners' sugar in a glass jar with 2 vanilla beans cut up into 1-inch sections. Close the jar tightly, and put it away for at least two weeks before sifting and using the quantity of sugar you need. Put the beans that might be in the sifter back into the jar. Replace the beans and replenish the sugar every 3 or 4 months.

SWISS CHARD. See SPINACH AND OTHER LEAFY VEGETABLES.

THINNING SLICES OF MEAT. Use a meat mallet or the blade of a cleaver to pound the slices down to the thinness desired. For large chunks of meat, see TURKEY BREAST.

TOMATOES. To peel tomatoes, drop them into a pot with boiling water and let them boil for 1 minute. With a slotted spoon, transfer into a bowl with icy water. The peel will crack, and will be easily pulled away.

TOMATO ROSES. For perfect roses, use only firm tomatoes. With a very sharp knife, cut a thin film of peel in a spiral about 1 inch wide. Discard the tomato itself (or reserve it for a soup or a salad) and use the peel. Roll the peel loosely around itself, place it on a flat surface standing, then flatten down the first, outer round; lightly open the rest and shape in the fashion of a rose. Use a metal spatula to transfer the rose to the desired spot on your plate.

TURKEY BREAST. Sometimes you need to shape a turkey breast — or any other piece of meat — into a large, thin sheet. If your butcher is not willing to butterfly it for you, you can do it yourself this way: place the piece of meat on a flat surface. With a very sharp long knife in your preferred hand and with the other hand pressing the piece of meat firmly down, slice the meat horizontally halfway down from the top, without cutting through. Open it like a book, and flatten it down with the blade of a cleaver or a meat mallet. If the piece of meat is quite thick, you might want to thin it twice. After the first cut is done one third down from the top, turn the meat upside down so that the cut side faces in the opposite direction and again cut one third down starting on the uncut side, still without cutting through, then open the "Z" and flatten down.

VANILLA-FLAVORED SUGAR. See SUGAR.

VEGETABLE BROTH. Make an excellent vegetable broth by boiling together a variety of vegetables (always including a potato, a carrot, and an onion) with water to cover and salt to taste for 1/2 hour, then strain. The vegetables, seasoned with salt, pepper, olive oil and vinegar, make a tasty side dish.

VINEGAR. Although kosher vinegar in its plain or aromatic forms can be easily found in the American marketplace, I have not been able, so far, to find kosher balsamic vinegar. So I use my own recipe, a mock balsamic vinegar. To make it mix 2 cups of an excellent red wine vinegar with 1/4 cup of red grape juice. 1/4 cup of prune juice and 1 tablespoon of raw sugar in a saucepan. Bring to a boil. Add 1/2 teaspoon rosemary leaves, 1/2 teaspoon of fennel seeds and after 1 minute turn the heat off. Let cool to room temperature, then filter and pour into a bottle.

WATER STEAM. See COLD WATER STEAM.

I Menu delle Feste

HOLIDAY MENUS

SHABBAT

INSALATA DI ACCIUGHE DI MARCELLA
Marcella's Anchovy Salad
or
ANTIPASTO DI PESCE E OLIVE
Fish and Olive Antipasto Platter
BRODINO IN TAZZA
Cup of Chicken Soup
or
MINESTRA DI PATATE
Potato Soup
CHAZIRELLO
Stuffed Breast of Veal
CARCIOFI RITTI
Standing Artichokes
INSALATA MISTA
Mixed Salad Leaves
PANE DEL SABATO COL LIEVITO CASALINGO
Sourdough Challa Bread
CROSTATA CON PASTA DI MANDORLE
Almond Tort

ROSH HASHANA

DENTICE LESSO
Boiled Red Snapper
TORTELLINI IN BRODO
Tortellini Soup
POLPETTONE DI TACCHINO
Turkey Roll
ZUCCHINI TRIFOLATI
Zucchini Truffle Style
ZUCCA SFRANTA IN FORNO
Baked Mashed Squash
INSALATA DI FAGIOLI CALDA
Warm Bean Salad
PANE DI ROSH HASHANA
Rosh Hashana Challa
DOLCE DI MIELE
Honey Cake
MELAGRANE, FICHI FRESCHI, MELE
Pomegrate, Fresh Figs, Apples

EREV YOM KIPPUR

BOCCETTE ROMANE
Roman Little Bowls
SOGLIOLE AI FUNGHI
Fillets of Sole with Mushrooms
ROTOLO DI CARNE RIPIENO
Stuffed Flank Steak
or
BRASATO DI MANZO
Brazed Beef
PISELLI COLLA LATTUGA
Peas with Lettuce
PATATE NUOVE CONDITE
New Potato Salad
CHALLA
FICHI FRESCHI, PERE, UVA
Fresh Figs, Pears, Grapes

SUKKOT

POMODORI RIPIENI DI RISO
Tomatoes Stuffed with Rice
CIMALINO ARROSTO
Pan-roasted Calicle
FAGIOLI COLLA LATTUGA
Beans and Romain Lettuce Salad
SPINACI ALL'AGRO
Lemon Spinach
PANE AI QUATTRO GRANI
Four-grain Bread
PIZZA ROMANA
Jewish Fruit Pie
FRUTTA DI STAGIONE
Fruits in Season

CHANUKA

CROCCHETTE DI MELANZANE
Eggplant Croquettes
COTOLETTE IMPANATE
Breaded Veal Chops
PATATE FRITTE A TOCCHETTI, CARCIOFI FRITTI
Cubed Fried Potatoes, Fried Artichockes
RADICCHIO BRASATO, SPINACI ALL'EBRAICA
Brased Radicchio, Spinach Jewish Style
INSALATA RICCIOLINA
Chicory Salad
FRITTELLE DI RISO PER CHANUKA
Chanuka Rice Fritters
PIZZARELLE DI FARINA DOLCE
Chestnut-flour Latkes
ARANCE, MANDARINI, KIWI
Oranges, Tangerines, Kiwi

ROSH HASHANA LEILANOT

CREMA DI CECI E TAHINA
Humus and Tahina
TORTELLI DI ZUCCA ALLA SALVIA
Squash Ravioli with Sage Oil
SCALOPPINE AL MARSALA
Scaloppine with Marsala wine
ARANCE CONDITE
Orange Salad
CIAMBELLE, GRISSINI TORINESI
Bagels, Turin Bread Sticks
TORZETTI DELL'ABBREI
Torsetti of the Jews

SHABBAT B'SHALLACH

CONCIA DI MELANZANE
Marinated Eggplant
TAGLIOLINI COLLA CROCIA AI FUNGHI
Crusty Fettuccine with Mushroom Sauce
ROLLATA DI SPINACI E PATATE
Spinach and Potato Roll
PUNTARELLE
Catalonian Chicory Salad
TORTA DI INES
Ines's Cake

PURIM

TORTELLINI DI CARNE AI FUNGHI
Meat Tortellini with Mushroom Sauce
POLLASTRINI ALLA GRIGLIA
Broiled Cornish Hens
BROCCOLI STUFATI
Stewed Broccoli
MISTICANZA
Salad Mixture
ROSELLINE, PANFORTE, CIAMBELLINE

PASSOVER

POLPETTE DI PESCE
Fish Balls
SFOGLIETTI AL SUGO
Sfoglietti with Meat Sauce
or
MAZZAGNE AL SUGO
Matza Lasagna with Meat Sauce
AGNELLO IN FORNO CON PATATE
Roast Lamb with Potatoes
or
POLPETTINE DI AGNELLO COI FUNGHI
Lamb Balls with Mushrooms
SPINACI ALL'EBRAICA
Spinach Jewish Style
or

MELANZANE ALL' EBRAICA
Eggplant Jewish Style
INSALATA DI CARCIOFI FINOCCHI E ASPARAGI
Artichoke Fennel and Asparagus Salad
TORTA DI CIOCCOLATA
Passover Chocolate Cake
or
TORTA DI NOCI
Passover Walnut Cake

SHAVUOT

PASTICCINI DI PESCE
Fish-filled Pastry
PANZOTTI DI SPINACI CON SALSA DI NOCI
Spinach Panzotti with Walnut Sauce
or
POLENTA BIANCA PASTICCIATA
White-corn Polenta Baked with Cheese
PASTICCIO DI SOGLIOLE E CAVOLFIORI
Sole and Cauliflower Bake
or
BUDINO DI PESCE
Fish Pudding
CROCCHETTE DI PATATE
Potato Croquettes
TIRAMISU'
or
LATTE ALLA PORTOGHESE
Milk Portuguese Style
FRUTTA DI STAGIONE
Fruit in season

Le Ricette

RECIPES

Antipasti e Uova

APPETIZERS AND EGGS

THIS SECTION SHOULD not be overlooked by the serious cook, not only because it contains many wonderful new ideas for hors d'oeuvres but also because it includes a host of main dishes which are fit, and indeed desirable, for luncheons, suppers, and buffet dinners alike.

Eggs have been a nutritious staple for mankind since time immemorial, and are used by cooks the world over in every category of dishes from appetizers to desserts. Here, of course, I do not mention the many soups and pasta dishes or desserts that make use of eggs, since these are described in their apposite categories. But I do include egg dishes that are meant to be prepared as main courses.

Another important aspect of this section is that here, more than in any other category, I have made use of leftovers to prepare new delicious dishes. The idea of using leftovers combined with a sauce and/or other ingredients to make a new dish is by no means peculiar to Italian Jewish cuisine. But as Jews we have had to be more inventive in order to create dishes that are tasty without combining ingredients that would make them unkosher.

Finally, the majority of recipes in this section can (and in some cases must) be prepared ahead of time, and even frozen, giving the hosts the very advantageous possibility of serving an unusual and delectable meal without having to fuss and get overly tired on or around the day they entertain guests.

CARCIOFI IN PINZIMONIO

Raw Artichokes with Oil Dip

This can be an unusual appetizer, but you will have to find the freshest and most tender of artichokes to serve raw; otherwise a bitter aftertaste will remain. At the time when appetizers always were served at the dinner table--either as antipasto at the beginning of a meal or as *tramezzi*, between two main courses to stimulate a second round of appetite--a small bowl with the seasoning and a large dish for the discarded leaves was placed at each table setting. Even now that appetizers frequently are served around the coffee table or with people standing, I suggest that these raw artichokes be served — as in times past — at the dinner table in place of soup.

6 to 12 medium tender artichokes
1 1/4 cup extra virgin olive oil
3 teaspoons salt
2 tablespoons lemon juice
*1 tablespoon balsamic vinegar**
Black pepper in a mill

Discard the small outer leaves from the artichokes. Trim the stem and cut the bottom flat so you can arrange each artichoke standing on a serving plate. Combine 2 tablespoons oil, 1/2 teaspoon salt, 1 teaspoon lemon juice, 1/2 teaspoon vinegar, and pepper from a turn or two of the mill in each individual small bowl. Serve one bowl of sauce with each serving of artichokes.

Carciofi in Pinzimonio are eaten this way: pull one leaf at a time, dip the whitest part in the oil mixture, and eat only what's tender, discarding the remaining tough part. When you've eaten the leaves using your fingers, cut whatever remains of the stem and bottom into the bowl and eat with a fork. **Serves 6.**

* See instructions on page 46.

TORTINO DI CARCIOFI CLASSICO
Classic Artichoke Omelet

Artichokes are a staple with the Italian Jews, who invented a good many ways to prepare them, especially during Passover when these buds are tender and in season. The brilliant technique for trimming artichokes devised by the ancient Roman Jews is indispensable for the preparation of most artichoke dishes. *Tortino Classico* is a delightful main course for luncheons and suppers, and a desirable addition to any buffet dinner.

*4 medium, tender artichokes, trimmed**
1 lemon
Salt
Freshly ground black pepper
1/2 cup unbleached flour
Olive oil
6 eggs
Nutmeg

Cut each trimmed artichoke lengthwise into 1/4-inch thick slices and return to lemon water. Drain and dry with paper towel. Lightly season with salt and pepper and dredge in flour, shaking off excess.

Place 4 tablespoons of oil in a large skillet over medium heat. Add artichoke slices, possibly in a single layer, and brown on both sides.

Slightly beat the eggs with salt and pepper to taste and a dash of nutmeg. Pour over browned artichokes and cook over very low heat, without turning, until the bottom is firm and the top still moist. Use a spatula to slide the omelet onto a warm dish. **Serves 4.**

* See instructions on page 36.

CONCIA DI MELANZANE
Marinated Eggplant

Eggplant, which is considered in this country the Italian food par excellence, was not known in Italy until the Jews brought it from the Near East a little over a century ago. It is a staple in Jewish cooking, especially among those who practice vegetarianism.

3 medium eggplant
Olive oil
Salt
Freshly ground black pepper
Garlic, minced
Fresh basil leaves, shredded
*Balsamic vinegar**

Trim eggplant and cut lengthwise into 1/2-inch slices. Spread over paper towels and let dry in a ventilated place overnight.

Heat about 1/2 cup oil in a large skillet; add only enough eggplant slices to fit in single layer. Fry, turning occasionally, until slices are browned on both sides and give out the oil they have absorbed during the first stage of frying. Transfer to a glass, porcelain, or plastic container and season each layer with salt, pepper, garlic, basil, and a sprinkle of vinegar. Repeat until you have exhausted the eggplant, adding fresh oil to the pan as necessary.

* See instructions on page 46.

Cover the container and store in the refrigerator for at least a few hours before serving. Serve at room temperature as an appetizer or as a side dish. **Serves 12.**

NOTE: There are no proportions for the seasoning because marinated eggplant can be prepared more or less piquant according to taste. Remember, however, that with insufficient salt this dish will not keep for too long. Refrigerated, it will last a few days; tightly covered, it can be frozen for several months.

FIORI DI ZUCCA
Squash Flowers

People who live in large cities are not likely to find squash blossoms too easily as yet. But once the demand begins to grow, more and more of the finer grocery stores will carry them at a reasonable price. However, even for those who live in the country or in suburbia and can grow squash plants without limitations, the enjoyments derived from this abundance are not without a price.

Squash flowers, whether from zucchini, butternut, acorn or any other member of the squash family, must be picked early in the morning because as the day grows older, so do the flowers, and eventually they wilt and become inedible. But mainly, as soon as the morning warms up, the home grower who doesn't use pest control has to contend with zucchini bugs, bees, and slugs, who like the flowers as we do. The first are innocuous pretty coleopterons which can be shaken away or, when persistent, washed away. The bees are not so innocuous. They get angry with you for taking their food and if you are not careful they might sting. The slugs are the grower's true arch-enemies. They are not content with eating the pollen: they eat the whole flower, or bruise it so badly that you can no longer use it except for the compost pile. Then why bother! Because whether you grow your own (even in a box on a sunny balcony or on the rooftop of a penthouse) or buy them, zucchini blossoms, prepared in a variety of ways, are a true delicacy you wouldn't want to miss.

How many flowers can you pick without weakening the plant? Of the male type — the first ones to appear as soon as the plant is well established and long before it is ready to bear its fruits — as many as come into bloom. There is a popular misconception as regards the picking of squash flowers. But the fact is that the more flowers you pick, the more you strengthen the plant, which will use its nutrients to produce new flowers and eventually the fruit itself — the squash. Each plant produces a great number of male, or sterile flowers, which will continue to bloom during the entire life of the plant. The female flowers come later, attached to a tiny squash which will take quite a while to grow to maturity. Leave these flowers alone. Pick the former ones which you will recognize because they have long stems: they have no tiny squash attached, and never will they grow one.

So, do buy squash blossoms whenever and wherever you find them; or grow your own, pick to your heart's content and enjoy the spoils of your morning battles.

CONCIA DI FIORI DI ZUCCA
Marinated Squash Flowers

For every 12 squash flowers, you will need:
- *3 tablespoons olive oil*
- *1 medium fresh basil leaf, shredded*
- *1 small garlic clove, minced*
- *1/8 teaspoon salt*
- *2 dashes freshly ground black pepper*
- *1 teaspoon wine vinegar*

Wash the squash flowers a few at a time holding them by the stems and letting cold water run over and inside them for a few seconds. Cut the stems down to about 1/2 inch.

Heat 3 tablespoons of oil in a frying pan, then add the flowers fanned out like the rays of a wheel, with the stems at the center. Place the pan over a small burner set at medium heat and fry until the flowers are wilted and golden on one side.

Turn the flowers one by one, keeping them in a wheel, and fry until golden on other side.

Remove from heat and arrange in layers in a glass, porcelain, or plastic container, seasoning each layer with small amounts of basil, garlic, salt and pepper, and a sprinkle of excellent vinegar. Repeat until you have exhausted the flowers. Cover the container and store in the refrigerator, where concia will keep for about a week. For longer storage, freeze.

Serve at room temperature as an appetizer alone, with other antipasti, or to garnish Humus and Tahina (page 70).

FRITTELLE DI FIORI DI ZUCCA
Squash Flowers Pancake

36 squash flowers
1 1/2 cups unbleached flour
1 1/2 teaspoons baking powder
3/4 teaspoon salt
2 tablespoons freshly chopped chives
1 tablespoon shredded basil leaves
1 tablespoon freshly chopped Italian parsley
Olive oil
1 cup cold water

Wash the flowers a few at a time, holding them by the stems and letting cold water run over and inside them for a few seconds. Shred the flowers and set aside.

In a shallow bowl sift together flour, baking powder, and salt. Add shredded flowers, chives, basil, parsley, 2 tablespoons oil, and 3/4 cup cold water. Mix to combine. If mixture is too thick add the remaining water a bit at a time.

Heat 1 cup of oil in a medium-sized frying pan to 375 °F on a deep frying thermometer. Drop a few rounded tablespoonfuls of mixture into the oil and fry, turning, until golden on both sides, 3 to 4 minutes. Transfer to paper toweling, and continue to fry the remaining mixture, adding fresh oil to the pan as it becomes necessary. Serve immediately, or reheat in a 300 °F oven for 10 to 15 minutes before serving. **Serves 6.**

FRITTATA DI FIORI DI ZUCCA
Squash Flower Omelette

18 large squash flowers
Olive oil
1 medium onion, minced
Salt
Freshly ground black pepper
10 eggs, slightly beaten
1 tablespoon finely chopped Italian parsley

Wash the flowers, holding a few at a time by the stems and letting cold water run over and inside them for a few seconds. Pat dry.

In a large skillet, heat 4 tablespoons of oil with onion, and saute for about 1 minute. Shred the flowers directly into the skillet with onion. Season with small amounts of salt and pepper and fry over moderately high heat, stirring occasionally, until the onion is soft and the flowers are wilted and lightly browned.

With a fork, transfer the sauted onion and flowers to the bowl with beaten eggs (reserve the oil). Add parsley and salt and pepper to taste and stir to combine. Reheat the oil in the skillet and pour in the egg mixture. Reduce the heat and cook until the omelette is firm on one side. With the help of a dish, turn the omelette* and cook the other side until firm. If necessary, add a tablespoon or two of fresh oil to the pan when you turn the omelette. Serve immediately. **Serves 6.**

* See instructions on page 42.

CAVOLFIORI SOTT'OLIO
Cauliflowers in Olive Oil

1 medium cauliflower
2 cups white vinegar
1 cup water
2 tablespoons salt
1 teaspoon whole black peppercorns
Olive oil

Discard outer leaves and core from cauliflower and separate the small florets. Bring vinegar, water and salt to a boil into a saucepan (avoid metallic pans). Add florets and cook for 5 or 6 minutes. Drain and cool thoroughly. Add peppercorns and toss.

Place into a glass jar and add olive oil to cover. Let the jar stand until all the bubbles of air have escaped through the top. Place the lid on and close it tightly. Store in the refrigerator for up to two weeks, or in the freezer for a longer storage. **Yields approximately 2 pints.**

PEPERONI SOTT'OLIO
Sweet Peppers in Olive Oil

3 pounds sweet red and/or yellow peppers
1/2 cup red wine vinegar
Salt
Freshly ground black pepper
2 large cloves garlic, quartered
Olive oil

Wash the peppers and place them in a large baking sheet where they can fit in a single layer. Bake in 550 °F oven for 15 minutes or until the peel begins to burn and blister. Drop in a basin with cold water, then try to remove as much of the peel as possible. Remove and discard stems, core, and seeds and cut peppers into strips.

Bring vinegar with 1 teaspoon salt to a boil in a non-metallic saucepan. Add pepper strips and cook 3 minutes stirring frequently. Remove from heat and let cool. Drain, and season with salt and pepper to taste. Add garlic, and toss. Place in a glass jar with oil to cover. Let rest until all bubbles of air have escaped through the top. Close the jar tightly and keep refrigerated if using within a week, or freeze for longer storage. Because of their bright color and their unique taste, *peperoni sott'olio* are an excellent complement and garnish to any antipasto platter.

Yields approximately 2 pints.

FAGIOLINI SOTT'OLIO
Green Beans in Olive Oil

2 pounds fresh, stringless green beans
2 cups white vinegar
1 cup water
2 tablespoons salt
2 cloves garlic, coarsely cut up
1 teaspoon whole black peppercorns
Olive oil

Trim the green beans at both ends, wash them, and place in a non-metallic saucepan with vinegar, water and salt. Bring to a boil and cook uncovered for 5 minutes. Drain and cool thoroughly. Add garlic and peppercorn and toss to combine.

Place in a glass or plastic container and pour oil over them to cover. Store in refrigerator for a few days to two weeks; freeze for longer storage. **Yields approximately 2 pints.**

POMODORI VERDI MARINATI
Marinated Green Tomatoes

If you have access to green tomatoes, you'll find this recipe invaluable. There is a time, before the deep frost comes to destroy all your crop, when tomatoes are beautifully grown, but still totally green. Most home growers pick them, wrap them in paper and let them slowly ripen. This is fine, but after a full season of eating just-picked ripe tomatoes, these are a bit of a letdown. Why not try to preserve them in this delicious form? It is easy, and you can begin to eat tomatoes thus prepared 5 days after you make them, and they will remain delicious for at least 5 months — if you have enough!

3 pounds green tomatoes
Salt
White wine vinegar
3 large cloves garlic, minced
2 tablespoons fennel seeds
2 tablespoons oregano
*2 tablespoons balsamic vinegar**
6 tiny hot red peppers
Olive oil

Wash tomatoes and without drying, slice thin over a dish so you don't lose the moisture. Arrange in layers in a large bowl, sprinkling each layer abundantly with salt. Add whatever liquid you find where you sliced the tomatoes. Place a dish slightly smaller than the bowl directly on top of the tomatoes, and place a weight on the dish. (A tightly-closed jar filled with water will do.) Let pickle for 4 to 5 hours.

* See instructions on page 46.

Drain thoroughly. Add white wine vinegar to cover, and let pickle for another 4 hours, then drain thoroughly once again.

Place in a glass jar in layers, sprinkling each layer with small amounts of garlic, fennel seeds, oregano, and a few drops of balsamic vinegar. Distribute the 6 hot red peppers here and there throughout the jar. Pour olive oil to cover, and replenish as the bubbles of air come to the surface. Cover tightly and store in a cool place or refrigerator.

Yields approximately 2 pints.

BRUSCHETTA
Garlic Bread

Bruschetta — so called in Rome, but also known as *fettunta* in Florence and *pancrocino* in Pitigliano — is a hearty garlic bread, which can be served as is or with any number of different toppings. It is always a favorite, whether it is served as an appetizer or as part of a buffet dinner. Here are a few examples, beyond which one's imagination is the only limit to the ways this delicacy can be prepared.

12 slices day-old Tuscan or four-grain bread
3 large cloves garlic
Coarse kosher salt
*Coarsely crushed black pepper**
Extra virgin olive oil
2 large ripe tomatoes
1 tablespoon shredded basil
1 small onion, chopped
or one of the following:
Sweet peppers in olive oil (page 65)
Marinated eggplant (page 61)
Cauliflowers in olive oil, chopped (page 65)
Marinated green tomatoes (page 66)

Toast the bread under the broiler until nicely browned on both sides. Rub one side with garlic, then season with salt and pepper to taste, and an abundant sprinkle of extra virgin olive oil.

Serve as is, or top with one of the garnishes. If you choose fresh, ripe tomatoes, dice them into a bowl; add basil and onion, lightly season with salt, pepper and oil and spoon over bruschetta. If you prefer one of the other garnishes, just place a couple of strips of peppers, a slice or two of eggplant, a spoonful of chopped cauliflowers, or 2 slices of green tomatoes on each bruschetta and serve.

Serves 6.

* See instructions on page 43.

OLIVE VERDI INDOLCITE

Cured Fresh Green Olives

The High Holiday season coincides with the harvest time for, among many other fruits and vegetables, green olives. Recently I have noticed that some vegetable stores, including the produce section of many supermarkets, carry raw green olives. Few people know what to do with them, but those who do are in for a treat. In Pitigliano, where the land was almost entirely covered with vineyards and olive groves, we used to cure olives by the tens of kilos. We had an enormous wooden tub for the purpose. In America, I make two or three pounds at a time during their peak and my family feasts on them.

I have one strong word of caution: since the curing agent is pure lye, a poisonous and highly corrosive substance (it is used to drain clogged pipes!), and since it can cause severe burns when it touches the skin, it should be handled with extreme care. Lye can be found in hardware stores or in any supermarket in the housecleaning section.

2 tablespoons pure lye (sodium hydroxide)
1 quart cold water
2 pounds fresh green olives
2 one-quart glass jars
2 tablespoons salt

In a large glass bowl, dissolve 2 tablespoons lye with 1 quart of cold water. Add the olives very carefully, so you do not touch the lye solution (I use oven mittens or heavy rubber gloves). Stir with a long wooden spoon every 2 hours until all the olives have sunk to the bottom. This will take from 7 to 10 hours.

Carefully drain and discard the solution, then rinse the olives many times with running cold water. When they are thoroughly rinsed, leave the olives in the bowl with fresh water to cover. Renew the water when it becomes rusty (about 3 times a day).

After 4 days of this treatment, drain the olives and place them into two glass jars. Add 1 tablespoon of salt to each jar; fill the jars with fresh water and shake to dissolve the salt. Store in refrigerator with loosely fitted lids.

Yields 2 quarts.

NOTE: Texture and taste are best if the home-cured olives are consumed within one week or two.

ANTIPASTO DI PESCE E OLIVE
Fish and Olives Antipasto Platter

1 small onion, minced fine
1/3 cup black caviar
3 hard-boiled eggs, separated*
1/2 pound smoked herring fillets
1/2 pound sliced smoked salmon
2 6-oz cans anchovy fillets, flat or rolled around capers
1 pound oil-cured black olives
1/2 lemon, sliced lengthwise very thin
1 cup green olives
1 cup peppers in olive oil
*Coarsely ground black pepper***
Extra virgin olive oil
Sourdough crackers (page 234)

At the center of a serving plate, pack a medallion of minced onion and spread caviar over it. Pass the yolks through a vegetable mill with its large-hole sieve attached and arrange in a ring around the onion. Pass the white through the same mill and make a ring around the yolks.

Cut the herring fillets into 1/2-inch pieces and the salmon slices into small strips, and arrange with the anchovy fillets around the center piece.

Mix black olives and lemon slices and arrange around the fish, alternating with green olives and marinated red or yellow peppers.

Sprinkle with pepper and abundant extra virgin olive oil. Serve with sourdough crackers. **Serves 12 to 20.**

* See instructions on page 38.
** See instructions on page 43.

INSALATA DI ACCIUGHE DI MARCELLA
Marcella's Anchovy Salad

This mixture, simple in its ingredients but very tasty, can be served as an appetizer, as does my sister Marcella who invented it, or as a condiment for poached eggs, as I sometimes do.

For the purpose of economy, you may buy the salted anchovies in large cans, available at some Italian grocery stores, and do the cleansing and boning yourself. If cost is no object, the anchovy fillets you find in any supermarket in small 6-ounce cans will save you a lot of time and energy. They come as flat fillets or rolled around capers. Either will do.

1 cup anchovy fillets, coarsely chopped
1 cup peeled carrots, finely shredded
1/2 cup finely chopped onion
2 cloves garlic, minced
1 cup coarsely chopped Italian parsley
1/4 cup red wine vinegar
1/2 teaspoon crushed red pepper
Olive oil

In a serving bowl alternate layers of anchovies with carrots, onion, garlic, and parsley, sprinkling the parsley layers with vinegar and pepper. When you have exhausted all the ingredients, pour enough oil to cover. Set aside to rest for several hours before serving. Serve with thin slices of Tuscan bread or with unsalted crackers.

Serves 12 or more.

CREMA DI CECI E SESAMO
Humus and Tahina

Humus is a chick-pea puree you can make from scratch or from canned peas. Tahina, or tahini, is a sesame-seed butter which you can find canned in many supermarkets, or in bulk in most health-food stores. Whether you are familiar with this dish or it is a new concept to you, try my version and your family and guests will fall in love with it.

1 large clove garlic
2 cups cooked chick peas with some of their liquid*
1/2 lemon with peel, cut up (optional)
1 teaspoon salt
1/8 teaspoon ground red pepper
3/4 cup tahina
Oil-cured black olives
Marinated squash flowers (page 63)
Peppers in olive oil (page 65)
Other marinated vegetables

Place garlic (and lemon if you opt for it) in a food processor and process for 5 seconds.

Add cooked chick peas and 2 tablespoons of their liquid and continue to process until smooth and fluffy.

Add tahina, salt and pepper and process to mix. Should the paste appear to be too thick, add a few drops of the remaining liquid at a time until you reach the desired consistency. Pour over a flat serving dish and garnish with oil-cured black olives, marinated squash flowers, peppers in olive oil, and other marinated vegetables, if desired.

Serves 6 to 12.

NOTE: If you use lemon, make sure to finish the humus within a day or two since the lemon will cause it to perish quickly.

* See instructions page 40 for dried beans

SUPPLI' AL TELEFONO CON FUNGHI

Rice Mushroom Croquettes

Suppli' al Telefono, so called because while eating each croquette you are supposed to spin a "wire" of cheese, is a classic Roman dish made with rice, tomato sauce, and mozzarella cheese. This version with mushrooms is an improvement on the original, especially if dried imported *porcini* mushrooms are used.

1/4 ounce imported porcini mushrooms
4 1/2 cups warm water
10 ounces white mushrooms, washed and sliced thin
Olive oil
1 clove garlic, minced
1 tablespoon freshly chopped Italian parsley
Salt
Freshly ground black pepper
1 rounded tablespoonful tomato paste
2 cups Italian rice
1/4 cup minced onion
3 tablespoons grated Italian Parmesan cheese
2 eggs, slightly beaten
1 pound mozzarella cheese, cut into 24 1/4x1/4x1-inch pieces
Seasoned bread crumbs

Soak porcini in 1/2 cup of warm water for about 10 minutes. Lift them from their bath with a fork, reserving the water. Remove any parts with dirt still attached, chop and place in a saucepan with the fresh mushrooms, 3 tablespoons olive oil, garlic, parsley, 1/2 teaspoon salt, the pepper and the tomato paste. Place over moderately high heat and cook, uncovered, 5 minutes, stirring frequently.

Add reserved water from soaked mushrooms, pouring carefully so that any remaining sand stays at the bottom of the cup.* Cook over high heat five minutes longer, then set aside.

Place the rice in a 2-quart saucepan with 2 tablespoons olive oil and the onion. Saute over moderate heat, stirring occasionally, 2 or 3 minutes. Add the cooked mushrooms and 4 cups warm water, and cook 20 minutes, covered, without stirring. Uncover and continue to cook, stirring, until the rice looks quite dry. Remove from heat and cool for 15 or 20 minutes, stirring from time to time. Add Parmesan cheese and eggs and mix well.

With damp hands shape heaping tablespoons of the cooked rice into croquettes the size of large eggs; insert a piece of mozzarella in each croquette, making sure that the piece of cheese is completely coated with rice. Roll in bread crumbs and fry a few at a time in hot oil until golden brown on all sides. Serve immediately or wrap tightly in foil and freeze. Reheat at 300 °F for 20 minutes before serving. **Serves 6.**

NOTE: Serve *suppli'* piping hot, and don't be bashful to let your guests know that they should hold them with their fingers. It is the string that spins between your mouth and the piece held in your fingers that gives them the name "*al telefono*".

*See instructions on page 43.

CROSTINI DI FEGATINI PICCANTI
Spicy Chicken Liver Toasts

1 pound chicken livers
4 tablespoons olive oil
1 small onion, chopped fine
8 anchovy fillets
1 tablespoon tiny capers, drained
1 tablespoon freshly chopped Italian parsley
Salt
Freshly ground black pepper
36 diagonally cut thin slices one-day-old Fruste *bread (page 228)*
1 1/2 cups clear chicken broth

Discard skins, fat, or any discolored parts from chicken livers. Soak in cold water and rinse until water is free from any trace of blood. Grind or chop uncooked livers until they become like a paste.

Heat oil in a skillet, add onion and saute 1 minute. Add chicken livers and saute, stirring frequently, 3 more minutes. Add anchovies and cook, stirring, 1 or 2 minutes longer. Add capers and parsley and remove from heat. Season with salt and pepper to taste and mix well.

Toast bread slices until lightly browned on both sides. Dip each slice in the broth very quickly (toast should be moist but still crunchy). Spread chicken liver mixture on each canape and arrange on serving plate. Serve immediately or at room temperature. **Serves 8 to 12.**

PASTICCINI DI CARNE
Meat-filled Pastry

My Aunt Delia, the wife of the late *chazan* of Pisa who was in office during the period that included the two World Wars, was a famed cook of budget Jewish specialties. Of these, one of my favorite was *pasticcini.* I had no idea of their composition, but a few years before she died, Aunt Delia revealed her secret to me. "When you have meat or fish leftovers," she said, "save them to make these delicious pasticcini and everyone will praise you." The following are her authentic recipes.

1/4 ounce imported dry porcini mushrooms
3/4 cup warm water
1 1/2 cup leftover meat or chicken, chopped fine
1/4 cup walnut meats, coarsely chopped
1 tablespoon freshly chopped Italian parsley
1/4 pound non-dairy margarine
Unbleached flour
2 egg yolks
Dash or two nutmeg
Salt
Black pepper
2 tablespoons brandy
Oil for frying

Soak mushrooms in 3/4 cup warm water for 10 minutes. Lift from their bath with a fork, discard any parts with dirt still attached, and chop fine. Pour the mushroom water in a small pan, taking great care to leave any sand at the bottom of the cup,* and keep warm.

Place the meat in a bowl with mushrooms, walnuts and parsley. In a small pan heat 2 tablespoons margarine with 2 tablespoons flour and saute until the flour turns lightly brown. Add the warm water from the soaked mushrooms all at once and stir vigorously with a wire wisk. Cook three minutes, stirring occasionally, then add to the meat bowl. Add 1 egg yolk, nutmeg, salt and pepper to taste, mix well, and set aside.

In a small bowl, make a pastry with 1 1/2 cups flour, 6 tablespoons margarine, 1 egg yolk, 1 teaspoon salt, the brandy and add enough cold water, a few drops at a time, to keep everything together. Do not manipulate too much. Pour onto a floured working surface and roll down to approximately 1/16-inch thickness.

Cut into 3-inch disks (if you don't have a cookie cutter of this diameter use a glass or a cup), place 1 level tablespoon of the mixture on each disk, moisten the edge, and fold over in half. With the prongs of a fork press the semi-circular edge to seal it, then poke a few holes on the top. Fry in hot oil until golden on both sides. Drain and serve. **Serves 6.**

* See instructions on page 43.

PASTICCINI DI PESCE
Fish-filled Pastry

1 1/2 cups boneless cooked fish
*1/4 cup slivered blanched almonds, toasted**
1 tablespoon freshly chopped Italian parsley
1/4 pound butter
Unbleached flour
1/2 cup hot milk
2 egg yolks
Dash or two nutmeg
Salt
White pepper
2 tablespoons brandy
1/4 cup cold water

Place fish, almonds and parsley into a bowl. In a small skillet heat 2 tablespoons butter with 2 tablespoons flour and saute until the flour begins to attain a light brown color. Add hot milk all at once and stir vigorously with a wire wisk. Cook, stirring occasionally, 3 minutes, then add to fish bowl. Let cool for a while, then add 1 egg yolk, nutmeg, and salt and pepper to taste. Mix well and set aside.

In a small bowl combine 1 1/2 cups flour, 6 tablespoons butter, 1 egg yolk, 1 teaspoon salt, brandy and enough water, a few drops at a time, to keep everything together. Do not manipulate too much. Pour onto a floured working surface and roll down to approximately 1/16-inch thickness. Cut into 2 1/2-inch disks, fill each disk with a rounded teaspoonful of the fish mixture, moisten the edge, and fold over in half. With the prongs of a fork press the semi-circular edge to seal it, then poke a few holes on the top. Fry in hot oil, drain and serve.

Serves 6.

* See instructions on page 36.

PASTICCINI DI PESCE SENZA LATTE

Non-Dairy Fish-filled Pastry

1 1/2 cups boneless cooked fish or 3/4 pound boneless raw fish
3/4 cup cold water
1 clove garlic, minced
4 sprigs Italian parsley
1 tablespoon olive oil
Salt
White pepper
1/4 pound non-dairy margarine
Unbleached flour
2 egg yolks
Dash or two nutmeg
2 tablespoons brandy
Oil for frying

If you don't have leftover fish, place the raw fish in a saucepan with 1/2 cup water, garlic, parsley stems (reserve and finely chop the leaves), olive oil, small amounts of salt and pepper, and cook for 6 minutes. Discard garlic and parsley stems, drain fish and shred into a bowl (reserve 1/2 cup of the liquid and keep it hot).

In a small skillet heat 2 tablespoons margarine with 2 tablespoons flour and saute until the mixture is lightly browned. Add the fish liquid all at once and stir vigorously with a wire wisk. Cook 3 more minutes, stirring occasionally, then add to the fish bowl. Let cool for a while before adding the chopped parsley leaves, 1 egg yolk, nutmeg, and salt and pepper to taste. Mix well and set aside.

In a small bowl combine 1 1/2 cups of flour, 6 tablespoons margarine, 1 egg yolk, 1 teaspoon salt, brandy, and enough water, a tablespoon at a time, to keep everything together. Do not manipulate too much. Pour onto a floured surface and roll down to approximately 1/16-inch thickness. Cut into 2 1/2-inch disks, fill each with a rounded teasponful of fish mixture, moisten the edge and fold in half. With the prongs of a fork, press the semicircular edge to seal it, then poke a few holes on the top. Fry in hot oil, drain and serve. **Serves 6.**

POLPETTE DI PESCE PER PESACH

Passover Fish Balls

Gefilte fish is traditionally served on Passover and other festivities in the home of the Ashkenazim. In Italy we had never heard of gefilte fish, even though fish was very much part of our festive meals. The following recipe is as close as we got to gefilte fish for the Passover Seder.

1 pound boneless raw fish
1/2 cup cold water
1 clove garlic
6 sprigs Italian parsley
2 tablespoons olive oil
Salt
White pepper
Dash or two nutmeg
2 tablespoons pinoli *(pine nuts)*
2 tablespoons non-dairy margarine
*3 tablespoons Passover flour**
1 egg, slightly beaten
1/2 cup matza meal
Oil for frying

Cook the fish for 6 minutes with water, garlic, parsley stems (reserve the leaves and chop them fine), 2 tablespoons olive oil, and salt and pepper to taste. Discard parsley stems and garlic, drain well (reserve the liquid and keep it hot), and place in a bowl with chopped parsley, nutmeg and *pinoli*. In a small skillet heat margarine and flour and cook, stirring, for a minute or two. Add the reserved hot liquid from the fish all at once and stir vigorously with a wire wisk. Cook 3 minutes, then add to fish bowl. Stir to cool a little, then add egg and mix well.

Spread the matza meal on a piece of waxed paper. Form small balls with the fish mixture and roll in matza meal. Fry in hot oil until golden brown.

Yields 3 to 4 dozen.

* See comments on page 42.

UOVA AL POMODORO
Eggs with Tomatoes

Olive oil
1 clove garlic, minced
2 tablespoons freshly chopped Italian parsley
6 medium ripe peeled tomatoes or*
2 cups canned peeled tomatoes
1 teaspoon salt
1/4 teaspoon crushed red pepper
12 eggs
Peppercorns in a mill

In a very large skillet heat 4 tablespoons of oil with garlic and half the parsley. Saute for 1 minute.

Cut the tomatoes into small strips and add, with their juice, to the skillet. Add salt and red pepper and shake the skillet to mix. Cook uncovered, shaking frequently, for 5 minutes or until most liquid has evaporated.

With a small ladle make 12 depressions in the sauce and sprinkle the depressions with oil. Break the eggs and drop them directly into the little craters in the sauce. Cook over low heat, covered, for 5 to 7 minutes, or until the eggs are firm but not too hard. Spoon eggs out into individual warmed dishes and place the cooked tomatoes around them. Top the eggs with the remaining parsley and with pepper from a few turns of the peppermill.

Serves 6.

* See instructions on page 45.

FRITTATINE IN TRIPPA
Egg Pancakes Tripe Style

During the first few months following the end of World War II, when our resources were very meager, this budget dish, prepared without such luxuries as black pepper, and with more bread crumbs and water than eggs, was our staple. We got to like it and even when our economic situation improved, it remained, with slight variations, in our culinary repertoire.

Salt
Water
2 tablespoons flour
11/2 tablespoons bread crumbs
4 jumbo eggs
Olive oil
2 tablespoons tomato paste
1 large clove garlic, minced
2 tablespoons freshly chopped Italian parsley
1 teaspoon chopped basil
1/2 teaspoon grated lemon peel
Dash black pepper

Place 1/2 teaspoon salt, 3 tablespoons water, flour and bread crumbs in a bowl and mix to form a paste. Let rest for a few minutes, then add the eggs and beat to homogeneity.

Heat 2 tablespoons of oil in a large skillet. Add batter by the tablespoonful to form separate little pancakes. When firm on the bottom, turn and cook on low heat until firm on the other side. Continue to make pancakes, adding oil to the pan if it becomes necessary. When all the pancakes are done, cut them into strips.

Dilute tomato paste in 2 cups of water and place in a large skillet with 2 tablespoons oil, garlic, parsley, basil, lemon peel, 1/2 teaspoon salt, and pepper. Cook for 1 minute, then add the pancake strips and allow to simmer 2 to 3 minutes before serving. **Serves 4.**

FRITTELLE DI SPINACI
Spinach Pancakes

2 pounds small-leaved bulk spinach
Salt
2 tablespoons olive oil
1 small clove garlic, minced fine
Black pepper
8 eggs, slightly beaten
1/2 cup seedless raisins
1/4 cup pinoli *(pine nuts)*
Olive oil or other vegetable oil

Remove stems and roots from spinach and discard or save for later use in a vegetable soup. Rinse spinach leaves in as many washes of cold water as needed to rid them of any sand. Place in a large pot with no water other than what leaves retain in washing. Add a pinch of salt and cook, covered, 5 to 10 minutes, depending on size of leaves.

Drain* and place over a piece of cheese cloth; wait until spinach is cool enough to handle, then wring to squeeze as much liquid out as possible. Chop fine.

Heat 2 tablespoons of olive oil in a skillet; add garlic and small amounts of salt and pepper, and saute for 1/2 minute. Add spinach and stir for another minute or two. Transfer to a bowl and let cool a little; then add eggs, raisins, *pinoli,* and salt (if needed) and mix to combine.

Drop by the rounded tablespoonful in hot oil and fry until browned on both sides. **Serves 6.**

*See instructions on page 44.

FRITTELLE DI SPINACI E RICOTTA
Spinach and Ricotta Pancakes

2 10-oz. packages frozen chopped spinach
Olive oil
1 tablespoon finely chopped onion
1/4 cup fine bread crumbs
2 tablespoons grated Parmesan cheese
*2 cups ricotta, moisture-reduced**
4 eggs, slightly beaten
Salt
Ground black pepper
Dash ground clove

Let frozen spinach stand at room temperature for a couple of hours before cooking. Cook according to directions with half the amount of water recommended.

In a medium-sized skillet heat 2 tablespoons olive oil with onion and cook, stirring, until onion is soft — about 2 minutes. Drain the spinach,** add to the skillet with onion, and saute, stirring frequently, until moisture is substantially reduced.

Remove from heat and after a while add bread crumbs, Parmesan cheese, ricotta, eggs, salt and pepper to taste, and clove. Mix well.

Drop by the rounded tablespoonful in hot oil and fry until well browned on both sides. Serve immediately.

Serves 4 to 6.

* See instructions on page 43.
** See Instructions on page 44.

FRITTELLE DI RISO PER CHANUKAH
Chanukah Rice Pancake

Although rice pancakes are traditionally made for Chanukah, I like to serve them throughout the year. They are a delightful alternative to plain rice as a side dish (try them with *Pollastrini alla Griglia*), and they make a delicious breakfast, luncheon, or snack. Rolled in sugar or sugar and cinnamon, they can be served as a dessert.

1 cup Italian rice
2 1/2 cups water
1 teaspoon salt
1 cup dark, seedless raisins
1/2 cup pinoli *(pine nuts) or slivered almonds*
2 teaspoons freshly grated lemon rind
6 eggs, slightly beaten
1 cup olive or other vegetable oil for frying
Granulated sugar and cinnamon (optional)

Place the rice in a saucepan with 2 1/2 cups of water and the salt and bring to a boil. Lower the heat to simmer, cover, and cook, without stirring, for 30 minutes, or until the rice is well done and quite dry. Remove from heat, add raisins, nuts, and lemon rind, and stir. Cool for at least 1/2 hour before adding the eggs; mix well.

Heat half the oil in a large frying pan. Drop the rice mixture into the hot oil by the rounded tablespoonful. Fry 2 to 3 minutes, turn and fry another 2 minutes or until frittelle are golden brown on both sides. Transfer to a serving plate lined with paper toweling. Place another piece of paper over them, and keep on stacking frittelle with paper between layers. Add the remaining oil as necessary, until the mixture is used up. When you're through with frying, remove the paper toweling and serve hot, plain, or rolled in sugar and cinnamon. **Serves 6.**

MIGLIACCINI AI FUNGHI
Crepes with Mushrooms

1 pound firm white mushrooms
1/4 ounce imported dried porcini *mushrooms*
1/2 cup hot water
1 tablespoon freshly chopped Italian parsley
1 small clove garlic, minced
2 tablespoons olive oil
Salt
Black pepper
1/2 cup shredded Pecorino Toscano or Muenster cheese*
Butter
Unbleached flour
Milk
3 eggs, slightly beaten

Wash the white mushrooms in cold water, chop them fine and place in a non-metallic saucepan. Soak the dried mushrooms in 1/2 cup of hot water for 10 minutes. Lift them from their bath with a fork, reserving the water; chop and add to the saucepan. Carefully add reserved mushroom water, making sure that any sand remains at the bottom of the cup.** Add parsley, garlic, oil, and small amounts of salt and pepper, and cook over moderate heat for 5 or 6 minutes, stirring occasionally. Remove from heat, drain (reserve the liquid), and place into a bowl with the cheese.

Heat 2 tablespoons butter in a small saucepan with 4 tablespoons flour and cook 2 minutes. Add enough milk to reserved mushroom liquid to obtain 1 cup. Pour into the saucepan with the flour mixture all at once, while stirring with a wire whisk. Cook, stirring frequently, another 3 minutes. Add to the bowl with mushrooms and cheese and stir to combine.

Make a batter with 1/2 cup flour, 1/2 cup milk, 3 eggs, 1/2 teaspoon salt and a dash of pepper.

Heat a 4-inch skillet; brush the bottom with butter. Pour 2 to 2 1/2 tablespoons batter into the skillet, tilting to spread the batter evenly. Cook 2 minutes or until bottom is done but top is still somewhat moist. Place 1 tablespoon of mushroom mixture off center on crepe; fold the other half on top, and seal the open semicircular edge with a fork.

Turn *migliaccini* onto an ungreased baking sheet as you make them. Bake in preheated 450 °F oven for 5 or 6 minutes and serve immediately. **Serves 6.**

* Pecorino Toscano is a delicate, soft cheese not to be confused with Pecorino Romano or Sardo, which are hard and salty. If Toscano is not available in your region, Muenster is an acceptable substitute.

** See instructions on page 43.

Minestre Chiare, Minestroni e Zuppe

SOUPS

BOCCETTE ROMANE
Roman Little Bowls

This is an ancient Roman-Jewish recipe which our mother, who specialized in Jewish food from her native Rome, made to boost our energy after a cold or a flu.

1 1/2 pounds lean beef, cubed or extra lean ground beef
2 tablespoons olive oil
3 quarts water
2 tablespoons bread crumbs
Salt
Black pepper
1 celery stalk
1/2 medium onion, studded with 3 whole cloves
2 carrots, peeled and cut up
2 large bay leaves
2 1/2 pounds beef bones

If you own a food processor, by all means buy cubed meat and grind it yourself after having removed any fat, gristle and skin. Add oil, 2 tablespoons water, bread crumbs, and small amounts of salt and pepper, and process to combine. Make little balls out of this mixture and set aside in the refrigerator.

In a stockpot place the bones, all the vegetables, the water and 2 teaspoons salt. Bring to a rapid boil, then lower the heat to minimum and simmer very gently, covered, for approximately 2 hours.

Strain and defat* the broth, bring again to a rapid boil, and add *boccette*. When boiling resumes, lower the heat to medium-low and cook 1 1/2 hours. Serve hot as a festive soup, or as a main dish for everyday meal.

Serves 6.

* See instructions on 40.

BRODO DI PESCE
Fish Broth

For this tasty soup all you need is the heads and bones of any fine fish such as striped bass or red snapper. You can save these scraps in your freezer each time you have some fish filleted for you, or obtain them simply by asking the people at a fish store to save them for you. Generally the bones, the scraps and the heads are thrown away, but if you tell the person who serves you that you are willing to pay, he will remember to save some for you. Make sure that the heads are cleaned of the gills.

Olive oil
1 medium onion, chopped
1 6-inch celery stalk, chopped
1 medium carrot, peeled and sliced
1 large ripe tomato, cut up
1 teaspoon salt
1/4 teaspoon crushed red pepper
1 tablespoon coarsely chopped Italian parsley
1/4 cup dry white wine
2 pounds or more fish heads and bones
8 cups cold water
*Bread croutons or 4 ounces fresh tagliolini**

Place 2 tablespoons oil, onion, celery, and carrot in a 4-quart pot and saute, stirring occasionally, 2 minutes. Add tomato, salt, pepper, and parsley, and cook 5 minutes over moderately high heat, stirring occasionally. Add wine and raise the heat to let the alcohol evaporate. Add fish scraps and water, and simmer, covered, 30 to 45 minutes.

Strain and discard fish scraps and vegetables. Serve with fried bread croutons or with tagliolini cooked in it.

Serves 6.

* See instructions on page 41.

BRODO VEGETALE
Vegetable Broth

2 all-purpose potatoes, peeled and quartered
3 large carrots, peeled and cut up
2 celery stalks, washed and coarsely cut up
1 large onion, quartered
Stems from a bunch of parsley
3 medium zucchini, trimmed, washed and cut up
2 medium turnips, peeled and quartered
2 medium parsnips, peeled and cut up
1/2 pound string beans, trimmed and cut up
1/2 small hot red pepper or 1/4 teaspoon crushed red pepper
2 large bay leaves
2 quarts cold water
1 tablespoon salt

Place all the ingredients into a large stockpot and bring to a boil. Lower the heat and simmer, covered, for approximately 1/2 hour. Strain through a fine strainer.

Serves 6.

MINESTRA DI PATATE
Potato Soup

In spite of its pedestrian name, this is an elegant soup one should not hesitate to include in a formal dinner menu. We used to serve it as an alternative to puffed-pastry nut soup, which was often served on Erev Shabbat.

1 1/4 pounds potatoes
4 eggs, slightly beaten
3 tablespoons fine bread crumbs
3 tablespoons flour
Salt
White pepper
2 dashes cinnamon
1 tablespoon finely chopped parsley
4 cups boiling water
8 cups chicken soup

Steam the potatoes until tender. Peel, mash, and after cooling a little, combine with eggs, bread crumbs, flour, salt and pepper to taste, cinnamon, and parsley. Gather the mixture over a piece of cheesecloth, wrap the cheesecloth around it, and tie the two ends with a string. Flatten down.

Bring 4 cups of water with 1 tablespoon of salt to a boil in a large skillet, gently add the potato loaf and simmer, covered, for 20 minutes. Transfer to a tray, cover with an inverted flat dish, and place a weight over it (a tightly closed jar filled with water will do). Cool thoroughly.

Remove and discard cheesecloth wrap and cut the potato loaf, using a sharp knife, into small cubes. Bring the soup to a gentle boil, drop the potato cubes into it and heat through. Avoid overboiling lest the cubes fall apart.

Serves 6.

VELLUTINA DI SPINACI
Cream of Spinach Soup

1 10-oz. package chopped frozen spinach
2 cups hot chicken broth
2 tablespoons non-dairy margarine
2 tablespoons unbleached flour
1/2 cup chopped onion
2 tablespoons olive oil
1 cup chopped fresh mushrooms
1 clove garlic, minced
1 tablespoon chopped parsley
1 cup cold chicken broth
Salt
Freshly ground black pepper

Cook spinach in 1 cup of hot chicken broth (for cooking time, follow manufacturers' directions). Let cool a little, then pour spinach and its liquid into a blender. Place margarine in a skillet, add flour and saute 2 minutes, stirring. Add the remaining cup of hot broth all at once, stirring vigorously with a wire whisk. Cook 5 minutes, then add to the blender.

Heat the oil in a small saucepan. Add onion, mushrooms, garlic, and parsley, and saute 5 minutes stirring frequently. Add to blender with 1 cup of cold broth and blend until velvety and creamy. Taste for salt and pepper and correct if necessary. Blend another few seconds.

Serves 4 to 6.

VELLUTINA DI SPINACI ALLA CREMA
Cream of Spinach Soup — Dairy

1 10-ounce package frozen spinach
3 cups vegetable broth (page 84)
4 tablespoons butter
2 tablespoons unbleached flour
2 cups hot light dairy cream
1/2 cup chopped onion
1 clove garlic, minced
1 cup chopped mushrooms
1 tablespoon chopped parsley
Salt
Freshly ground white pepper
Sour cream
1 tablespoon freshly chopped chives

Cook spinach in 1 cup of broth following manufacturer's directions and set aside. In a small skillet, place 2 tablespoons butter with 2 tablespoons flour and cook 2 minutes stirring. Add 1 cup hot cream all at once and stir vigorously with a wire whisk. Cook 3 more minutes.

In a small saucepan place the remaining butter, onion, garlic, mushrooms, and parsley, and saute for 5 minutes stirring frequently. Place spinach and its liquid, white sauce, mushrooms, and the remaining broth in a blender or processor and blend until velvety and creamy. Pour into a tureen. Add the remaining cream, salt and pepper to taste, and stir to combine.

Serve hot or at room temperature garnished with a dollop of sour cream and a sprinkle of chopped chives.

Serves 4 to 6.

MINESTRA DI LENTICCHIE
Lentil Soup

2 cups lentils
2 1/2 quarts warm water
2 sage leaves
Salt
1 clove garlic, husk on
1 clove garlic, minced
1/4 cup olive oil
2 tablespoons minced onion
1 tablespoon chopped Italian parsley
1/4 teaspoon crushed red pepper
2 tablespoons tomato paste diluted in 2 cups water
1 cup tubettini pasta

Pick any stones or debris from lentils and rinse twice in warm water. Place in a large pot with 2 quarts of warm water, sage leaves, 1 whole garlic clove, and 1 teaspoon salt. Bring to a boil, then lower the heat to minimum, and simmer for 10 minutes.

In a small skillet, heat the oil with onion and saute for 2 minutes; add minced garlic, parsley, red pepper, and 2 teaspoons salt and saute, stirring, 1 more minute. Add the diluted tomato paste, stir to combine, then pour the content of skillet into the pot with lentils. As soon as boiling resumes, add 1 cup tubettini and cook 10 minutes or until pasta is tender. **Serves 6.**

NOTE: Lentils, unlike other legumes, cook very quickly. Overcooking will result in a mushy, pureed product.

MINESTRONE DI RISO

Rice Minestrone

Pick all stones and debris from beans and rinse twice in warm water. Place in a pot with 1 1/2 quarts of hot water and 1 teaspoon salt. Bring to a rapid boil; decrease heat to very low and gently simmer, covered, for 1/2 hour. Add garlic and sage and simmer another 1/2 hour, or until beans are tender but not mushy.

Meanwhile, place onion and oil in a large pot and cook over moderately high heat 2 minutes, stirring frequently. Add all other vegetables and cook, stirring, another 5 minutes. Add rice and small amounts of salt and pepper and saute 5 minutes, stirring occasionally.

Remove and discard garlic and sage from beans and add beans and their liquid to the pot with vegetables and rice. Cook stirring frequently for about 15 minutes, or until rice is done *al dente*. Remove from heat, add parsley, and correct salt and pepper if necessary. Stir and let stand 5 minutes before serving. Excellent also at room temperature. **Serves 8.**

* See instructions on page 36.

1/2 cup dried Great Northern beans
1 1/2 quarts hot water
Salt
1 clove garlic with husk on
2 sage leaves
1 medium onion thinly sliced
4 tablespoons olive oil
1 stalk celery, chopped
1 medium artichoke trimmed and sliced or 2 small zucchini, trimmed and diced*
1 potato, peeled and diced
1 medium carrot, peeled and sliced
1/2 cup broccoli florets
Crushed red pepper
1 cup Italian rice
1 tablespoon coarsely chopped Italian parsley

MINESTRONE GRASSO

Meat Minestrone

Place shank in a pot with water, 2 teaspoons salt, and half an onion studded with cloves and peppercorns. Add half a carrot and 1 celery stalk and bring to a boil. Cook until the meat feels tender and easily parts from the bones. Strain, discard the bones, dice the meat and set it aside. Defat the broth.*

* See instructions on page 40.

2 pounds beef shank
Salt
2 quarts cold water
1 1/2 medium onions
2 whole cloves
2 peppercorns
1 1/2 medium carrots, peeled
3 small stalks celery

Olive oil
1 medium potato, diced
2 small zucchini, diced
1 small wedge of savoy cabbage, shredded
1/2 cup shelled peas
*1/2 cup canned or fresh peeled tomatoes, ** drained*
1 cup cooked spinach or Swiss chard
Ground red pepper
1 cup broken-up fresh egg noodles

Dice the remaining onion, carrot, and celery stalks, and place in a large pot with 3 tablespoons of oil and the rest of the vegetables. Add small amounts of salt and red pepper and saute, stirring, approximately 10 minutes. Add the meat and saute 5 more minutes to bring the flavors together. Add the broth (you should have 4 to 6 cups of it), bring to a boil, and cook the pasta in it for 15 minutes. **Serves 6.**

** See instruction on page 45.

PAPPA COLLA RICOTTA
Ricotta Bread Soup

The gamut of bread soups is almost infinite. In Italy when the bread is cooked in the liquid, we call the soup *pappa*; when the bread is soaked without being cooked, the soup's name is *zuppa. Pappa colla Ricotta* is one of the most delicate among bread soups.

*1 teaspoon salt**
4 cups cold water
1/2 pound stale Tuscan bread, broken up
*3 cups ricotta at room temperature, drained***

In a 2-quart saucepan, place salt and water and stir a little. Soak bread in this solution for 10 minutes or until soft and swollen. Place saucepan over high heat and bring to a rapid boil. Cook rapidly for 3 to 4 minutes uncovered. Remove from heat and drain all the water that has not been absorbed by the bread. Add ricotta, mix lightly, and serve. **Serves 6.**

* Tuscan bread is absolutely salt-free. If you use other bread, use only 1/2 teaspoon salt.
** See instructions on page 43.

PAPPA COL POMODORO
Tomato Bread Soup

As I began to write this recipe, I realized that its unsophisticated name does not reveal what a delicacy this soup really is. Only for lack of a better name do I use this one, which is the literal translation of the Italian name.

3 medium onions, thinly sliced
4 tablespoons unsalted butter
6 large fresh ripe tomatoes, peeled and cut up*
Salt
Dash ground red pepper
1 cup Italian parsley, stems removed
3 1/4 cups cold water
12 1-inch slices Fruste *or French bread, stale*
*6 heaping tablespoons shredded Pecorino Toscano** or Muenster cheese*

In a large saucepan, place onions and butter and cook over moderate heat until onion is soft and translucent, but not browned. Add a few tablespoons of water, if necessary, before onion begins to turn golden. Add tomatoes, 2 to 3 teaspoons of salt, and parsley; raise the heat and cook 5 to 6 minutes. Remove from heat and set aside for 1 hour or longer, until completely cool.***

Twenty minutes before serving, add 3 1/4 cups cold water and stir. Correct salt to your taste, then add bread and soak for 8 to 10 minutes. Return to high heat, bring to a rapid boil, and cook 3 to 4 minutes.

Place 1 heaping tablespoon of cheese into each serving bowl; pour the soup over it, and serve immediately.

Serves 6.

NOTE: This is obviously a dairy dish. If you want to use this soup with a meat meal, substitute oil for butter, broth for water, and omit the cheese. Either way it is delicious.

* See instructions on page 45.
**See note on page 80.
*** Up to this point, the soup can be prepared as far as a day in advance and refrigerated. It can also be frozen and removed from freezer a few hours before finishing the preparation.

ZUPPA DI FAGIOLI
Bean and Bread Soup

Zuppe are best in summer when a large variety of vegetables are in season and one can mix a number of different flavors; however, *zuppe* made with dried beans, cauliflower, and other winter vegetables are delicious as well and can be enjoyed all year round.

1 1/2 cups dry red kidney beans
2 quarts hot water
Salt
1 large clove garlic, husk on
1 teaspoon dried sage leaves
Olive oil
1 medium onion, sliced very thin
2 celery stalks, diced
1 large carrot, peeled and diced
1 cup canned peeled tomatoes
Crushed red pepper
1/2 pound day old Tuscan bread

Remove any stones or debris from beans and rinse twice in warm water. Place in a large pot with 2 quarts of hot water and 2 teaspoons salt. Bring to a rapid boil; reduce heat and simmer, covered, for 1 hour. Add garlic and sage and cook 1/2 hour longer or until beans are tender and some have popped open.

Meanwhile, heat 4 tablespoons of oil in a medium skillet; add onion, celery, and carrot and cook over moderate heat approximately 10 minutes, stirring occasionally. Add tomatoes and small amounts of salt and pepper, and cook 5 more minutes.

Remove and discard garlic and sage from the pot with beans. Add the content of the skillet and simmer, covered, 10 to 15 minutes to bring the flavors together. Taste for salt and correct if necessary.

Into a large tureen, slice the bread paper thin. Pour the soup over it; cover with a clean kitchen towel and let steep 5 to 10 minutes before serving. **Serves 6.**

ZUPPA LOMBARDA
Lombard Soup

I first learned to enjoy this soup from one of our maids at the time when most of the foods we ate didn't have a name. Recently I was baffled to discover that in Tuscany this soup is called *Lombarda* even though it is a true Tuscan dish practically unknown in Lombardy. I have liked this peasant soup ever since I was a child and I still like it, its fancy name notwithstanding.

Remove all stones and debris from beans and rinse twice in warm water. Place in a large pot with 3 quarts of hot water, add 1 teaspoon salt and bring to a boil. Lower heat and gently simmer, covered, for half an hour; add one clove of garlic with husk on, and the sage and cook another half hour or until beans are tender but not mushy.

Toast the slices of bread until brown on both sides, then lightly rub the remaining cloves of garlic all over them. Place a toast on each of 8 individual soup dishes, then ladle the cooked beans and some of their liquid over the toast. Season with abundant oil, salt and pepper to taste, and, if desired, a sprinkle of vinegar. **Serves 8.**

1 pound dry white beans
3 quarts hot water
Salt
3 large clove garlic
3 sage leaves
8 3 1/2x5x1/2-inch slices Tuscan Bread
Extra virgin olive oil
*Coarsely ground black pepper**
*Balsamic vinegar*** *(optional)*

* See instructions on page 43.
** See instructions on page 46.

IL CROSTINO
Cauliflower and Bread Soup

This is one of the soups I learned from the peasants who gave us shelter during World War II. I make it to remember and honor them, but also because I like it very much.

With a sharp knife separate florets from the main core of cauliflower. Divide the large florets into 4 sections and the rest in half. Place in a saucepan with 3 cups cold water and 1 teaspoon salt; bring to a boil and cook 8 to 10 minutes. Drain, transfer to a warm bowl (reserve the water), and season with oil, lemon juice, and salt and pepper to taste.

Toast the bread slices until brown on both sides, then lightly rub the garlic all over them. Dip in reserved cauliflower water until thoroughly soaked and arrange in a tureen. Season toast with oil, vinegar, and salt and pepper to taste. Top with cauliflower and its seasoning and serve. **Serves 6.**

1 large white cauliflower
3 cups cold water
Salt
Extra virgin olive oil
Juice of 1 large lemon
*Coarsely ground black pepper**
6 3/4-inch-thick slices Tuscan bread
1 large clove garlic
*2 tablespoons balsamic vinegar***

* See instructions on page 43.
** See instructions on page 46.

IL BRODINO
Clear Chicken Soup

The difference between *Brodino* and any ordinary chicken soup is that the latter is generally made with the addition of vegetables, herbs and spices. If the chicken used to make this broth is fresh, as it should be, no other flavors are necessary in order to have a very tasty broth. The very best broth, when I was growing up, was made with an old chicken, since as the proverb went, *gallina vecchia fa buon brodo*, old chicken makes for a good broth. However, the young fowl I find here is good enough.

It is said that chicken soup contains a substance that inhibits the common cold. Just to be on the safe side, I make *brodino* whenever the symptoms of an incipient cold are present, and often the development of the annoying ailment is averted.

1 fresh fowl
3 quarts water
Salt

Remove and discard as much fat as you possibly can from the cavities of the fowl. Wash thoroughly and place in a stockpot with cold water to cover. Add 1 tablespoon of salt and bring to a boil. Lower the heat and simmer very gently, covered, for 2 1/2 hours without uncovering or turning. Thereafter, begin to test with a fork the tenderness of the meat every 15 minutes.

Transfer the fowl to a plate,* and strain the broth. Defat with the apposite vessel**, or refrigerate for several hours, then completely remove the coagulated fat. Serve clear or with pastina, capellini, fine egg noodles, or *meat tortellini* (page 117) cooked in it.

Yields approximately 2 1/2 quarts.

* Use boiled chicken as an entree with one or more of the marinated vegetables in the appetizers section or *Salsa Verde (page 217)*, or make *Pasticcini* or, in summer, make delightful *Pollo Freddo.*

** See instructions on page 40.

MINESTRA DI PASTA E CECI
Pasta and Chick Pea Soup

The traditional pasta and chick pea soup is preferably made with homemade egg pasta scraps. However, if you do not have homemade pasta scraps, as an alternative use ditalini, the commercial cut pasta which is also traditionally used for this soup.

1 cup dried chick peas
2 1/2 quarts hot water
Salt
1 clove garlic with husk on
1 small branch rosemary or 1 teaspoon rosemary leaves wrapped in a piece of cheese cloth
4 tablespoons olive oil
1 medium onion, sliced very thin
1 clove garlic, minced
1 tablespoon chopped Italian parsley
1 stalk celery, diced
1 small carrot, peeled and diced
Crushed hot red pepper
1 cup homemade pasta scraps or store-bought ditalini

Remove any stones or debris from chick peas and rinse twice in warm water. Place in a large pot with 2 1/2 quarts hot water and 2 teaspoons salt. Bring to a boil; then reduce the heat and simmer, covered, for 1 hour. Add the whole clove of garlic and rosemary and cook 1 more hour or until chick peas are tender. (Cooking time depends on the quality and freshness of the chick peas.*)

In a small skillet place oil, onion, minced garlic, parsley, celery, and carrot. Lightly season with salt and pepper and cook over moderate heat, uncovered, for 5 or 6 minutes, stirring frequently.

Remove and discard garlic and rosemary from chick peas and add the content of the skillet to the pot. Taste for seasoning and correct if necessary. Bring to a boil and cook a couple of minutes to bring all the flavors together. Add pasta scraps and cook, uncovered, 3 to 4 minutes or, if ditalini are used, according to manufacturer's directions. **Serves 6.**

• see instructions on page 40.

ACQUA COTTA
Cooked Water

As the name indicates, this was a soup invented by the poor who would pour boiled water over a few pieces of stale bread. But some could afford a piece of onion, some salt and oil, and already the "cooked water" would have acquired a better taste. Eventually, as people became less indigent, *uova di giornata*, eggs that were laid the same day the soup was made, were added, and this was the stage of evolution in which I found this soup when I first became acquainted with it. Since most of us do not have access to such a luxury as *uova di giornata*, I have modified the recipe to accomodate store-bought eggs, the freshness of which we cannot know. In the original recipe, eggs were cracked open and dropped raw into the boiling soup; the heat was immediately turned off, and the soup dished out over the toast— the eggs still quivering. My directions call for poached eggs.

1/4 cup chopped mushrooms
1/4 cup minced onion
1 tablespoon freshly chopped Italian parsley
4 tablespoons olive oil
1/8 teaspoon ground red pepper
2 cups scallion greens cut into 2-inch pieces
4 1/2 cups cold water
6 eggs, poached
6 medium slices Tuscan bread

In a large skillet, place mushrooms, onion, parsley, and oil and saute 2 minutes. Add salt, pepper, scallion greens and 4 1/2 cups cold water and bring to a boil. Lower heat and simmer 5 minutes. Add poached eggs and simmer 3 more minutes to heat the eggs through.

Toast the bread until brown on both sides. Place one slice of toast in each soup dish. Place one egg on each slice of toast; ladle the soup over it and serve. **Serves 6.**

Riso

RICE

WHEN ITALIAN RICE WAS a rarity and its cost accessible only to a lucky few here in America, my directions for *risotti* and some of the other rice recipes might have called alternatively for short-grain rice, which is inexpensive and resembles Italian rice somewhat. Because of the emphasis advertisers have put on long-grain rice, whose grains remain separate, it is now difficult to find the good old short-grain rice whose grains clump together. This characteristic, which short-grain rice shares with most Italian rices, is desirable not only for *risotti* but also for most rice desserts, such as *frittelle* or puddings, in which the rice grains are supposed to stick together.

The kind of Italian rice one chooses to buy depends on the use one wants to make of it. Most Italian rices have on their packages the description of what they are best suited for. However, Arborio seems to meet most needs.

When recipes call for rice without any specifications, this means that the type of rice one uses does not really matter and depends only on individual tastes.

Rice for desserts should be cooked until quite soft. However, risotti, like *paste asciutte*, taste better and are more easily digested *al dente*.

RISOTTO IN BIANCO
Dairy Rice

This risotto is very popular as a first course in a dairy meal. If prepared with care, *risotto in bianco* is delicious despite its simplicity. You may skimp on quality for other risotti; for this risotto, however, I highly recommend the finest Italian rice you can find and afford.

1 1/2 quarts water
2 cups Italian rice
2 teaspoons salt
1/2 cup unsalted butter
2 dashes white pepper
1 cup freshly grated Italian Parmesan cheese

Bring 1 1/2 quarts of water to a boil. Add rice and salt and lightly stir. When boiling resumes, lower the heat and cook, with the lid a little bit askance, for 12 to 15 minutes without stirring. Make sure risotto is only cooked *al dente.**

Uncover, stir, and spoon out any excess water. (If you prefer, you may drain the rice in a colander, but be sure it remains moist.) Add butter, pepper, and half the cheese and mix with a fork. When serving, pass the remaining cheese in a separate dish. **Serves 6.**

NOTE: For an elegant side dish, cook the rice in 5 cups water and drain quite dry, then shape into a ring and fill the center with buttered artichokes (page 186).

*See instructions on page 36.

RISOTTO VERDE
Green Risotto

1 pound small-leaved bulk spinach
1/4 cup olive oil
2 scallions, including greens, chopped fine
1 6-inch celery stalk with leaves, chopped fine
1 1/2 teaspoons salt
1/8 teaspoon white pepper
Hot water
1 1/2 cups Italian rice
1 tablespoon freshly chopped Italian parsley

Remove all the stems and use only the leaves of spinach. Rinse thoroughly in many changes of water until any trace of sand is gone. Drain, then chop very fine. Reserve the liquid that forms in chopping.

Heat the oil in a 2-quart saucepan. Add scallion, celery, salt, and pepper, and cook 2 minutes stirring. Add chopped spinach and cook, on moderately high heat, 6 or 7 minutes, stirring frequently.

Add enough hot water to the reserved liquid from the chopped spinach to make 2 cups. Add rice and liquid to saucepan and bring to a boil. Reduce heat, cover pan, and cook 15 minutes without stirring. Add a few tablespoons of hot water if rice becomes too dry. Just before serving, add parsley and mix well. **Serves 4 to 6.**

NOTE: For an elegant presentation of this rice, and for a complete protein dish, I spoon it out around the edge of a large serving platter forming a ring of green rice "eggs". Then I fill the center with *Ceci Conditi* or *Insalata di Fagioli Calda*.

RISOTTO CON LE VERDURE DI GINO
Gino's Vegetable Risotto

Olive oil
1 medium onion, diced
2 cloves garlic, sliced
3 celery stalks, coarsely chopped
2 large carrots, peeled and diced
1/2 pound spinach or Swiss chard, thoroughly washed and coarsely chopped
1 small bunch Italian parsley, coarsely chopped
Salt
Crushed red pepper
1 1/2 cups Italian rice
Hot water
1 tablespoon shredded basil leaves

In a medium-sized pot, place 2 tablespoons of oil with the onion and saute for 1 minute. Add garlic, celery, carrots, and spinach or Swiss chard, and saute, stirring frequently, 6 or 7 minutes. Add half the parsley, 1 teaspoon salt, 1/8 teaspoon red pepper, 2 tablespoons oil, and the rice, and stir. After 1 minute add 1/2 cup of boiling water and lower the heat. Cook gently, stirring occasionally, and keep on adding water, 1/2 cup at a time, until the rice is half way done, about 10 minutes. Taste for salt and pepper and correct if necessary. Add basil and remaining parsley, and finish cooking, keeping the rice *al dente** and moist.

Serve hot or, in summer, at room temperature.

Serves 4 to 6.

* See instructions on page 36.

RAPE E RISO
Rice with Turnips

To be really good, turnips should be small, firm, and very fresh. Turnips that have become soft and porous lose their lovely bittersweet flavor and are hard to digest.

1 pound small fresh turnips
1 medium onion, thinly sliced
5 tablespoons olive oil
1 1/2 teaspoons salt
1/4 teaspoon freshly ground black pepper
3 cups hot water
1 1/2 cups rice

Peel turnips and slice thin. Place in a 2-quart saucepan with onion, oil, salt, and pepper. Cook 3 or 4 minutes over moderate heat, stirring occasionally. Add 3 cups of hot water and cook, covered, another 10 minutes. Add rice; stir once and cook, covered, for 9 or 10 minutes. Taste for salt and correct if necessary. Stir and cook 5 minutes longer, or until rice is *al dente.** **Serves 4 to 6.**

* See instructions on page 36.

RISOTTO DEL CAPITANO
The Captain's Rice

1 slice (about 3/4 pound) fresh salmon
3 1/2 cups water
Salt
Olive oil
2 tablespoons minced onion
1 carrot, peeled and shredded
1 clove garlic, minced
1/8 teaspoon ground red pepper
1 tablespoon freshly shredded basil leaves
1 tablespoon finely chopped Italian parsley
1/2 cup dry white wine
1 1/2 cups Italian rice
2 tablespoons extra virgin olive oil

Carefully skin and bone the salmon and place skin and bones in a saucepan with 3 1/2 cups of water and 1 teaspoon salt. Bring to a boil and cook 1/2 hour. Strain and keep the stock warm.

In a 2-quart saucepan, heat 2 tablespoons of oil with onion, carrot, garlic, pepper, basil, and half the parsley, and saute 2 minutes. Dice the salmon, add to saucepan, and saute 2 more minutes, stirring. Add wine and raise the heat to let the alcohol evaporate completely. Add warm fish stock and rice and cook 15 minutes. Taste for salt and correct, if necessary. When rice feels done to you, add the remaining parsley and 2 tablespoons of fresh virgin olive oil, stir and serve. **Serves 4 to 6.**

MELANZANE E RISO
Rice with Eggplant

Trim eggplant and peel only if you are not sure of its freshness. Dice and place in a 2-quart saucepan with garlic, oil, salt, pepper, and basil. Cook for 5 minutes over moderately high heat, stirring frequently. Add rice and saute, stirring, 5 minutes. Add hot water, lower heat, and cook, covered and without stirring, another 10 minutes. Taste for salt and correct if necessary; stir and cook just until rice is *al dente.** **Serves 4 to 6.**

1 pound eggplant
1 large clove garlic, minced
5 tablespoons olive oil
1 1/2 teaspoons salt
2 dashes ground black pepper
1 tablespoon shredded basil leaves
1 1/2 cups rice
3 cups hot water

* See instructions on page 36.

RISO COI PISELLI
Rice with Peas

Place 1/2 cup water, oil, onion, 1/2 teaspoon salt, pepper, and parsley in a small saucepan. Bring to a boil and cook for 3 minutes. Add peas and cook, over moderately high heat, uncovered, 5 minutes.

Bring 3 cups of water with 1 teaspoon salt to a boil. Add rice and stir a little. As soon as boiling resumes, reduce heat and cook, covered, 10 minutes. Add peas with all their juice and cook an additional 5 minutes. Mix well and serve. **Serves 4 to 6.**

3 1/2 cups water
6 tablespoons olive oil
*1 tablespoon dehydrated minced onion**
1 1/2 teaspoons salt
2 dashes freshly ground black pepper
1 tablespoon freshly chopped Italian parsley
2 cups shelled fresh peas or 1 10-ounce package frozen June (tiny) peas
1 1/2 cups rice

* Dehydrated onion is preferred for cooking peas because it adds sweetness to the naturally sweet peas.

RISOTTO COI FEGATINI
Rice with Chicken Livers

1 pound chicken livers
1/4 cup olive oil
1/2 cup onion, minced
1/8 teaspoon savory
1 tablespoon freshly chopped Italian parsley
Salt
Freshly ground black pepper
1 1/2 cups Italian rice
3 cups chicken broth

Discard skins, fat, or any discolored parts from chicken livers. Soak in cold water and rinse until no trace of blood is visible. Chop very fine.

In a 2-quart saucepan, heat the oil with onion and saute until the onion is golden brown. Add the chopped livers, savory, parsley, small amounts of salt and pepper and cook, over moderately high heat, 2 to 3 minutes, stirring frequently. Add the rice and saute 2 minutes longer. Add 3 cups of broth and bring to a boil; then lower the heat and cook, covered, 15 minutes. Add a few tablespoons of water if the rice becomes too dry. Stir and serve. **Serves 4 to 6.**

FRITTATA DI RISO
Rice Omelette

1 1/4 cups rice
3 cups water
2 1/2 teaspoons salt
2 teaspoons freshly grated lemon rind
1 teaspoon vanilla extract (optional)
1/2 cup dark, seedless raisins
1/2 cup pinoli *(pine nuts)*
9 eggs, slightly beaten
4 tablespoons vegetable oil
1/2 cup honey heated with 1 table-spoon lemon juice (optional)

Cook rice in water with 1 teaspoon salt for 20 to 30 minutes, or until very soft. Let cool for a while, then add grated lemon rind, vanilla extract, raisins, pinoli, eggs, and 1 teaspoon salt, and mix well.

Heat 2 tablespoons of oil in a large iron or non-stick skillet. Carefully pour in all the rice mixture and level with a spatula. Cook on medium-to-low heat, keeping the skillet on the edge of the range and rotating it to make sure the omelette doesn't burn at the center. Shake the skillet from time to time to prevent sticking at the bottom.

When the bottom seems firm, turn the omelette with a dish,* adding 2 tablespoons of fresh oil to the skillet before returning the omelette. Cook another few minutes on this side, then turn again and cook another minute before sliding it onto the serving plate.

Serve as is, or if opting for vanilla, topped with honey and lemon mixture. **Serves 6.**

NOTE: Since this is an enormous omelette, you might want to make two smaller and more manageable ones out of this mixture.

* See instructions on page 42.

RISOTTO AL TONNO
Tuna Rice

If you are tired of serving tuna salad, use the can of tuna in your pantry to try this risotto. It is not a pretentious dish, but a very tasty one.

1 6-ounce can solid white tuna fish
2 anchovy fillets
1 large clove garlic
2 large sprigs Italian parsley
3 large basil leaves
Olive oil
1/4 teaspoon crushed red pepper
1/2 cup dry white wine
1 tablespoon tomato paste
Salt
1 1/2 cups rice
3 cups hot water

Drain tuna and coarsely chop together with anchovies.

Chop garlic, parsley, and basil together very fine, and place half of the mixture in a 2-quart saucepan with 3 tablespoons oil and the red pepper. Saute on moderate heat until garlic is golden brown but not burned. Add tuna and anchovies and saute, stirring, 2 to 3 minutes. Add the wine and raise heat to let the alcohol evaporate completely. Add tomato paste and a small amount of salt and saute, stirring, one more minute.

Add rice and water, stir and bring to a boil. Lower heat and cook, covered, 15 minutes without stirring. A moment before removing from heat, add the remaining garlic, parsley, and basil mixture and 3 tablespoons of fresh oil.

Stir and serve immediately. **Serves 4 to 6**.

Pasta, Gnocchi, Polenta, Crespelle

PASTA, DUMPLINGS, POLENTA, CREPES

THE WORD PASTA in Italian has different meanings. The term can be used for dough, paste, single piece of pastry (such as an eclair, or a napoleon), cake, and macaroni, among other things. When the Italians talk about pasta in the sense that this term has come to mean here in America — any variety of macaroni from egg noodles to penne, cooked in salted water, drained, and dressed with a sauce — they say *pasta asciutta,* dry pasta (to distinguish it from pasta in a soup).

Pasta asciutta is divided into two main types: *pasta fatta in casa o pasta all'uovo,* which is homemade pasta or fresh egg noodles, and *pasta comprata,* or store-bought hard pasta. The latter can be *lunga,* such as spaghetti and linguine, or *tagliata,* cut pasta, such as ziti and cannelloni.

This is not the place for a detailed description and discussion on the various types and cuts of pasta, since plenty has been said elsewhere. However, I do want to emphasize that even though all the hard pasta is made with the same durum flour, the texture and even the taste change greatly from one cut to another. Therefore, the cuts are not always interchangeable. When a recipe calls for pasta cooked *al dente,* it means slightly underdone, although not quite hard. Pasta that is not mushy is not only more pleasant to the palate, but definitively more digestible.

I am happy to see that the staple of all my life in Italy has become so popular in America, because it is a nutritious and healthful food, besides being inexpensive and delicious.

CAPELLINI AL BURRO
Capellini with Butter Sauce

Capellini, or fine hair, is the thinnest pasta in the spaghetti family. Capellini in Italy is generally used as a pastina in soups, but it is also delicious as a *pasta asciutta* dressed with a delicate sauce.

4 quarts water
1 pound capellini
2 1/2 tablespoons salt
3/4 cup unsalted butter, melted

Bring 4 quarts of water to a rapid boil. Add the pasta and the salt at the same time. With a long two-prong fork stir and lift the pasta to prevent clumping and sticking until rapid boiling resumes. Cook over moderately high heat, uncovered, for 2 to 3 minutes. (Some manufacturers make capellini thicker than others, so make sure you do not overcook this fine pasta.)

Pour half the butter in a heated serving bowl. Drain the pasta not too dry* and add it to the bowl. Pour over the remaining butter and toss quickly just until all pasta is coated with butter. Serve immediately.

Serves 4 to 6.

* See instructions on page 42.

VERMICELLI PRIMAVERA

This dish has become so popular in America that it doesn't require any translation. You can use any pasta with primavera sauce, but I find that the marriage between such a delicate sauce and vermicelli, or fidelini, or even capellini, is the most successful. The vegetables one chooses to use also can vary according to season and taste. Below is only one example.

Heat the butter in a large skillet. Add the vegetables and small amounts of salt and pepper, and saute for 1 minute, stirring frequently. Add the flour, stir, and cook another 2 minutes. Add the hot milk all at once and stir to prevent lumps. Cook 3 more minutes, stirring occasionally.

Bring the water to a rapid boil. Add the pasta and 2 tablespoons of salt at the same time. Stir and cook 1 to 6 minutes (depending on cut of pasta) or until pasta is *al dente.* Drain very well* and transfer to the skillet with primavera sauce. Add half the cheese and toss over the heat until well coated. Serve immediately with the remaining cheese in a separate dish. **Serves 4 to 6.**

*See instructions on page 42.

6 tablespoons unsalted butter
1/2 cup small cauliflower florets
1/2 cup small broccoli florets
1/2 cup shredded carrots
1/4 cup shelled tiny peas
1/4 cup diced pink tomato
Salt
White pepper
1 1/2 tablespoons unbleached flour
1 1/2 cups hot milk
1/2 cup freshly grated Italian Parmesan cheese
4 quarts water
1 pound vermicelli, fidelini, or capellini

TAGLIOLINI COI CARCIOFI
Thin Egg Noodles with Artichokes

Trim artichokes as described on page 37, making sure to remove any choke. Cut the trimmed artichokes into very thin wedges. Heat the oil in a large skillet and add artichokes. Season with salt and pepper to taste.

Cook over moderately high heat, stirring frequently for approximately 5 minutes. Lower the heat to medium and cook, stirring occasionally, another 5 to 10 minutes, depending on the freshness of the artichokes.

Roll dough thin and cut into *tagliolini* as fine as possible.

Bring water with 2 tablespoons salt to a boil. Add tagliolini and stir. When boiling resumes, cook 2 minutes.

Drain** and transfer to the skillet with the artichokes. Toss until tagliolini are coated with oil and artichokes are well distributed. **Serves 6.**

* See instructions on page 41

**See instructions on page 42

6 medium artichokes
1/2 cup olive oil
Salt
Freshly ground black pepper
*Homemade pasta made with 4 eggs and 2 1/2 to 3 cups flour**
6 quarts water

LINGUINE AL POMODORO E BASILICO
Linguine with Tomato and Basil Sauce

4 tablespoons olive oil
2 large cloves garlic, crushed
2 pounds ripe, firm tomatoes, peeled, cut up or 1 2-lb. can peeled plum tomatoes, drained and cut up*
Salt
Dash or two ground red pepper
1/4 cup firmly packed whole tiny or shredded large basil leaves
4 tablespoons exta virgin olive oil
4 quarts water
1 pound linguine

Heat 4 tablespoons of oil in a large saucepan. Add the garlic and saute until golden, then discard.

Add tomatoes, 1 1/2 teaspoons salt and a dash or two red pepper, and cook over moderately high heat, stirring frequently, 6 or 7 minutes.

Add basil and cook 1 minute longer. Remove from heat and add the extra virgin olive oil.

Meanwhile bring 4 quarts of water to a rapid boil. Add the pasta and 2 tablespoons salt at the same time. Stir until boiling resumes. Cook over moderately high heat for 10 minutes or until desired tenderness.

Place the tomato and basil sauce into a heated serving bowl. Drain linguine very thoroughly** and add to the bowl with sauce. Toss until all pasta is coated with sauce and serve. **Serves 4 to 6.**

* See instructions on page 45.
** See instructions on page 42.

PENNE ALL'ARRABBIATA
Penne With Angry Sauce

4 quarts water
2 tablespoons salt
1 pound penne lisce
2 cups angry sauce (recipe follows)
1/2 cup grated Romano cheese (optional)

Bring 4 quarts of water to a boil. Add penne and salt and stir until boiling resumes. Cook, uncovered, 7 minutes, stirring occasionally. Meanwhile place the sauce in a large pot and heat through.

Drain penne thoroughly and add to the pot with sauce. Cook, stirring from time to time, 5 additional minutes, or until pasta is slightly underdone and coated by a thick sauce.

If you opt for the cheese, use less salt or no salt at all in the cooking water since Romano is quite salty itself. Add half the cheese a moment before removing from the heat and stir to mix. Serve immediately with the remaining cheese in a separate dish. **Serves 6.**

SALSA ARRABBIATA
Angry Sauce

Arrabbiata, angry, in this case means spicy and hot. The sauce is so "angry" that it bites your tongue.

1/2 cup olive oil
1/2 to 1 teaspoon crushed red pepper
1/2 teaspoon salt
1/4 teaspoon oregano
1/4 teaspoon powdered sage
2 large cloves garlic, passed through a garlic press or minced
6 anchovy fillets
1/2 cup very dry red wine
2 cups peeled ripe tomatoes or canned peeled tomatoes, drained and coarsely chopped*

Heat the oil in a saucepan over moderate heat; add pepper, salt, oregano, sage, garlic, and anchovies, and stir a little. When the garlic looks golden (but not browned!) and the anchovies are almost melted, add the wine and raise the heat to let the alcohol evaporate.

Add tomatoes and cook, over medium heat, for 10 to 15 minutes, stirring occasionally. Use immediately, or cool before storing in a tightly covered jar in refrigerator where it keeps for several weeks without the need to freeze it.

Yields approximately 2 cups.

* See instructions on page 45.

SPAGHETTI AL PESTO
Spaghetti with Pesto Sauce

4 quarts water
2 tablespoons salt
1 pound spaghetti
1 1/2 cups pesto sauce (page 213)
1/2 cup freshly grated Italian Parmesan cheese

Bring 4 quarts of water to a rapid boil. Add salt and spaghetti at the same time to prevent water from slowing down. Cook *al dente.*

Meanwhile, warm a serving bowl and place half the sauce into it. Drain spaghetti not too dry* and transfer into the bowl with sauce. Add remaining sauce and toss quickly to combine. Serve immediately with Parmesan in a separate dish.

Serves 4 to 6.

*See instructions on page 42.

SPAGHETTI AL MASCARPONE
Spaghetti with Mascarpone

4 quarts water
Salt
1 pound spaghetti
2 tablespoons olive oil
1 sweet red pepper, cored and diced
1 small white onion, minced
Dash white pepper
1/2 pound mascarpone cheese at room temperature
2 tablespoons freshly chopped Italian parsley

Bring 4 quarts of water to a rapid boil. Add 2 tablespoons salt and spaghetti at the same time to prevent boiling water from slowing down. Cook *al dente.*

Meanwhile, heat the oil in a skillet and stir-fry sweet pepper and onion in it for 3 minutes or until tender. Transfer vegetables to a warmed serving bowl, leaving the oil behind. Add half the mascarpone and stir to combine.

Drain the pasta not too dry* and add to the bowl. Add the remaining mascarpone and the parsley and toss to combine. Serve immediately. **Serves 4 to 6.**

*See instructions on page 42.

TIMBALLO DI MACCHERONI
Macaroni Timbale

Unbleached flour
1/4 cup sugar
Salt
1/4 cup butter, chilled
1 egg, slightly beaten
2 egg yolks
1 pound firm white mushrooms, washed and sliced
1 tablespoon coarsely chopped Italian parsley
Freshly ground black pepper
1 small clove garlic, minced
Olive oil
1/2 cup water
2 teaspoons dehydrated minced onion
1 cup freshly shelled or frozen tiny peas

Sift together 1 1/4 cups flour, 1/4 cup sugar, and 1/4 teaspoon salt. Shred chilled butter over mixture, then add 1 egg and 1 egg yolk; quickly mix and form into a ball. Place in a small dish, cover with an inverted dish, and let rest in the refrigerator for at least 1/2 hour.

Place mushrooms, parsley, garlic, small amounts of salt and pepper, and 2 tablespoons of oil in a saucepan. Cook covered over moderate heat approximately 10 minutes, stirring occasionally.

In a separate saucepan, place 1/2 cup of water, onion, 2 tablespoons of oil, and small amounts of salt and pepper. Bring to a boil and cook 2 minutes. Add peas, cover, and cook over moderately high heat 5 more minutes.

Cook macaroni according to manufacturer's directions. Drain not too dry* and place in a bowl. Add cooked mushrooms and cooked peas with all their juices, and toss to combine.

Heat 3 tablespoons butter with 2 tablespoons flour in a small skillet. Cook 2 minutes, stirring with a wire whisk. Add hot milk all at once and stir vigorously. Cook 4 minutes longer, stirring occasionally.

Take half the pastry from refrigerator, form into a ball, and roll it into a disk about 14 inches in diameter. Line a buttered 10-inch pie dish with pastry. Add alternate layers of macaroni and white sauce, sprinkling each layer with the two cheeses. Roll the remaining pastry thin and adjust loosely over the macaroni. Nicely seal and crimp the two disks of pastry together along the border. With a sharp knife make a few slits on top to allow the steam to escape during baking. Beat the remaining yolk with 1 teaspoon water and brush the top with mixture. Bake in preheated 350 °F oven for 30 minutes, or until the top is nicely browned. Serve hot. **Serves 6.**

1/2 pound elbow macaroni, short ziti, or rigatoni
Butter
1 1/2 cups hot milk
1/4 cup grated Parmesan cheese
1/2 cup shredded Mozzarella cheese

* See instructions on page 42.

TAGLIOLINI COLLA CROCIA AI FUNGHI
Crusty Fettuccine with Mushroom Sauce

Roll dough not too thin and cut into fettuccine.

Bring 6 quarts of water to a boil. Add pasta and salt; when boiling resumes, cook for 1 minute.

Drain well, place in a large bowl with the mushroom sauce, and toss quickly to distribute the sauce evenly. Loosely cover with a clean towel and set aside for a few hours.

Heat 3 tablespoons of oil in a large frying pan. Pour half the dressed fettuccine in the pan and flatten down with a spatula. Cook over very low heat, shaking the pan from time to time, until a golden crust is formed at the bottom. Turn with a dish** and cook until golden on the other side. Repeat with the other half of fettuccine. **Serves 6 to 8.**

*Homemade pasta made with 4 eggs and 2 1/2 to 3 cups flour**
6 quarts water
3 tablespoons salt
3 cups mushroom sauce (page 215)
Olive oil

* See instructions on page 41
** See instructions on page 42 for omelettes.

TAGLIATELLE ALL'EBRAICA
Tagliatelle Jewish Style (Noodle Kugel)

Homemade pasta made with 2 eggs and 1 1/2 cups flour or 3/4 pound fresh fettuccine*
3 quarts water
1 1/2 tablespoons salt
2 tablespoons sugar
2 eggs, slightly beaten
1 cup milk
*2 cups ricotta, moisture reduced***
1/2 cup dark, seedless raisins
1/2 cup pinoli *(pine nuts)*
Grated rind of 1 lemon
1/4 teaspoon cinnamon
Dash ginger
4 tablespoons butter
1/4 cup fine bread crumbs

Roll dough thin and cut into tagliatelle with the largest cutter. Bring 3 quarts of water to a boil. Add tagliatelle and salt. As soon as boiling resumes, drain pasta well and place in a large bowl. (If you use store-bought fresh egg noodles cook half the time recommended by manufacturer.) Add all the other ingredients except butter and mix well to combine.

Butter an oven proof lasagna dish and coat it with bread crumbs. Transfer tagliatelle into it, flatten with a rubber spatula, and dot with butter. Bake in preheated 350 °F oven for approximately 30 minutes. Serve hot or at room temperature. **Serves 6.**

* See instructions on page 41.
.** See instructions on page 43.

TAGLIATELLE COLLE NOCI
Tagliatelle with Walnut Sauce

This pasta was traditionally made by our Christian neighbors on the Friday preceding Christmas, when they refrained from eating any meat. Out of respect for our Christian maids, our mother would make it too.

Homemade pasta made with 4 eggs and 3 cups flour or 1 1/2 pounds fresh fettuccine*
6 quarts water
6 tablespoons salt
1/2 teaspoon cinnamon
2 1/2 cups walnut sauce (page 216)
1/4 cup granulated sugar

Roll dough thin and cut into tagliatelle with the largest cutter.

Bring 6 quarts of water to a boil. Add tagliatelle and salt and cook 2 minutes. (For store-bought noodles follow manufacturer's directions.) Place half the walnut sauce in a warmed serving bowl. Drain tagliatelle and add to bowl. Sprinkle with cinnamon and sugar. Add the remaining sauce, toss to combine and serve. **Serves 6.**

*See instructions on page 41.

I TORTELLI DELLA PORA ADELE
Adele's Homemade Ravioli

Adele was a Christian girl who lived in the Jewish Ghetto and had always worked as a mother's helper in Jewish families. Even after she had grown up, had married, and had children of her own, she was willing to help Mamma whenever she was asked. One day, a few weeks before we set out for the woods to escape the Nazi-fascists, she knocked at our door with a bundle hidden under her shawl. Upon entering the kitchen, she cautiously walked toward the table and lay her bundle on it. Then she painstakingly unfolded the large cloth napkin and revealed an enormous plate of steaming homemade ravioli.

It was a punishable crime to help the Jews at that time, and a double crime to provide them with food other than what was allotted by the rationing system. Yet Adele knew that we often went hungry, and, bless her, she cared for us. She wouldn't have been able to enjoy the special meal she had prepared for her family had she not shared it with us. We dove upon the plate like vultures, oblivious of Adele who stood there watching us with her sweet satisfied smile.

When we came back from our odyssey nearly one year later, Adele was no longer among the living — a victim of the bombings. Even though tortelli prepared in this manner are by no means Adele's invention, in honor of her generous gesture we have called them "Adele's Tortelli" ever since.

1 pound small-leaved bulk spinach
Salt
Olive oil
1 small onion, chopped fine
Freshly ground black pepper
*2 cups ricotta, moisture reduced**
1 tablespoon freshly chopped Italian parsley
*1/2 cup shredded Pecorino Toscano** or Muenster cheese*
1 egg, slightly beaten
1 egg yolk
*Homemade pasta made with 4 eggs and 3 cups flour ****
6 quarts water
3 cups tomato sauce (page 218)
Dash or 2 nutmeg

Use only the leafy part of spinach discarding all stems. Wash in cold water as many times as needed so that no trace of sand remains. Place in a pot with no water other than the water retained from washing. Add a pinch of salt and cook, covered, 5 or 6 minutes. Lift with a fork and squeeze all water out. (It helps to wrap the spinach in a piece of cheese cloth and then to wring it.) Chop spinach very fine.

Heat 2 tablespoons of oil in a skillet with the onion, and saute for about 1 minute. Add spinach and small amounts of salt and pepper. Cook over low heat, stirring frequently, approximately 2 minutes, or until spinach is quite dry. Transfer to a bowl and combine with ricotta, parsley, Pecorino or Muenster cheese, egg, egg yolk, and nutmeg. Taste and correct seasoning if necessary.

Take 1/4 of the dough, roll it thin, and place over a floured cloth. With a pastry brush dipped in cold water, lightly brush the top of the sheet to maintain moisture. Take half the filling mixture and place mounds of it on the sheet in straight lines about 2 inches apart, measuring from the center of mounds. You should obtain 4 or 5 dozen of them. Roll out another 1/4 of the dough and place loosely over the mounds. Press the dough around the mounds with your fingers. With an Italian pastry wheel, press along the furrows, cutting and sealing at the same time. Continue to make ravioli with the remaining pasta and filling.

Bring 6 quarts water to a boil. Add ravioli and 3 tablespoons salt. Stir gently until boiling resumes. Cook, uncovered, 4 to 5 minutes, or until desired tenderness. Drain well and dress with hot tomato sauce.

Serves 6 to 8.

*See instructions on page 43.
** See note on page 80.
*** See instructions on page 41.

TORTELLI DI ZUCCA ALLA SALVIA
Squash Ravioli with Sage Oil

2 1/2 pounds butternut squash
1/2 cup chopped onion
Olive oil
Salt
Freshly ground black pepper
6 quarts water
1 tablespoon freshly chopped Italian parsley
1 egg, slightly beaten
1 egg yolk
*Homemade pasta made with 4 eggs and 2 1/2 to 3 cups flour**

Peel squash and cut in half, lengthwise. Remove all seeds and scrape to remove stringy parts as well. Cut into approximately 1-inch cubes and place in a skillet with onion, 2 tablespoons oil, 1 teaspoon salt, and a dash or two of pepper. Add 1/4 cup water and cook over moderate heat, covered, for 15 minutes. Uncover and continue to cook, stirring, until most liquid has evaporated and squash is reduced to a coarse puree.

Remove from heat and let cool a little. Add parsley, egg and egg yolk, and stir to combine. Return to a very low heat and stir until the egg has lost its rawness and the puree has thickened.

Take one-fourth of the pasta from the refrigerator and roll it thin. Place it over a floured cloth and lightly brush the surface with a pastry brush dipped in cold water to maintain moisture. Take half the filling and place mounds of it in straight lines about 2 inches apart. Roll thin another fourth of the pasta and place it loosely over the mounds. Press around the mounds with your fingers. With an Italian pastry wheel, press along the furrows, cutting and sealing at the same time. Repeat with the remaining pasta and filling.

Place 3/4 cup oil, the sage, and small amounts of salt and pepper into a large skillet. Heat the oil and saute the sage for 1 minute or two. Sprinkle with wine and cook until wine has completely evaporated. Remove and discard sage, but retain the salt and pepper together with the oil.

Bring the water with 3 tablespoons of salt to a boil. Add ravioli and cook 5 minutes or until desired tenderness. Drain thoroughly and add to skillet with the sage oil. Stir until all ravioli are coated with oil and serve.

Serves 6 to 8.

1/4 cup firmly pressed sage leaves
1/4 cup dry white wine

* See instructions on page 41.

TORTELLINI DI CARNE
Meat Tortellini

Heat 2 tablespoons of oil in a medium skillet with onion and garlic. When the garlic becomes lightly golden, add the meats and small amounts of salt and pepper and cook over moderate heat about 10 minutes, stirring occasionally. Remove from heat and chop very fine. Transfer to a medium bowl and combine with the other filling ingredients. Taste and correct seasoning if necessary.

Take half the pasta and roll it thin. Cut into 2-inch squares. Spread 1/4 teaspoon filling diagonally on each square; fold into a triangle along the line of the filling, and fold once more. Lift the little stuffed roll and wrap it around your finger; squeeze the farthest points together. Toss over a large floured cloth where tortellini can fit without touching. Continue until you have finished the first half of pasta, then repeat with the second half until you have used up either pasta or filling or both.

Yields about 15 dozen.

Olive oil
1/2 medium onion, sliced
1/2 clove garlic, sliced
1/2 chicken breast, cubed
1/4 pound lean veal, cubed
Salt
Freshly ground black pepper
2 boiled chestnuts (page 254), mashed
1 teaspoon Bac-O, crushed
2 tablespoons beef bouillion
2 tablespoons bread crumbs
1 egg, slightly beaten
*Homemade pasta made with 4 eggs and 3 cups flour**

* See instructions on page 41.

TORTELLINI VEGETARIANI
Vegetarian Tortellini

1 pound fresh green beans
Olive oil
2 cloves garlic
Salt
Freshly ground black pepper
3/4 cups water
Dash or two nutmeg
1 tablespoon freshly chopped Italian parsley
3/4 cup walnut meats, chopped fine
3/4 cup freshly grated Italian Parmesan cheese
*Homemade pasta made with 4 eggs and 3 cups flour**

Trim and wash green beans and place in a saucepan with 1 tablespoon oil, garlic, salt, pepper, and water. Cook over moderate heat, uncovered, for 5 to 10 minutes, depending on the quality and freshness of the beans. Let cool for a while, then place in the cup of a blender or processor and process until you have a puree. Transfer to a medium-sized bowl and add nutmeg, parsley, walnuts and Parmesan cheese. Mix to combine.

Take half the pasta and roll it thin. Cut into 2-inch squares. Spread 1/4 teaspoon filling diagonally on each square; fold into a triangle along the line of the filling and fold once more. Lift the little stuffed roll and wrap it around your finger; squeeze the farthest points together. Toss on a large floured cloth where tortellini fit without touching. Continue until you have finished the first half of pasta, then repeat with the second half until you have used up either pasta or filling or both.

Yields approximately 15 dozen.

* See instructions on page 41.

TORTELLINI DI CARNE AI FUNGHI
Meat Tortellini with Mushroom Sauce

15 dozen tortellini di carne (page 117)
6 quarts boiling water
3 tablespoons salt
Mushroom sauce (page 215)

Drop tortellini into a large pot with 6 quarts of rapidly boiling water. Add salt and stir gently. When boiling resumes, lower the heat and cook, uncovered, 5 to 6 minutes.

Meanwhile, heat the sauce in a very large skillet. Drain tortellini and transfer them to the skillet with the sauce. Shake the skillet, then gently stir until tortellini are well coated with sauce. Serve immediately.

Serves 6.

TORTELLINI ALLA PANNA
Tortellini in Heavy Cream

15 dozen tortellini vegetariani (page 118)
6 quarts boiling water
3 tablespoons salt
1 pint heavy dairy cream
1 cup freshly grated Italian Parmesan cheese

Drop tortellini into a large pot with 6 quarts of rapidly boiling water. Add salt and stir gently. When boiling resumes, lower the heat and cook, uncovered, 5 to 6 minutes. Drain well.

Heat the cream in a large skillet, but do not allow it to boil. Add the drained tortellini and gently stir over moderate heat, until most of the cream has been absorbed by the tortellini. Turn off the heat, add half the Parmesan cheese, and stir to combine. Serve immediately with the remaining Parmesan cheese in a separate dish. **Serves 6.**

PANZOTTI DI SPINACI
Spinach Panzotti

Panzotti look like overgrown tortellini. Like tortellini they are somewhat laborious to prepare because they require wrapping by hand one by one. However, you can master this art with a little practice, and the reward will be great.

2 pounds small-leaved spinach
Salt
2 tablespoons butter
1 small onion, chopped fine
1 small clove garlic, minced
1/4 teaspoon powdered marjoram
*2/3 cup ricotta, moisture reduced**
2/3 cup freshly grated Italian Parmesan cheese
2 eggs, slightly beaten
*Homemade pasta made with 4 eggs and 3 cups flour***

Use only the leafy parts of spinach. Rinse in cold water as many times as necessary to rid the leaves of any sand. Place in a large pot with no water other than the water retained by the leaves from washing. Add a pinch of salt and cook covered over high heat for 5 or 6 minutes. Drain and squeeze all water out.*** Chop spinach very fine.

Heat the butter in a skillet and saute onion and garlic in it for approximately 1 minute. Add spinach, marjoram, and 1 teaspoon salt, and cook, stirring, 2 minutes more or until spinach looks quite dry. Transfer to a bowl and combine with ricotta, Parmesan cheese and eggs. Taste and correct seasoning if necessary.

Roll pasta to medium thinness (one half at a time). Cut into 3-inch squares. Fill each square with 1 teaspoon of filling mixture, and fold diagonally into triangles. When the triangles are all lined up, take one and fold once more in the same direction; then pick up the two ends and bring them together. Press firmly to seal. Repeat with the rest of the stuffed triangles until they have all become panzotti, big bellies. **Yields 7 or 8 dozen.**

* See instructions on page 43.
.** See instructions on page 41.
*** See instructions on page 44.

PANZOTTI DI SPINACI AL BURRO E PARMIGIANO
Spinach Panzotti with Butter and Parmesan Cheese

Some purists coat boiled panzotti by holding in one hand a stick of butter and passing it over the steaming panzotti one by one. I find this orthodoxy unnecessary and actually undesirable, since by the time all the panzotti are coated with butter they have become cold. My method is less tedious and works just as well.

6 quarts rapidly boiling water
7 or 8 dozen panzotti (see preceding recipe)
3 tablespoons salt
1/4 pound unsalted butter at room temperature
1 1/2 cups freshly grated Italian Parmesan cheese

Add panzotti and salt to the pot with 6 quarts of rapidly boiling water and cook, uncovered, 3 to 4 minutes or until desired tenderness. Warm a large serving bowl and slice half the butter into it. Add 1/4 cup of boiling water from cooking panzotti and stir a little.

Drain panzotti well and add to the bowl. Slice the remaining butter over them and toss gently just until all the panzotti are coated. While tossing, sprinkle half the Parmesan cheese so that the panzotti are coated with cheese as well. Serve immediately with the remaining grated cheese in a separate dish. **Serves 6 to 8.**

PANZOTTI DI SPINACI CON SALSA DI NOCI
Spinach Panzotti with Walnut Sauce

Add panzotti and salt to the rapidly boiling water, and cook, uncovered, 3 to 4 minutes or until desired tenderness.

Warm a large serving bowl and place half the sauce into it. Drain panzotti and add to the bowl. Add the remaining sauce and toss gently just until all the panzotti are coated. Serve immediately. **Serve 6 to 8.**

6 quarts rapidly boiling water
7 or 8 dozen panzotti (page 119)
3 tablespoons salt
2 1/2 cups walnut sauce at room temperature (page 216)

LASAGNE ALL'ARANCIA
Lasagna with Orange Sauce

Heat 4 tablespoons butter in a saucepan. Add flour and cook, stirring, until the mixture acquires a light-brown color. Add the orange juice all at once and stir vigorously to avoid lumps. Add 1/2 teaspoon salt and cook 5 minutes, stirring occasionally. Remove from the heat, add the orange sections and the walnut meats and mix.

Beat the ricotta with the sugar until light and fluffy. Add the raisins and orange rind, and stir to combine.

Roll the pasta thin and cut into strips about 5x8 inches. Bring 6 quarts of water with 3 tablespoons salt to a boil. Cook a few strips of dough at a time for 2 minutes, uncovered. Remove from boiling water and drop into a bowl with cold water. Drain and spread over a lightly damp cloth.

Coat the bottom of a large lasagna dish with butter. Starting with pasta, make layers, alternating pasta with orange sauce and ricotta mixture, and ending with orange sauce. Bake in 400 °F oven for 20 minutes or until edges begin to brown. **Serves 8 to 12.**

Unsalted butter
4 tablespoons unbleached flour
2 1/2 cups orange juice
Salt
1 cup orange sections, peeled and diced
1/2 cup coarsely chopped walnut meats
2 pounds whole milk ricotta
2 tablespoons sugar
1/2 cup dark seedless raisins
1 tablespoon grated orange rind
*Homemade pasta made with 5 eggs and 3 cups flour**
6 quarts water

* See instructions on page 41.

LASAGNE CON SPINACI E RICOTTA
Lasagna with Spinach and Ricotta

2 pounds small-leaved bulk spinach
Salt
3/4 cup butter
2 tablespoons finely chopped onion
Freshly ground black pepper
Dash or two nutmeg
*Homemade pasta made with 5 eggs and 3 cups flour**
6 quarts water
*2 pounds ricotta, moisture reduced***
1 1/2 cups freshly grated Italian Parmesan cheese

Use only the leafy part of the spinach. Rinse in cold water as many times as necessary to rid the leaves of any trace of sand. Place in a large pot with no water other than what clings to the leaves. Add a pinch of salt and cook, covered, for 5 or 6 minutes. Drain well*** and chop fine.

Heat 4 tablespoons butter in a large skillet; add onion, and saute 2 or 3 minutes. Add spinach and small amounts of salt, pepper, and nutmeg. Cook over moderate heat for 4 or 5 minutes, stirring frequently. Transfer to a bowl and add ricotta and 1/4 cup Parmesan cheese. Mix lightly, taste for salt and correct if necessary, and set aside.

Roll pasta thin and cut into strips about 5x8 inches. Bring 6 quarts of water to a boil with 3 tablespoons salt. Cook a few strips of dough at a time for 2 minutes, uncovered. Remove from boiling water and drop into a basin with cold water. Drain and spread over a slightly damp cloth.

Coat the bottom of a large lasagna baking dish with butter. Starting with pasta, make alternate layers with spinach mixture. Dot the spinach layer with butter and sprinkle it with Parmesan cheese; end with pasta, butter and Parmesan cheese. Bake in 400 °F oven for approximately 20 minutes. Serve with remaining cheese in a separate dish. **Serves 8 to 12.**

* See instructions on page 41.
** See instructions on page 43.
*** See instructions on page 44.

MAZZAGNE CON RAGU E SALSA DI FUNGHI
Matza Lasagna with Meat Ragu and Mushroom Sauce

Passover lasts eight days, and given the limitations imposed by the dietary laws, one has to use imagination in order to have variety during this period. Using his imagination is just what my brother Mario, a mathematician at the University of Parma, did when he devised *mazzagne.* As the name suggests, mazzagne is a lasagna made with store-bought matzot instead of the characteristic wide noodles.

Cover the bottom of a lasagna baking dish with a thin film of oil. Make alternate layers of sauces and uncooked matza, ending with a sauce. Pour the broth over the prepared matza lasagna, cover with aluminum foil, and let rest in the refrigerator for 1 hour, or until matza is quite soaked.

Place in preheated 350 °F oven, covered, for 10 minutes. Remove the foil and bake another 10 to 15 minutes. **Serves 6 to 8.**

Olive oil
2 cups mushroom sauce (page 215) and 1cup ragu (page 218)
8 egg matzot
1 cup beef or chicken broth

MAZZAGNE AL PESTO

Matza Lasagna with Pesto Sauce

Coat the bottom of a deep square baking dish slightly larger than the matza with pesto.

Make alternate layers with uncooked matza, pesto sauce with dollops of ricotta sauce. Continue to make layers until you have exhausted all the ingredients. End with the ricotta sauce. Pour all the milk over the prepared mazzagna, cover with aluminum foil, and bake in preheated 350 °F oven for 30 minutes. Serve hot or at room temperature. **Serves 6 to 8.**

2 cups pesto sauce (page 213)
8 egg matzot
2 cups ricotta sauce (recipe follows)
1 cup milk

SALSA DI RICOTTA PER PESACH

Passover Ricotta Sauce

Heat the butter and flour in a saucepan and cook 2 minutes, stirring frequently. Add the milk all at once, and cook another 2 minutes, stirring vigorously with a wire whisk.

Add ricotta and simmer, stirring, until ricotta is almost completely melted. **Yields approximately 2 cups.**

4 tablespoons unsalted butter
*6 tablespoons Passover cake flour**
1 1/2 cups hot milk
1 cup ricotta

* See page 42 for comments on this flour

SFOGLIETTI PER PESACH AL RAGU
Passover Sfoglietti with Meat Sauce

Sfoglietti is a homemade pasta which can be used during the eight days of Passover. Pasta, in general, is not allowed on Passover. However sfoglietti — which was devised by the Italian Jews, who would not give up their taste for pasta even during Passover — differs from other pastas in two ways. It is made with the same flour that is used to make matzot, and it is baked as soon as it is rolled thin to prevent leavening. Pasta that has been prebaked has a different texture from ordinary pasta, and this difference provides a delightful gourmet experience.

4 eggs, slightly beaten
*3 cups Passover flour**
4 quarts water
2 tablespoons salt
3 cups hot ragu sauce (page 218)

Mix eggs with enough flour to make a rather hard dough. Divide into 16 pieces. With rolling pin or with machine rollers, roll each piece very thin, toss on baking sheet and bake immediately in 550 °F oven (higher if your oven goes to more than 550 °F) for approximately 2 minutes. Turn over and bake 1 minute longer. Sfoglietti should be well dried but not browned. Remove from oven, cool, and break into large, uneven pieces.

Bring 4 quarts of water to a boil; add sfoglietti and salt and cook, uncovered, 3 to 4 minutes. Drain and dress with hot sauce. Serve immediately. **Serves 6.**

NOTE: Sfoglietti can be prepared ahead of time and stored for later use in a plastic bag after they are thoroughly cooled and broken up. They will keep fresh for the eight days of Passover and beyond.

* See comments on page 42.

GNOCCHI DI PATATE ALLA CAPRESE
Gnocchi Capri Style

3 pounds baking potatoes
1 egg, slightly beaten
Salt
2 1/2 cups unbleached flour

Boil or steam potatoes until very soft. Peel while still hot, and mash or force through a sieve (do not use blender or food processor). After the potatoes cool a little, add eggs and 1/2 teaspoon salt and stir to combine. Add enough flour to make a soft dough and pour onto a floured surface. Divide into 6 or 8 pieces, then roll each piece into a rope, 3/4-inch thick. Cut ropes into 1-inch pieces and roll in flour to prevent sticking.

For a more elegant appearance, roll each *gnocco* over the teeth of a fork or in the under part of a cheese grater; otherwise just make a depression at center of each one with your finger.

Oil a large baking dish and sprinkle with some sauce.

Bring 4 quarts of water with 2 tablespoons salt to a boil. Add 1/4 of the gnocchi. As soon as boiling resumes and gnocchi come to the surface, remove with a slotted spoon and transfer to the baking dish. Sprinkle with tomato sauce, top with 1/4 of the mozzarella, dust with small amounts of oregano and pepper, and drizzle with oil. Repeat with the remaining gnocchi and condiments.

Bake in preheated 400 °F oven for 15 to 20 minutes. **Serves 6.**

4 quarts water
Olive oil
1 cup tomato sauce (page 218)
3/4 pound mozzarella di bufala, shredded
Oregano
Freshly ground black pepper

GNOCCHETTI DI PATATE AL GORGONZOLA

Small Potato Dumplings with Gorgonzola Cheese

Gnocchetti is one of the many culinary inventions of Giovanna's. Yet Giovanna is not a professional cook. She is one of those amazing persons who can do anything well. Giovanna is a professor of English literature in the English department at the University of Bologna; as a literary critic specializing in the Gothic and the Romantic novel, she has published many acclaimed works in the field, in Italian as well as in English. And as a native Bolognese, she has an innate flair for cooking.

Giovanna is not Jewish, but she knows about the Jewish dietary laws, and when I asked her for a contribution for my new book, she came up with this delightful dish.

3 pounds baking potatoes
2 1/2 cups unbleached flour
1/4 cup freshly grated Italian Parmesan cheese
1 egg, slightly beaten

4 quarts water
Salt
1 pint heavy cream
1/4 pound Gorgonzola cheese, crumbled
1/3 cup chopped walnut or pecan meats

Boil or steam potatoes until very soft. Peel while still hot and mash or force through a sieve. (Do not use blender or food processor.) Add Parmesan cheese and stir to cool a little. Add egg and stir to combine. Add enough flour to make a soft dough. Knead 2 minutes on a floured board. Cut into 6 or 8 pieces. Roll each piece into a 1/2-inch rope. Cut ropes into 1/2-inch bits, sprinkling with flour to prevent sticking.

Bring 4 quarts water with 2 tablespoons salt to a boil. Add one-fourth of the gnocchetti. As soon as boiling resumes and gnocchetti float to the surface, remove with a slotted spoon and place in a colander to drain. Continue with the remaining gnocchetti.

Heat the heavy cream in a large skillet without letting it boil. Add gnocchetti and gently stir until they have absorbed the cream. Remove from heat, sprinkle Gorgonzola over gnocchetti, and stir once more. Pour on a heated serving plate, sprinkle top with chopped nuts and serve.

Serves 6.

POLENTA

Polenta, a staple among the Italian peasants, used to be served in the homes of city dwellers only on occasion. In recent years, however, polenta has found its way among people with more sophisticated palates both in Italy and in America, and it is finally recognized for the true delicacy it is.

Some people, here in America, think that they don't like polenta because they associate it with corn mush. But aside from their corn derivation, the two dishes have very little in common as far as texture, versatility, and even flavor are concerned.

In my parents' household polenta was very rarely served. I learned to like it when I was living with the peasants who sheltered us from the Nazi-fascists during World War II, and since then it has been one of my most favorite foods.

In America, as a married woman, I got into the ritual of making polenta when the first snow whitened the grounds, and made it again once or twice during the cold season. It was a laborious task I could not afford to undertake too often. Eventually I devised a simpler method of cooking it than the one used by the Italian peasants, and I now enjoy polenta in its many forms quite often.

Below is the basic recipe for making polenta followed by a few classic polenta dishes. Other recipes involving polenta may be found in the meat and in the fish sections.

3 cups yellow cornmeal
6 cups water
1 tablespoon salt

Mix 2 cups of cornmeal with 2 cups of cold water. Bring 4 cups of water with 1 tablespoon salt to a boil. Gradually drop the corn mixture into the boiling water while stirring with a large wooden spoon.* Continue to stir until boiling resumes. Simmer for 10 minutes, stirring frequently. Add the remaining cornmeal a handful at a time while stirring vigorously. Cook 10 minutes more, stirring occasionally, to ensure no burning or sticking of polenta to the bottom of the pot.

Remove from heat. With a flat wooden spatula dipped in cold water, separate the mass of polenta from the walls of the pot, gently tapering it towards the center. Dip the spatula in cold water very frequently, so that the polenta doesn't stick to it.

Return the pot to the burner and raise the heat very high for 1 or 2 minutes without stirring. The hot steam will separate the polenta from the bottom of the pot, although some will stick to the bottom at this point.**

Holding the pot firmly, turn it over a wooden board in one swift motion. A cheese-like round cake of polenta will come down. Cover with a clean kitchen towel and let rest 2 or 3 minutes before slicing.

To slice freshly made polenta, hold a 20-inch piece of white string at tension between your thumbs and forefingers. Slide it under the cake of polenta to the thickness of the slice you want to cut (generally 1/2 to 2 inches). Still holding the string with both hands, pull it upward so that, in passing through, it cuts one slice. Give one slice at a time and keep the remaining polenta covered to maintain heat.

Serve with *Ciccio and Cavolo Riccio, Spezzatino, Gulyas, Baccala' colla Cipolla, or Ricotta.* **Serves 6 or more.**

NOTE: Cutting polenta with a string is part of the fun. After it gets cold and firm, however, you must use a sharp knife. Keep leftover polenta refrigerated no longer than a day; you may freeze it for longer periods, but although the flavor remains more or less the same, the texture is definitely no longer like the fresh one.

* I brought a special wooden spatula from Italy. If you can't find one in specialty stores, use a 20-inch section from a new, unpainted wooden broomstick, washed with bleach and rinsed thoroughly.

** As soon as you have poured the polenta, place the pot under the faucet and half fill it with cold water. When you are ready to clean the pot, you will find that the polenta that stuck to it will easily peel off.

POLENTA COL CACIO
Polenta with Cheese

Cacio is the generic term for cheese. In this case, however, the term cacio had a very specific connotation. It meant cheese that was freshly made from sheep milk, and used before it had a chance to form a crust. This cheese is formally called *Pecorino fresco,* not to be confused with *Pecorino Romano* or *Sardo,* which are both aged and very sharp. Pecorino fresco is not treated to last. It is mild, soft, and has a delicious creamy consistency. If finding pecorino fresco is a bit of a problem, Muenster cheese is a satisfactory substitute.

1 cake freshly made polenta (page 126)
1/4 unsalted butter, melted
4 cups shredded Pecorino fresco or *Muenster cheese*

As soon as polenta has been turned onto the wooden board, cover it with a clean kitchen towel for a couple of minutes. Then, as described in the preceding recipe, cut 1/2-inch slices with the string. When you have cut the first slice, pull it gently with your fingers toward you to separate it from the rest of the cake, and quickly place it in a large heated and buttered serving plate. Repeat until you have made a first layer of slices. Brush with melted butter and smother with cheese. Continue to make layers until you have finished all the ingredients.

Serve immediately. **Serves 6.**

NOTE: For a more rustic polenta, omit the butter, serve each slice coated with cheese individually, and pass the pepper mill.

POLENTA BIANCA PASTICCIATA PER SHAVUOT

Shavuot Baked White-corn Polenta

3 cups white corn meal
6 cups cold water
1 tablespoon salt
Unsalted butter
4 tablespoons unbleached flour
2 cups hot milk
1 pound mozzarella di bufala, shredded
1 cup freshly grated Italian Parmesan cheese

Prepare polenta as described on page 126. Let it cool for several hours or overnight.

Make a white sauce with 4 tablespoons butter, 4 tablespoons flour, and the hot milk.*

With a sharp knife, cut the polenta into 1/2-inch slices. Place 1/3 of the slices in a well-buttered baking dish and smear with one third of the white sauce. Sprinkle 1/3 of the shredded cheese and continue to make layers until you have used up all the ingredients (except for the Parmesan cheese). Dot with butter and place in 350 °F oven for 30 minutes or until the top begins to brown. Serve hot with the Parmesan cheese in a separate dish. **Serves 8.**

* You can prepare the white sauce the traditional way: saute the butter and flour for a couple of minutes, then add the hot milk all at once while stirring vigorously with a wire whisk and cook a few more minutes. Or, you can use the blender white sauce of page 216.

POLENTA ABBRUSTOLITA
Toasted Polenta

1 cold cake of polenta (page 126)
2 tablespoons butter
4 cups ricotta at room temperature
1 cup honey, hot

With a sharp knife cut polenta into 1/2-inch slices. Line up on a well-buttered baking sheet. Place on the rack closest to the broiler and broil for 6 minutes or until the tops get dark brown. Turn slices and brown the other side.

Transfer to a hot serving plate. Spread ricotta over slices, then pour the hot honey over ricotta. Serve immediately. **Serves 8.**

NOTE: You can serve the toasted polenta, ricotta, and hot honey separately, so that the family or the guests may help themselves to as much ricotta and honey as they wish.

POLENTA FRITTA
Fried Polenta

1/2 cake day-old cold polenta (page 126)
1 cup olive or other vegetable oil for frying

Cut polenta into 1/2-inch slices with a sharp knife. Heat the oil in a frying pan (preferably non-stick) and fry the slices, in a single layer, for 5 to 6 minutes on each side, or until a golden crust is formed. Transfer to a paper towel to drain excess oil. Sprinkle with salt and serve as a snack. **Serves 4 to 6.**

NOTE: For a more elegant *Polenta Fritta* to be served as a side dish, make polenta as described on page 126 up to when polenta is ready to be removed from heat. Instead of making a bulky cake out of it, spread it 1/2 inch thick over an oiled surface. When it is cold, cut with cookie cutters into disks, diamonds, stars, etc., and proceed as above. Omit the salt.

CRESPELLE ALLA FIORENTINA
Crepes Florentine

These crepes taste better if you can make them with *Pecorino fresco* — a sweet cheese made from sheep milk — which differs from region to region according to pasture and local taste. In Florence, of course, we used *Pecorino Toscano.* If you don't find it, Muenster cheese is an acceptable substitute.

2 pounds small-leaved bulk spinach or 2 10-ounce packages frozen spinach
3 tablespoons olive oil
1 medium onion, chopped fine
1/2 pound finely chopped white mushrooms
2 tablespoons freshly chopped Italian parsley
Salt
Freshly ground black pepper
Dash nutmeg
Milk
Unbleached flour
Unsalted butter
1 1/2 cups shredded Pecorino fresco or Muenster cheese
6 eggs, slightly beaten

Remove stems from spinach and wash leaves until no trace of sand remains. Cook without any additional water other than the water retained from washing. Drain, get rid of most liquid*, and finely chop.

Heat the oil in a large skillet. Add onion and saute 2 minutes. Add spinach, mushrooms, and parsley; lightly season with salt, pepper, and nutmeg and saute 3 more minutes. Remove from heat.

Make a white sauce by heating 6 tablespoons butter with 6 tablespoons flour. Add 2 cups hot milk all at once and stir vigorously with a wire whisk while cooking for 4 or 5 minutes. Take 1 cup of white sauce and 1/2 cup of cheese and add to the spinach mixture; stir and set aside.

Make a batter combining eggs, 1 1/2 cups milk, 1 1/2 cups flour, and 1 teaspoon salt. Heat 1 tablespoon butter in a 8-inch skillet. Add 1/3 cup batter and tilt the skillet in a rotating motion to spread the batter evenly. Cook for 1 or 2 minutes or until firm, with bottom slightly brown. Invert on a clean, damp cloth on the table. Repeat, using less butter to grease the pan, until you have used up the batter (12 or more crepes.)

Divide the spinach mixture among the crepes, spread over each one, and roll up. Arrange in a well buttered oven-proof dish in a single layer.

Add 1 cup milk to the remaining white sauce, mix in the remaining cheese, and pour over the crepes. Bake in preheated 375 °F oven for 1/2 hour. Remove from oven and let stand 5 to 10 minutes before serving.

Serves 6.

* See instructions on page 44.

Carne

BEEF, VEAL, LAMB, POULTRY

BUE
Beef

POLPETTONE DI MANZO
Meat Loaf

2 pounds lean ground beef
2 eggs, slightly beaten
Seasoned bread crumbs
Salt
Freshly ground black pepper
*2 hard-boiled eggs, shelled**
1/2 cup olive oil
1 1/2 cups tomato sauce (page 218)
1/2 cup warm water
1 large clove garlic, sliced
1 tablespoon freshly chopped Italian parsley

In a large bowl, combine meat, beaten eggs, 1/4 cup bread crumbs, and salt and pepper to taste. Mix well. Spread half the mixture over an oiled piece of plastic wrap. Place 1 hard-boiled egg at the center. With the help of the plastic wrap, enclose the egg inside the meat, trying to avoid pockets of air, and form a large, egg-shaped loaf. Roll in bread crumbs. Repeat with the remaining meat mixture and egg.

Heat 4 tablespoons of oil in a large non-stick skillet and fry the two loaves in it until nicely browned on all sides. Remove to a fish poacher or large saucepan. Add tomato sauce and warm water and cook over moderate heat, covered, for 30 minutes, turning loaves occasionally. Make sure the loaves don't stick to the bottom of the pan. Add the remaining oil, garlic, and parsley and cook 5 minutes longer. Remove from heat and let cool for 5 or 6 minutes.

Slice carefully so that the egg remains in its place. Arrange the slices on a hot serving plate and pour the gravy over them. **Serves 6 to 8.**

* See instructions on page 38.

SCALOPPINE ALLA PIZZAIOLA
Beef Scaloppine Pizzaiola

Olive oil
1 1/2 pounds lean beef, sliced very thin
1 teaspoon salt
2 cloves garlic, sliced
*1 1/2 cups fresh or canned peeled tomatoes**
1/8 to 1/4 teaspoon crushed hot red pepper
1 teaspoon oregano
1 tablespoon freshly chopped Italian parsley

In a large skillet, heat 3 tablespoons of oil. Add the meat and quickly brown over high heat for approximately 1 minute on each side. Remove from heat, transfer the meat to a warmed dish, and season with salt on both sides.

Wipe the skillet clean with a paper towel. Add the remaining 3 tablespoons of oil and the garlic and place over moderate heat until garlic is lightly browned. Add tomatoes; raise the heat and cook 2 to 3 minutes stirring frequently. Return meat to the skillet. Add pepper, oregano, and parsley and simmer, covered, for 5 minutes. **Serves 4.**

* See instructions on page 45.

NOTE: Scaloppine pizzaiola may be prepared as much as two or three days ahead of time and refrigerated. Reheated just before serving, they will actually taste better.

ROTOLO DI CARNE RIPIENO
Stuffed Flank Steak

Olive oil
1 small onion, chopped fine
1 small carrot, peeled and shredded
1 5-inch celery stalk, chopped fine
1 slice day-old bread
1/4 cup beef stock or water
1/2 pound ground veal
1 egg slightly beaten
1/4 cup coarsely chopped walnut meats
1 1/2 teaspoons salt
1/4 teaspoon black pepper
1 1/2 pounds flank steak
1 clove garlic, slightly crushed

Place 2 tablespoons of oil, onion, carrot, and celery in a small saucepan over medium heat, and cook 2 minutes, stirring. Remove from heat and add bread and stock or water. After a minute or two, place over high heat and cook 2 minutes, or until most liquid has evaporated. Transfer to a bowl. Add ground veal, salt and pepper, and mix to combine.

Remove all fat and skin from the flank steak. Rub with garlic on both sides and lay it on a working surface. Shape the ground-meat mixture into an oval ball about as long as the width of the steak; place at the center of the steak. Roll the steak and place in an oiled loaf pan with seam side down. With a sharp knife, gash the top against the grain, brush it with oil and place in a 375 °F oven for 1 to 1 1/2 hours, or until fork tender. **Serves 6.**

ARROSTO DI MANZO
Roast Beef

3 pounds boneless rib roast, trimmed
1 clove garlic, crushed
1 teaspoon salt
1/4 teaspoon freshly ground black pepper
1/8 teaspoon ground clove
1/2 teaspoon rosemary leaves
1/2 cup dry white wine
1 cup olive oil
1 1/2 cup sliced zucchini, mushrooms or artichokes

Rub crushed garlic all over the meat. Evenly season with salt, pepper, clove, and rosemary. Place in a small bowl, add wine and let rest in a cool place for several hours or overnight, turning once.

Transfer the meat to a small saucepan where it fits snugly. Reserve the marinate-the wine and the spices left in the bowl. Add all the oil to the meat and cook over high heat, turning, until well browned on all sides. Add the reserved marinate. After 2 or 3 minutes, lower the heat and cook, uncovered, 20 minutes longer, turning occasionally. If meat becomes too dry, add a few drops of water. Remove from heat, pour most of the oil into a skillet and reserve. Cover the pan and let rest for a few minutes.

Meanwhile, quickly stir fry sliced vegetable in the reserved skillet with oil. Slice the roast and strain the gravy over it. Serve surrounded by the stir-fried vegetable.

Serves 6.

GULYAS COLLA POLENTA
Gulasch with Polenta

2 1/2 pounds boneless beef shank
1/2 cup olive oil
1 clove garlic, crushed
2 bay leaves
1 teaspoon rosemary leaves
1 cup diced onion
Salt
1/4 teaspoon crushed red pepper
1 6-ounce can tomato paste
2 cups beef stock or water
2 quarts water
2 cups coarse corn meal

Cut the meat into 1-inch cubes. Place oil, garlic, bay leaf and rosemary leaves in a large skillet. Saute, stirring, until garlic is browned. Sprinkle with water a couple of times to release the flavors from the herbs. With a fork, remove and discard the herbs. Add the onion and saute until soft. Add the meat, 2 teaspoons salt, and the pepper, and brown, stirring, 5 minutes. Add the tomato paste and saute, stirring, another 2 minutes. Add 1 cup of beef stock or water and cook, covered, 2 hours, adding more liquid as necessary. Keep cooking while polenta is being made.

Start polenta by bringing two quarts of water with 1 tablespoon salt to a rapid boil. Lower heat, add corn meal all at once, and stir vigorously. Cook 20 minutes, stirring frequently to prevent sticking. Spoon polenta directly into each individual dish and top with a portion of gulasch.

Serves 6 to 8.

CIMALINO BRASATO
Brazed Calicle

Combine salt and pepper on a piece of waxed paper. Roll the meat over the mixture until completely coated. Place in a pan with oil, onion, carrots, and celery. Brown thoroughly on all sides. Add wine, and after 1 minute lower the heat. Cover tightly and simmer for approximately 1 hour. Check the liquid and add a few tablespoons of water, if necessary. Tightly cover again and cook another hour.

Temporarily transfer the meat to a dish and strain the gravy and vegetables through a sieve. Add flour to gravy and mix to combine. Return meat and gravy to the pan; add parsley and simmer, covered, until fork tender — approximately 1/2 hour. Serve sliced, topped with its own gravy. **Serves 6 to 8.**

2 teaspoons salt
1/4 teaspoon freshly ground black pepper
2 to 3 pounds calicle, trimmed
6 tablespoons olive oil
1 medium onion, sliced
2 carrots, peeled and sliced
2 stalks celery, cut up
1/2 cup red wine
1 tablespoon unbleached flour
1 tablespoon freshly chopped Italian parsley

LUGANEGA
Venetian Beef Sausage

This beef sausage is not intended to be preserved for long periods as other sausages are: it should be consumed within four or five days. However, it tastes better if kept for three or four days in the refrigerator before using it. It is not necessary to stuff it into casing and it is, therefore, very easy to prepare.

In a meat grinder or food processor, grind the meat (together with fat if desired). Add seasoning and process a few more seconds to combine.

Roll out in the form of a rope, or make small balls with it. Arrange over a large plate in a spiral, or, if you make balls, spread in a single layer. Store, uncovered, in the refrigerator, where it will keep four or five days without spoiling. During this period turn it once to allow the bottom side to dry.

Serve as an appetizer in an antipasto platter or cooked with a vegetable as in the following recipe. **Serves 6.**

*The original recipe, given to me by a Venetian Jew whose family has resided in Venice for centuries, called for fat. However, I never use fat in my ground meat, and the flavor of my version, if not the texture, is superior.

2 pounds lean beef cubes
1/2 pound white beef fat (optional)*
1 clove garlic, passed through a garlic press
1 1/2 tablespoons salt
1 teaspoon freshly ground black pepper
1/8 teaspoon ground clove

LUGANEGA COI FAGIOLI
Venetian Beef Sauce and Beans

1 cup dried white beans
5 cups hot water
1 teaspoon salt
1 clove garlic, husk on
2 large sage leaves
Olive oil
Luganega *of the preceding recipe*
2 heaping tablespoons tomato paste, diluted in 1 cup warm water

Remove stone or any debris from beans. Rinse twice in warm water. Place in a large saucepan with 5 cups of hot water and 1 teaspoon salt. Bring to a boil; then reduce heat and simmer, covered, for 45 minutes.

Add garlic and sage. After 5 minutes add 4 or 5 tablespoons of olive oil, luganega cut into bite-size pieces, and the diluted tomato paste. Simmer, uncovered, shaking the pan from time to time, for 1/2 hour or until the sausage is fork tender and the beans are done but not mushy. The sauce should be thick and savory. Remove garlic and sage before serving. **Serves 8.**

ZUCCHINE RIPIENE
Meat-stuffed Zucchini

For this dish to be authentic, you would need *zucchine Fiorentine* which are very thin and straight. On the other hand, to remove the pulp from these tiny zucchini requires the use of a suitable instrument called *sgubbia* which I was never able to find in America. The second best choice is to use medium-sized zucchini which are more readily available in American markets, and can be cored with a small teaspoon or a sharp penknife.

12 small to medium zucchini
1 1/4 pounds lean ground beef
1 egg, slightly beaten
*2 thick slices stale bread, soaked and cooked into a pap**
1 tablespoon freshly chopped Italian parsley
1 teaspoon salt
1/4 teaspoon freshly ground black pepper
Dash nutmeg or cinnamon
2 cups tomato sauce
6 tablespoons olive oil

Gently core zucchini without breaking the outer shell. Reserve 2 tablespoons of the pulp, finely chopped.

Place meat, egg, pap, parsley, salt, pepper, nutmeg, and the reserved zucchini pulp in a bowl. Mix well to combine. Fill zucchini shells with this mixture and place in an oiled baking dish where they fit. Add tomato sauce and oil. Cover with aluminum foil and bake in 375 °F oven for 1 hour, or until zucchini are in a thick and savory sauce. **Serves 4.**

* See instructions on page 39.

CICCIO E CAVOLO RICCIO
Meats and Kale for Polenta

Ciccio (pronounced chee-cho) is another way of saying *carne,* meat, especially a variety of fried meats. *Cavolo riccio,* kale, generally accompanies the fried meats, but any green leafy vegetable such as spinach or dandelion also goes well with it.

2 pounds fresh small-leaved kale
1 cup water
Salt
Olive oil
12 bite-size frankfurters
12 balls or 1-inch pieces luganega *(page 135)*
6 1/4-inch slices kosher salami
6 chicken livers, soaked in cold water
1 clove garlic, minced
1 cake freshly made polenta (page 126)

Remove stems and larger leaves from kale. Rinse and place in a large pot with 1 cup water and 1/2 teaspoon salt. Cook over high heat, covered, for 10 minutes or until tender. Transfer to a colander to drain.

In a large skillet place 6 tablespoons of oil, frankfurters, luganega, and salami. Gently fry until meats are lightly browned.

Drain chicken livers. Remove and discard fat and discolored parts. Cut livers in half and add to skillet with meats. Fry an additional 5 minutes, stirring. Remove from heat and transfer the meats to a hot serving plate, leaving the oil in the skillet.

Add garlic to the skillet and saute until lightly golden. Add cooked kale and saute, stirring occasionally, 5 more minutes, or until kale is crisp and dry. Transfer to the plate with meats. Serve with hot slices of polenta.

Serves 6 to 8.

POLPETTINE DI CARNE E PATATE
Meat and Potato Patties

This dish was obviously born to make use of leftover meat. Its plebeian origin notwithstanding, it is a very pleasant dish you can serve with a soup and/or a tossed salad for lunch or even at dinner.

1 1/2 cups cooked meat, cubed
2 or 3 medium boiling potatoes, cooked, peeled, and mashed
2 eggs, slightly beaten

Grind the meat and combine with potatoes, eggs, parsley, garlic, and nutmeg. Add salt and pepper to taste and mix very well.

Spoon by the heaping tablespoon onto your oiled hands and shape into round patties. Roll in fine bread crumbs* and pat to remove excess.

1 tablespoon freshly chopped Italian parsley
1 small clove garlic, minced
Salt
Freshly ground black pepper
Dash nutmeg
1 cup fine bread crumbs (optional)
Vegetable oil for frying

Heat the oil in a large skillet and fry until golden brown on both sides. Serve immediately. **Serves 6 to 8.**

*This is exactly how the recipe was given to me. However, I have made these patties without rolling them in bread crumbs and they are fine that way as well.

VITELLO
Veal

SCALOPPINE AL MARSALA
Veal Scaloppine with Marsala Wine

1 1/2 pounds veal scaloppine, sliced very thin
1 teaspoon salt
1/8 teaspoon freshly ground white pepper
1/2 cup unbleached flour
Olive oil
1/2 cup imported dry Marsala wine
1/2 cup orange juice

Sprinkle scaloppine with salt and pepper; dredge with flour and pat to shake off excess.

Heat 4 tablespoons of oil in a large skillet and lightly brown scaloppine 1 1/2 to 2 minutes on each side over moderately high heat. Add Marsala and cook over high heat until all liquid has evaporated. Transfer scaloppine to a hot serving plate.

Add orange juice to skillet and simmer for 1 or 2 minutes, scraping the bottom. Pour this gravy over the scaloppine and serve immediately. **Serves 4 to 6.**

OSSIBUCHI COI PISELLI
Veal Shanks with Peas

Cut skin at 2 or 3 points around the circumference of the ossibuchi so that the skin, on shrinking, does not bunch the meat out of shape. Lightly flour shank pieces on all sides.

Chop garlic, parsley and basil together very fine and place half of this mixture in a large skillet together with onion, carrot and oil. Saute, stirring, 1 to 2 minutes. Add ossibuchi in a single layer and brown 2 minutes on each side. Add wine and raise the heat to let the wine evaporate completely. Add tomato paste and scrape the bottom of the skillet with a wooden spatula to loosen stuck particles. Add 1 cup of stock or water, shake pan, and simmer, covered, 1 1/2 hours, scraping the glaze occasionally.

Add the remaining liquid as it becomes necessary, but keep the ossibuchi in a thick, savory sauce at all times. When meat begins to separate from bone, add the remaining garlic mixture, lemon rind, and peas. Cook 10 more minutes, or until peas are tender but not mushy and the sauce is thick and flavorful. **Serves 4 to 6.**

6 slices veal shank (about 4 1/2 pounds)
Unbleached flour
1 clove garlic
2 sprigs Italian parsley
2 large basil leaves
1/4 cup chopped onion
1 carrot, peeled and diced
6 tablespoon olive oil
1/2 cup dry white wine
2 teaspoons salt
1/4 teaspoon freshly ground black pepper
2 dashes nutmeg
2 teaspoons tomato paste
2 cups beef stock or water
1 teaspoon grated lemon rind
2 cups freshly shelled or 1 10-oz package frozen sweet tiny peas

COTOLETTE IMPANATE
Breaded Veal Chops

Separate the rib bone from any attached meat or skin so that the rib is bare. Trim off all fat and gristle from the chops. With a meat mallet or the blade of a heavy cleaver, pound the meaty rosettes until they are considerably enlarged and very thin. Combine salt and flour and lightly coat the meat with the mixture. Holding by the bare rib, dip each chop in beaten egg and dredge with bread crumbs.

Heat the oil in a large, heavy skillet and fry the chops over moderately high heat for 2 minutes on each side or until golden brown. Transfer to a hot serving dish and garnish with parsley and lemon slices or wedges.

Serves 6.

6 rib veal chops, about 1 pound each
1 teaspoon salt
3 tablespoons unbleached flour
2 eggs slightly beaten
1 cup seasoned bread crumbs
3/4 cup olive oil
6 small sprigs parsley
1 lemon, sliced, or cut into 6 wedges

PIZZETTE DI VITELLA CON CAROTE
Veal Patties with Carrots

2 pounds lean veal for stew
2 small eggs, slightly beaten
*1 1/2 slices stale bread soaked in water and cooked into a pap**
1 tablespoon freshly chopped Italian parsley
1 teaspoon chopped chives
1 teaspoon salt
1/8 teaspoon freshly ground black pepper
3 tablespoons olive oil
1 large clove garlic, crushed
1/2 teaspoon rosemary leaves
1/2 cup dry white wine
3 cups stewed carrots (page 190)

Remove any fat or skin from veal and grind. Combine ground veal, eggs, pap, parsley, chives, salt, and pepper. Mix thoroughly. Shape this mixture into 12 oval patties.

Heat the oil with garlic and rosemary in a large skillet. Saute until garlic is browned, then discard both garlic and rosemary leaves. Fry the veal patties in this oil, over moderately high heat, until golden brown on both sides. Add wine and cook over high heat for 1 minute; then lower heat and simmer, covered, for 15 minutes. Add prepared carrots and heat 5 minutes to bring the flavors together. **Serves 6.**

*See instructions on page 39.

LINGUA E CIPOLLINE IN AGRO-DOLCE
Calf Tongue and Onions in a Sweet-and-Sour Sauce

2 1/2 pounds calf tongues
Olive oil
1 small carrot, peeled and sliced
1 stalk celery, coarsely chopped
2 bay leaves
1 large sprig Italian parsley, coarsely chopped
2 teaspoons salt
1/8 teaspoon ground cloves
1/4 teaspoon whole peppercorns
Hot water
2 pints pearl onions, peeled and soaked in cold water
1/2 cup dark seedless raisins
2 tablespoons raw sugar
1 tablespoon red wine vinegar

Trim the tongues of all fat that can possibly be removed. Place them under a broiler or in a toaster oven, turning once, until the skins begin to burn and blister. As soon as the tongues can be handled, peel them, then rinse thoroughly under cold water and pat dry.

In a pot just large enough to contain the tongues snugly, heat 3 tablespoons of oil. Add carrot, celery, bay leaves, and parsley, and saute 2 minutes. Add the tongues and season with salt and cloves. Lightly brown, turning once or twice, for 3 or 4 minutes. Add the peppercorns and enough hot water to cover and simmer, covered, for about 1 hour. Transfer the tongues to a cutting board and remove any peel that remains. Strain and defat* the broth and reserve.

Drain onions and place in a saucepan with 3 tablespoons oil. Brown, stirring frequently, for about 5 minutes. Add raisins, sugar, vinegar, and reserved broth to onions.

Slice the tongues and add to the saucepan. Cook, uncovered, for 1/2 hour or until most liquid has evaporated and meat and onions are in a dense, savory sauce. Excellent hot or at room temperature. **Serves 6.**

* See instructions on page 40.

PICCATA IN SALSA D'UOVO
Veal Scaloppine with Egg Sauce

2 pounds veal scaloppine, cut very thin
3 tablespoons unbleached flour
2 teaspoons salt
1/8 teaspoon freshly ground black pepper
4 tablespoons olive oil
1/4 cup hot chicken broth or water
Juice of 1 small lemon
1 egg, slightly beaten

With a meat mallet or the blade of a heavy cleaver, pound scaloppine until paper thin. Combine flour, salt, and pepper and lightly coat scaloppine with the mixture.

Heat the oil in a large skillet and add the scaloppine in a single layer. Brown over high heat approximately 1 1/2 minute on each side. Remove to a hot serving dish. Repeat until all scaloppine are browned.

Add broth or water to the skillet and simmer 1 minute while scraping the glaze with a wooden spoon. Lower the heat to minimum.

Mix lemon juice and egg and add to the skillet. Quickly stir until sauce begins to thicken (do not allow it to boil or the egg will curdle). Pour over the scaloppine and serve immediately. **Serves 6.**

LINGUA DI VITELLO FREDDA
Cold Calf Tongue

1 calf tongue (about 2 pounds)
1 tablespoon salt
1/4 teaspoon whole peppercorns
1/8 teaspoon ground cloves
2 bay leaves
Green Sauce (recipe follows)

In a saucepan just large enough to contain the tongue snugly, place tongue, salt, peppercorns, ground cloves, and bay leaves. Add enough warm water to cover and bring to a rapid boil. Cook, covered, over moderately high heat, for approximately 2 hours.

Transfer tongue to a cutting board. As soon as it is cool enough to handle, remove and discard the skin, and trim all the fatty parts. Cool thoroughly before slicing into thin slices.

Arrange on a serving plate; spread the sauce over it. Cover the plate with plastic wrap and place in refrigerator for several hours to allow the tongue to absorb the flavors of the sauce. **Serves 4 to 6.**

SALSA VERDE
Green Sauce

1 cup firmly packed parsley leaves
1 small clove garlic
1 tablespoon capers, drained
1 small hard-boiled egg, shelled
1 tablespoon bread crumbs
1 tablespoon lemon juice
1 tablespoon wine vinegar
1/4 cup olive oil
Salt and pepper to taste

Finely chop together parsley, garlic, and capers. Transfer to a sauce bowl. Mash the egg and add to the bowl. Add bread crumbs, lemon juice and vinegar and let stand for a few minutes.

Add oil and small amounts of salt and pepper to suit your taste, and mix well. **Yields about 1/2 cup.**

VITELLA IN FORNO
Oven-Roasted Veal

1 tablespoon salt
1/2 teaspoon freshly ground black pepper
1 clove garlic, minced
1 1/2 teaspoons rosemary leaves
2 pounds lean veal leg in one piece*
1 large onion, coarsely cut up
2 large carrots, peeled and coarsely cut up
Olive oil
1/2 cup dry white wine
1/2 cup warm water

Combine salt, pepper, garlic, and rosemary leaves on a piece of waxed paper. Roll the piece of meat over this mixture until it is evenly coated on all sides.

Oil a shallow baking dish and spread onion and carrots in it. Place the veal at center; slowly pour 1/2 cup of olive oil over the meat and vegetables. Place in 450 °F oven for 20 minutes.

Baste with wine and return to hot oven; after 3 minutes add 1/2 cup of warm water. Turn the heat down to 300 °F and bake another 1/2 hour or until fork tender. Remove from oven and cover with a damp towel for 5 to 10 minutes.

Slice the meat and arrange on a hot serving plate. Strain the gravy and vegetables through a sieve and serve over the slices of meat. **Serves 6.**

* See notes on kashrut on page 41.

CHAZIRELLO (PANCETTA DI VITELLA RIPIENA)
Piglet (Stuffed Breast of Veal)

Some time ago I received a telephone call from the widow of the historian Cecil Roth who asked me whether I knew why the Jews of Pitigliano called this delicious kosher dish *chazirello*, piglet. She and her late husband had found the recipe in ancient Italian-Judaeo dialect (which used Hebrew lettering) during one research trip they took many years ago to Pitigliano. I didn't know for certain, but I could imagine the reason. In early autumn, in the main piazza in Pitigliano, a big open-air fair took place in which almost everything — from shoes to dry fruit, from livestock to toys, from yard goods to wines, from earthenware to grains — was sold. In the middle of the square loomed a pushcart that sold hot slices of *porchetta*, a stuffed roasted piglet which sent forth delicious aromas. The Jews, who refrained from eating pork to obey their dietary laws, were envious of their fellow Pitiglianesi and invented this dish which of course doesn't use any pork, but is as fragrant and perhaps as tasty as its namesake.

4 pounds breast of veal
2 cloves garlic, crushed
Salt
Freshly ground black pepper
1 teaspoon fennel seeds
Dash or two nutmeg
1/2 boneless, skinless chicken breast
3/4 pound cubed lean beef
*2 thick slices stale bread, cooked into a pap**
1 egg, slightly beaten
1/4 cup raw, unsalted pistacchio *nuts or walnut meats*
1 teaspoon fresh or 1/2 teaspoon dried rosemary leaves

Open the pocket of the breast of veal completely as you open a book, or have your butcher do it. Painstakingly remove and discard as much fat as possible. Rub with garlic on both sides, then sprinkle with salt and pepper to taste. Spread the open breast, rib side down, over a working surface and sprinkle with fennel seeds.

Grind together the chicken breast and the beef. Combine ground meats with pap, egg, nuts, nutmeg, and salt and pepper to taste and mix well. Spread this mixture over the rib half of the open breast, then close the other half over it. Sew the sides closed using thread and needle, or fasten all around with a string. Sprinkle all over with rosemary leaves and place in a baking pan, rib side down. Bake in 350 °F oven for 2 1/2 hours or until quite browned and crisp.

Remove from oven, cover with clean kitchen towel, and let stand 10 minutes before slicing. **Serves 6.**

* See instructions on page 39.

VITELLA IN GELATINA
Jellied Veal

2 pounds boned veal shoulder
1 tablespoon salt
1/4 teaspoon freshly ground black pepper
2 tablespoons olive oil
1 clove garlic
1/2 calf foot
1 lemon, sliced or cut into wedges
4 or 5 sprigs American curly parsley

Sprinkle veal with salt and pepper and form into a roll. Tie all around with a string and place in a casserole with oil and garlic. Slowly brown on all sides, over moderate heat, for about 10 minutes. Discard garlic and add calf foot. Add water to cover and simmer, covered, for 1 1/2 hours or until veal is quite tender. Transfer the roll to a dish to cool.

Boil the calf foot another hour or until the broth is greatly reduced.

Remove the string from the roll and slice. Arrange the slices in a somewhat deep serving plate. Strain the broth through a fine sieve and pour over the slices. Place in refrigerator until firm. Garnish with lemon and parsley sprigs.

Serves 6.

NOTE: The calf foot is also delicious. You may want to cut the meaty parts and add them to the strained broth.

SPEZZATINO DI VITELLA
Veal Stew

2 pounds boneless leg of veal, cut into 1 1/2-inch cubes*
2 pounds veal breast, cut into 1 1/2-inch cubes
2 teaspoons salt
1/4 teaspoon ground red pepper
1 dash ground clove
2 dashes cinnamon
1 tablespoon unbleached flour
1/4 cup olive oil
1 medium onion, sliced thin
1 medium carrot, peeled and diced
1/2 cup dry white wine
1 1/2x2-inch piece lemon peel, shredded
*2 cups diced peeled tomatoes** with their juice, fresh or canned*
1 clove garlic, minced
1 tablespoon freshly chopped Italian parsley

Sprinkle veal cubes with salt, pepper, clove, cinnamon, and flour.

Heat the oil in a large saucepan with onion and carrot. Add veal and cook over moderately high heat, stirring, until all pieces of veal are browned. Add wine and cook over high heat 1 or 2 minutes.

Lower heat, add lemon peel and tomatoes and simmer, covered, for approximately 1 hour, stirring occasionally. (Should sauce become too dry, add a few tablespoons of water. However, this is unlikely to happen, and at any rate, veal should cook in a thick, flavorful sauce at all times.) A few minutes before removing the stew from the heat, add garlic and parsley and stir.

Serves 6.

* See notes on kashrut on page 41.
** See instructions on page 45.

AGNELLO
Lamb

AGNELLO IN FORNO CON PATATE
Roast Leg of Lamb with Potatoes

In the aftermath of World War II in Italy, when euphoria and reconstruction fervor swept through the country and everyone's motto was *carpe diem*, grab the day, my only ambition was to resume my formal education, abruptly interrupted against my will during the initial stage of the persecutions of the Jews several years earlier.

After I graduated from the British Institute in Florence with a proficiency diploma in English, I thought my proficiency would not be hurt if I spent a few months in England testing it. I answered an ad which a London family had placed in our local paper for a cook. Even though a cook I was not, and becoming a professional one was the last choice in the gamut of my aspirations, I did want to improve my English, so I tried to impress my interviewer with what I had observed in my mother's kitchen, and to my delight I was hired.

As it turned out, this aristocratic family of six came originally from French Switzerland and spoke only French at home. Luckily I could understand and speak French passably, so I had the double benefit of practicing French with them and English outside. Every morning, when the whole family went about their business, I was left with a menu, a set of recipes and the precise timing for serving each dish. And I mean *precise.* Every evening at 6:45 sharp the family sat at the dinner table and the mistress of the house would press a button under the table which rang in the kitchen signaling that it was time to serve the hors d'oeuvres. At 7:00

the bell rang for the soup; at 7:15 for the main dish, and so on.

One day the butcher delivered a huge leg of mutton. That day I noticed with dismay that my passport would expire unless I renewed it immediately. I had no choice but to run to the Italian Consulate and have it renewed. I quickly prepared the dessert, trimmed and dressed the mutton, and off I went. But I had not taken into account the phlegmatic attitude of some Italian bureaucrats abroad, and spent innumerable hours in that dark antechamber before being admitted to the passport office. On returning I barely reached the house ahead of the family, and only a half hour before the first course was to be served.

The recipe for the mutton called for 3 hours' cooking time at about 275 °F, but I only had one hour remaining, so I set the oven at maximum temperature and quickly shoved the pan with the mutton into it. I then prepared the hors d'oeuvres, the soup and the vegetables.

The bell rang for the first course; then for the second, which I brought with shaky legs. Finally it was time for the main dish. I had the vegetables nicely arranged on the sterling plate and at the very last minute I took the accursed mutton from the oven. It looked horribly charred. I laid it at the center of my beautiful vegetable display, took a deep breath, and carried the evidence of my guilt to the table. I ran back to the kitchen expecting to hear at any moment a furious bell calling me back to explain. Instead, the gentle, quiet voice of the man of the house who had never exchanged with me more than a "Bon jour," called my name.

I went into the dining room with brimming eyes, ready to confess. But the gentleman simply repeated my name, and after a brief pause added, "C'est delicieux."

1 leg of lamb (6 or 7 pounds) or 1/2 baby lamb, about the same weight*
12 medium potatoes
3 tablespoons olive oil
3 teaspoons salt
3/4 teaspoon freshly ground black pepper
1 small clove garlic, minced
1 teaspoon dried rosemary leaves
1 clove garlic, slightly crushed

Leave the lamb at room temperature. Peel the potatoes and cut lengthwise into 4 or 6 pieces each. Place in a bowl and season with 2 tablespoons of oil, 1 teaspoon salt, half the pepper, the minced garlic, and half the rosemary leaves. Toss well and set aside.

Remove excess fat from the lamb. Rub all its surface with the crushed garlic clove and then with the remaining tablespoon of oil. Season with the remaining salt, pepper, and rosemary leaves and place at the center of a large roasting pan. Distribute the seasoned potatoes around it and bake in 550 °F oven for 30 minutes. Decrease the temperature to 350 °F and hold for another 45 minutes.

Keep in mind that overcooked lamb acquires an unpleasant flavor and it is better — as it happened in my first experience quite by accident — to have it quite done on the surface, but slightly underdone on the inside.

Serves 6 to 8.

*See notes on kashrut on page 41.

ANIMELLE COGLI SPINACI
Sweetbreads with Spinach

2 pounds lamb sweetbreads
2 pounds small-leaved bulk spinach
Salt
2 cloves garlic, sliced
2 large sprigs Italian parsley, coarsely chopped
6 tablespoons olive oil
Dash nutmeg
Freshly ground black pepper
1/2 cup cold water

Lamb sweetbreads are a delicacy which you don't find very readily on the market. However, ask your butcher to save some for you because they are worth trying.

Place the sweetbreads in a bowl with cold water to cover and let them stay immersed for a few minutes. Meanwhile, rinse spinach thoroughly, and place in a large pot with no water other than what clings to the leaves. Cook on high heat, covered, for 3 minutes. Drain well.*

Drain the sweetbreads and place in a large saucepan with garlic, parsley, olive oil, nutmeg, 1 teaspoon salt, 1/4 teaspoon pepper, and 1/2 cup of cold water. Bring to a boil, then lower the heat and simmer, covered, 15 minutes. Remove lid and cook over moderately high heat until sweetbreads are fork tender and liquid has almost totally evaporated.

Add spinach, stir, and simmer 5 to 10 minutes to allow the flavors to come together. Serve hot or at room temperature. **Serves 6.**

* See instructions on page 44.

CIANCHETTI DI AGNELLO BRASATI
Brazed Lamb Shanks

6 meaty lamb shanks
Olive oil
Salt
Freshly ground black pepper
2 cloves garlic, minced fine
2 teaspoons rosemary leaves
1/2 cup dry white wine
1/2 cup hot broth or water

Wash shanks thoroughly and pat dry. Rub with olive oil, then sprinkle with salt and pepper, garlic, and rosemary. Set aside in a cool place, covered, for several hours.

Place in a large saucepan with 1/2 cup of olive oil and brown over moderate heat on all sides for 10 to 15 minutes. Add wine and raise the temperature for 1 minute, then lower to minimum, cover the pan tightly, and simmer for 1 hour, or until shanks are fork tender. Check every 15 minutes or so and add broth or water by the tablespoonful as it becomes necessary.

Transfer the shanks to a hot serving plate and strain the gravy over them before serving. **Serves 6.**

MEDAGLIONI DI AGNELLO E CARCIOFI
Lamb and Artichokes Medallions

12 medium-thick rib lamb chops
3 medium artichokes
2 lemons, juice and rind
Salt
Freshly ground black pepper
2 tablespoons freshly chopped Italian parsley
1 small clove garlic, minced
1 cup unbleached flour
3 eggs, slightly beaten with a pinch of salt and a dash of pepper
1 cup seasoned bread crumbs
Olive oil
Sauce for cutlets (recipe follows)

Use only the central rosettes of the ribs and reserve bones and scraps for the sauce. With a meat mallet or with the blade of a heavy cleaver, pound the meat rosettes thin. Arrange on a working surface in a single layer.

Clean and trim artichokes,* then cut each lengthwise into 4 slices (remove choke, if there is any), and spread out on the working surface next to the meat.

Lightly season meat and artichokes with small amounts of salt, pepper, parsley, and garlic. Combine one meat rosette with one artichoke slice, seasoned sides together, and gently press. Coat with flour, patting to remove excess. When all cutlets are ready, dip in beaten egg, roll in bread crumbs, and fry in hot oil for 2 minutes on each side or until golden on both sides. Serve as is or with the hot sauce on a separate sauce dish. **Serves 4 to 6.**

*See instructions on page 36.

SALSA PER MEDAGLIONI
Sauce for Medallions

Bones and scraps from previous recipe
Salt
2 1/2 cups water
4 tablespoons olive oil
3 tablespoons unbleached flour
2 tablespoons dry white wine
1/2 medium clove garlic, minced fine
1 tablespoon freshly chopped Italian parsley
2 egg yolks
Freshly ground black pepper
2 tablespoons lemon juice

Place lamb bones and scraps in a saucepan with 1 teaspoon salt and 2 1/2 cups of water. Bring to a boil, then reduce heat and simmer gently, covered, for 45 minutes to 1 hour. Strain and defat* the broth.

Heat the oil in a saucepan, add the flour and saute, stirring, 2 minutes. Add wine and lamb stock and stir vigorously to prevent lumps from forming. Cook 2 minutes.

Remove from heat and add garlic, parsley, pepper, and egg yolks, stirring after each addition.

Return to heat and cook 1 or 2 minutes longer, stirring frequently. Just before serving add the lemon juice and mix well. **Yields approximately 2 cups.**

*See instructions on page 40.

POLPETTINE DI AGNELLO COI FUNGHI
Lamb Balls with Mushrooms

*4 1/2 pounds lean boneless lamb**
Salt
Freshly ground black pepper
Olive oil
1/2 cup dry white wine
1 pound small white mushrooms sliced very fine
1/4 teaspoon savory

Grind lamb with 2 teaspoons salt and 1/8 teaspoon pepper. Shape into tiny balls.

Heat 1/2 cup of oil in a large skillet and fry half the balls, shaking the skillet frequently, until browned on all sides. With a slotted spoon transfer to a warm dish and set aside. Repeat with the remaining balls, adding fresh oil to the skillet as necessary. Pour most of the oil into a new skillet (reserve the one where you fried the balls). Add the mushrooms, the savory, and salt and pepper to taste, and stir fry over moderately high heat for 5 minutes.

Add wine to the old skillet and simmer for 1 minute or 2, scraping the glaze. Transfer balls and mushrooms to this skillet and heat through over moderately high heat, stirring frequently, until most liquid has evaporated.

Serves 6.

* See notes on kashrut on page 41.

TESTINE DI AGNELLO IN FORNO
Roast Lamb Heads

I include this recipe in my collection because it stirs memories of a truly delicious and unique dish. In Italy, when I was much younger, lamb heads were sold oven-ready, that is to say, already plucked of the fleece. Here, I must confess, I have never made *testine*, and therefore I never found out whether they are available, nor whether the old European practice of selling them oven-ready is still in existence. So, if you wish to try them, you must ask your butcher.

3 lamb heads, split in halves
Salt
2 teaspoons rosemary leaves
2 cloves garlic, minced fine
Freshly ground black pepper
Olive oil

Wash the heads in warm water thoroughly, especially around the tongue and ear holes.

Spread on a working surface skin side up. Sprinkle with all the rosemary and garlic and with small amounts of salt and pepper. Place skin side down into an oiled baking pan where the half heads fit snugly in a single layer. Sprinkle with small amounts of salt, pepper, and oil. Place in 350 °F oven for 1 to 1 1/2 hours, or until nicely browned. Serve hot.

Serves 3 to 6.

POLLASTRINI ALLA GRIGLIA
Broiled Young Roosters

In Pitigliano, where we had only charcoal ranges for all our cooking needs, marinated pollastrini were enclosed in a *gratella,* closed grill, and broiled directly over the range. Here, however, I have made them successfully using a modern broiler.

- *6 very young roosters or 6 cornish hens, cut lengthwise on the back*
- *1 large clove garlic*
- *Salt*
- *Freshly ground black pepper*
- *Olive oil*
- *Juice of 2 large lemons*
- *1 1/2 pounds firm white mushrooms, sliced thin*

Rub the garlic on the inside of the open birds. Sprinkle all over with salt and pepper and place in an oiled large baking pan with skin side down. Sprinkle 1 tablespoon of oil and 1 tablespoon of lemon over each bird and set aside to marinate for at least 1 hour. Place the marinated birds under the broiler for approximately 20 minutes, or until the higher bones begin to burn.

Meanwhile heat 1/2 cup of oil in a large skillet and add the mushrooms. Add 1 teaspoon salt, 1/8 teaspoon pepper, and the remaining lemon juice. Cook over high heat, stirring frequently, 5 to 6 minutes, or until moisture has evaporated.

Turn the birds and broil 10 to 15 minutes on the skin side. Serve with mushrooms. **Serves 6 to 8.**

POLLO ARROSTO RIPIENO
Stuffed Roast Chicken

Place sage and rosemary in a piece of cheesecloth and tie with a string.

In a medium skillet, heat 2 tablespoons of oil over moderate heat. Add onion, veal, and livers (previously soaked in water until no trace of blood is visible). Sprinkle with small amounts of salt, pepper, and nutmeg. Cook, stirring frequently, for 3 minutes. Add chicken broth and cheesecloth bouquet and simmer, covered, for 1/2 hour. Remove and discard bouquet and transfer contents of skillet to a bowl. Add toasted bread and let it soak thoroughly. Add celery, mushrooms, and egg, and mix well.

Rub the inside and outside of the chicken with garlic. Sprinkle the inside with fennel seeds and rub the outside with olive oil. Place the stuffing into the chicken cavity and season the outside with salt and pepper to taste.

Place in an uncovered roasting pan, breast side up, in a preheated 500 °F oven for 30 minutes. Lower the temperature to 350 °F and cook 1 1/2 hours longer.

Serves 6.

1 teaspoon dried sage leaves
1 teaspoon dried rosemary leaves
Olive oil
1 medium onion, chopped
1/2 pound lean ground veal
2 chicken livers, cut up
Salt
Freshly ground black pepper
Dash nutmeg
1 cup chicken broth
2 slices white bread, toasted
2 white celery stalks, diced
4 medium mushrooms, sliced
1 egg, slightly beaten
1 medium roasting chicken (about 4 pounds)
1 large clove garlic, slightly crushed
1 teaspoon fennel seeds

POLPETTINE DI POLLO E PATATE
Chicken and Potato Patties

Grind or chop the chicken very fine and combine with potatoes, eggs, parsley, garlic, and nutmeg. Add salt and pepper to taste and mix well.

With oily hands, shape mixture by the tablespoonful into round patties.

Heat 1/2 cup of oil in a large skillet and fry the patties, turning and adding oil if necessary, until they are golden brown on both sides. Serve immediately.

Serves 6.

2 1/2 cups cooked chicken, diced
1 pound all-purpose potatoes, steamed, peeled and mashed
3 eggs, slightly beaten
1 tablespoon freshly chopped Italian parsley
1/2 small garlic clove, minced
Dash nutmeg
Salt
Freshly ground black pepper
Olive oil for frying

POLLO ALLA CASALINGA
Chicken Home Style

1 small onion
1 small clove garlic
1 egg
1 large sprig Italian parsley
1/2 cup chicken broth
Salt
Freshly ground black pepper
Dash ground cloves
1/2 cup bread crumbs
1 pound lean ground beef
Olive oil
1 small chicken, whole
4 potatoes, peeled and cut up
1 turnip, peeled and cut up
1 large onion, cut up
2 carrots, peeled and cut up
4 firm tomatoes, quartered
2 large green peppers, cored and cut up
1 cup water

Place the small onion, garlic, egg, parsley, broth, 1 teaspoon salt, a dash pepper, and a dash cloves in a blender or processor and liquefy. Pour the liquid into a bowl. Add bread crumbs and ground meat and mix well. Let rest for a few minutes, then form into small balls.

Heat 3 tablespoons of oil in a large saucepan or dutch oven, add the meat balls and brown on all sides, shaking the pan. Temporarily transfer the balls to a dish reserving the oil.

Wash the chicken thoroughly and pat dry. Sprinkle all over with salt and pepper and brown on all sides in the reserved oil.

Return meat balls to the saucepan with chicken. Add all the vegetables and 1 cup of water and cook, covered, 1/2 hour or until chicken and vegetables are done.

Place the chicken on a serving plate surrounded by the meat balls. Serve the vegetables in a separate dish.

Serves 8.

COTOLETTE DI POLLO E CARCIOFI
Chicken and Artichoke Cutlets

6 medium fresh artichokes
2 lemons, juice and rinds
2 boneless chicken breasts (4 halves)
2 tablespoons freshly chopped Italian parsley
Salt
Freshly ground black pepper
1 cup unbleached flour
3 eggs, slightly beaten with a pinch of salt
1 cup fine bread crumbs
Olive or other vegetable oil for frying
1 lemon cut into 6 wedges

Clean artichokes* and slice lengthwise into 4 slices each.

Cut chicken breast into 24 small pieces and flatten down with the blade of a cleaver or a meat mallet. Line up on a working surface and season only the top side with parsley and small amounts of salt and pepper.

Cover the seasoned side of each cutlet with 1 artichoke slice and gently press down.

Coat with flour, patting to remove excess; dip in beaten egg, and roll in bread crumbs. Fry in hot oil, a few at a time, until golden on both sides. Serve with lemon wedges.

Serves 6.

*See instructions on page 36.

BOCCONCINI DI POLLO

Chicken Little Bits

Wash chicken breast and pat dry. Remove and discard all fatty parts and tendons and cut into 3/4-inch cubes. Place in a small saucepan with salt, pepper, rosemary leaves, and garlic. Toss to distribute the seasoning evenly. Add all the oil and set aside in the refrigerator for several hours or overnight.

Place on moderately high heat and brown for 10 minutes stirring frequently. Add the broth and let the steam bring the flavors together for 1 minute. Add lemon juice and remove from heat. Serve with its gravy and *spinaci all'agro* (page 178). **Serves 6.**

2 pounds skinless, boneless chicken breast
2 teaspoons salt
1/4 teaspoon ground white pepper
2 teaspoons fresh or 1 teaspoon dried rosemary leaves
2 cloves garlic, minced
1 cup olive oil
1/4 cup clear chicken broth
Juice of one lemon

POLLO FREDDO IN SALSA VERDE

Cold Chicken with Green Sauce

Chill the chicken in the refrigerator for several hours. Slice thin and arrange the slices on a platter. Sprinkle with small amounts of grated nutmeg, cover with plastic wrap, and return to the refrigerator.

Place the parsley in a processor and process until the parsley is chopped fine. Add capers and process a few seconds. Add bread crumbs, vinegar, and hard-boiled eggs and process just until eggs are chopped but not reduced to a puree. Add 1/4 to 1/2 cup oil and salt and pepper to taste. Blend for a second.

Take the chicken platter from the refrigerator and spread the sauce over the chicken, leveling with a rubber spatula. Garnish with *peperoni sott'olio* (page 65), or tomato roses.* Cover with wrap again and keep refrigerated until ready to serve. **Serves 6.**

*See instructions on page 45.

NOTE: If you opt for tomato roses, make them and place them on the plate a moment before serving, since they lose their crispness in the refrigerator.

1 boiled young fowl, boned
Nutmeg
1 cup firmly packed parsley leaves
2 tablespoons tiny capers, drained
2 tablespoons bread crumbs or matza meal
2 tablespoons wine vinegar
2 hard-boiled eggs
Olive oil
Salt
Freshly ground black pepper

COLLO DI POLLO RIPIENO
Stuffed Chicken Neck

I don't recall a holiday in my mother's household without stuffed chicken neck. It was served as an antipasto, as a *tramezzo* (between two main courses), or as part of a boiled chicken platter. But no matter when or how, it is no wonder that it was omnipresent, since it is indeed delicious!

- *3 whole neck skins from chickens, cut low at the shoulders*
- *1 clove garlic, slightly crushed*
- *3/4 pound boneless chicken breast*
- *1/2 pound boneless chicken thigh*
- *1/4 cup seasoned bread crumbs*
- *1 teaspoon salt*
- *1/8 teaspoon freshly ground black pepper*
- *2 dashes nutmeg*
- *1/4 cup shelled* pistacchio *nuts*
- *2 eggs slightly beaten*
- *3 quarts salted chicken soup*

After washing the neck skins, turn them inside out, pat them dry, and rub the garlic over the inside. Turn them again.

With a large needle and white thread, sew one opening of the necks closed and set aside. Grind the meat and place in a bowl with all the other ingredients, except for the soup, and mix very well.

Place this mixture rather loosely inside the skin sacks (the skins will shrink and burst if they are too stuffed), then sew the mouth of the little sacks closed. Poke the skins all over.

Bring the soup to a boil, gently add the necks, lower the heat, and cook for 1 to 1 1/2 hours.

Transfer the necks to a dish, place an inverted dish over them and a weight over the dish (a tightly closed jar filled with water will do) until they cool down to room temperature. Remove the threads and slice slantwise so that the slices are not too small. **Serves 4 to 6.**

TACCHINO ARROSTO MORTO
Pot-Roasted Turkey Drumsticks

A whole roasted turkey is the very symbol of affluence. When I was growing up in Italy, this luxury was known only to the royal family and a privileged few. All other people — those able to afford meat of any kind — bought turkey only by the parts. A wing was a desirable complement to other bony meats for a good broth; breast was used in place of veal for scaloppine; drumsticks made a tasty pot roast.

Combine salt, pepper, sage, rosemary, and garlic on a piece of waxed paper. Roll the turkey legs over the mixture to coat them evenly. Place in a fish poacher without the rack or in a large saucepan. Sprinkle the remaining salt mixture over the legs, then add 1 cup of olive oil. Set aside in refrigerator for several hours or overnight.

Place over high heat and brown on all sides. Reduce the heat and simmer, covered, for about 20 minutes, turning the legs occasionally. Add wine and cook, uncovered, until liquid is completely gone. Sprinkle with cold water to generate steam*. Repeat sprinkling as many times as needed for the meat to become fork tender. **Serves 6.**

*See directions on page 39.

3 teaspoon salt
1/2 teaspoon black pepper
1 teaspoon dried sage leaves
1 teaspoon dried rosemary leaves
1 clove garlic, minced
6 small turkey drumsticks (3 1/2 to 4 pounds)
Olive oil
1/2 cup dry white wine

PETTI DI TACCHINO IN SALSA D'UOVO
Turkey Breast with Egg Sauce

Cut turkey breast into small strips. Quickly roll in flour and pat to remove excess. Place in a casserole with oil, salt, and pepper and cook over moderately high heat, stirring, just until turkey pieces are lightly golden.

Add scallions, celery, carrot, lemon peel, and 1 1/2 cups warm water; cover the casserole and simmer for 1 to 2 hours, stirring occasionally.

Temporarily transfer the turkey pieces to a dish and strain the liquid and vegetables. Return turkey and sauce to the casserole and bring to a boil.

Mix together egg yolks and lemon juice. Pour the mixture over the turkey and immediately turn the heat off. Add parsley and stir gently to combine. **Serves 6.**

2 pounds young turkey breast
1/2 cup unbleached flour
3 tablespoons olive oil
1 teaspoon salt
1/8 teaspoon white pepper
3 scallions, coarsely cut up
3 2-inch-long celery stalks
1 medium carrot, peeled and coarsely chopped
1 small piece lemon peel
1 1/2 cups warm water
3 egg yolks
Juice of 1 lemon
1 tablespoon chopped parsley

POLPETTONE DI TACCHINO
Turkey Roll

1 1/2 pounds turkey breast
2 cloves garlic, minced
2 tablespoons chopped parsley
Salt
Freshly ground black pepper
1 pound ground dark turkey meat
*1/3 cup seasoned bread crumbs**
1 egg, slightly beaten
Chicken broth
2 tablespoons pistacchio *nuts*
2 sage leaves
1 teaspoon rosemary leaves
6 tablespoons olive oil
1/3 cup dry white wine

Slice the turkey breast open** and place on a working surface. Flatten it down with the blade of a large cleaver or with a meat mallet, then sprinkle with garlic, parsley, and small amounts of salt and pepper on both sides. Set aside.

Place ground meat, bread crumbs, egg, 2 tablespoons of chicken broth and *pistacchio* nuts into a bowl. Add 1/2 teaspoon salt and a pinch of pepper, and mix to combine.

Spread this mixture over the sheet of turkey breast, then roll the short way as you would for a jelly roll. Tie all around with a string and place into a pan with sage, rosemary and all the oil. Brown on all sides, then add the wine and raise the heat to let the alcohol evaporate. Add 1/2 cup broth and simmer, tightly covered, for about 2 hours, turning only once. Add more broth if necessary.

Remove the string before slicing. Serve with the pan juices strained over the slices. **Serves 6.**

* See note on next recipe.
** See instructions on page 45.

POLPETTONE DI TACCHINO II
Turkey Loaf

1 1/2 pounds ground dark turkey meat
1 cup seasoned bread crumbs
2 eggs, slightly beaten
1 teaspoon minced garlic
1 teaspoon salt
1/8 teaspoon ground red pepper
2 teaspoons dehydrated minced onion
1/2 cup olive oil
2 sage leaves
1 teaspoon rosemary leaves
1/4 cup dry white wine
2 tablespoons lemon juice

In a bowl place turkey, 1/3 cup bread crumbs, eggs, garlic, salt, red pepper, and onion and mix to combine. Spread the remaining bread crumbs over a piece of waxed paper. Divide the ground meat into two portions and form each into an egg-shaped loaf. Roll in bread crumbs until coated all over.

Heat the oil with sage and rosemary in a large skillet and place the two loaves in it. Thoroughly brown on all sides. Sprinkle a few drops of water to generate steam.* When the loaves feel firm they are done — about 30 minutes in all.

Remove from skillet to a heated serving plate. Add wine and lemon juice to the skillet and saute, scraping the bottom with a wooden spoon. Slice the loaves and pour the gravy over the slices. **Serves 6.**

* See instructions on page 39.

NOTE: For Passover, substitute matza meal for bread crumbs. However, since matza meal is not seasoned, you may want to mix it with 1/2 teaspoon Italian herb seasoning and 1/2 teaspoon garlic salt for a comparable flavor.

ANATRA ALL'ARANCIA
Duck in Orange Sauce

1 medium duck
1 clove garlic, slightly crushed
Salt
Freshly ground black pepper
1/4 cup orange marmalade
Olive oil
1/4 cup frozen orange juice
4 seedless oranges, 2 unpeeled and 2 peeled, sliced

Remove as much fat as possible from the bird. Rub inside and out with garlic; generously season with salt and pepper. Spread orange marmalade inside the cavity. Sprinkle the outside with olive oil and rub with your hands to coat evenly. Place in an uncovered roasting pan, breast side up, in preheated 450 °F oven for 30 minutes.

Baste with all the concentrated orange juice and arrange the unpeeled orange slices all around. Lower the temperature to 350 °F and bake 1 hour longer.

Arrange the peeled orange slices on top of the duck and bake just until the orange is heated through. **Serves 4 to 6.**

Pesce

FISH

BRODETTO
Fish Soup

Place onion and oil in a large skillet and saute, sprinkling with water from time to time, until onion is soft and translucent. Add 2 teaspoons salt, pepper to taste and parsley, and saute 2 or 3 minutes, stirring occasionally. Add vinegar and diluted tomato paste, and cook a few minutes longer to bring the flavors together.

Wash the fish, and without drying it, add to the skillet. Lower the heat to minimum, cover the skillet, and simmer 20 minutes, shaking the pan from time to time. Transfer the fish to a warm serving plate. Pour the liquid over the toast and serve on a separate dish. **Serves 6.**

1 medium onion, thinly sliced
1/2 cup olive oil
Salt
Freshly ground black pepper
3 tablespoons freshly chopped Italian parsley
1/2 cup white wine vinegar
2 rounded tablespoons tomato paste, diluted in 1/2 cup water
5 pounds assorted small fish, cleaned and gutted
12 slices 4-grain bread, toasted

DENTICE LESSO
Poached Red Snapper

Have the fish cleaned at the store, making sure the gills are removed from the head. Have the meat separated from the bones and head, but take everything home.

In a fish poacher or kettle, place the bones, the head, the fish fillet, the lemon slice, and cold water to barely cover. Bring to a boil, then simmer for 15 to 20 minutes, or until the fish flakes easily and the white hard sphere of the eye pops out. Remove from heat.

Carefully lift the meat, avoiding any bones, and transfer to a serving plate, skin side down. Season with salt and pepper to taste and drizzle with lemon juice. Sprinkle abundantly with extra virgin olive oil. Garnish with parsley and serve warm or at room temperature. **Serves 6.**

1 4- to 5-pound red snapper
1 slice lemon with peel
Salt
Coarsely ground black pepper
Juice of one lemon
Extra virgin olive oil
A few sprigs parsley

NASELLO LESSO COLLA MAIONESE
Boiled Young Cod with Mayonnaise

Have the fish cleaned and filleted at the fish store, but make sure to ask for the head (with the gills removed) and bones.

In a fish poacher or kettle, place onion, carrot, celery, lemon, salt, and peppercorns. Add water and the head and bones of the fish, and bring to a boil. Lower the heat and simmer, covered, for 30 to 45 minutes.

1 cod (4- to 5-pound)
1 small onion, sliced
1 carrot, sliced
1 stalk celery, coarsely cut
1 slice lemon with peel
1 teaspoon salt
1/4 teaspoon peppercorns
1 cup water
1 1/2 cups mayonnaise

2 tablespoons scallion greens, cut into 1/4-inch rings
1 tablespoon freshly chopped Italian parsley
1/2 cup Peperoni sott'olio
1/2 cup oil-cured olives

Strain the broth through a fine sieve and return to the kettle. Add the fish fillets and simmer 10 to 20 minutes or until the meat easily flakes. Drain and shred the fish into a bowl. Let it cool to room temperature, then add 1 cup of mayonnaise and the scallion greens and stir to combine.

Transfer to a serving plate, flatten with a spatula, and cover with the remaining mayonnaise. Sprinkle with parsley, and garnish with red peppers and black olives.

Serves 6.

FILETTI DI SOGLIOLE E CARCIOFI
Sole and Artichoke Casserole

1 lemon
9 medium fresh artichokes
1 clove garlic, minced
1 tablespoon freshly chopped Italian parsley
1 1/2 teaspoons salt
1/4 teaspoon freshly ground black pepper
1 1/2 pounds fillets of sole
1/2 cup olive oil
1/4 cup bread crumbs

Squeeze the lemon and place juice and rind halves into a basin with cold water. Trim the artichokes* and drop them in the acidulated water. Drain and cut the artichokes lengthwise into thin slices and remove choke if there is any. Place in a bowl and combine with half the garlic, half the parsley, half the salt, and half the pepper. Toss and set aside for a moment.

Wash fillets and pat dry with paper toweling. Cut into small strips, place in a bowl, and season with the remaining seasoning ingredients.

In an oiled baking dish, arrange artichoke slices and sole strips in alternate layers, sprinkling each layer with oil. End with fish, top with bread crumbs and a drizzle of oil. Bake, uncovered, in 400 °F oven for 30 to 45 minutes. (Baking time depends on size and freshness of artichokes; if they are crisp and tender, do not bake for more than 30 minutes.) Delicious hot or at room temperature. **Serves 6.**

* See instructions on page 36.

FILETTI DI SOGLIOLE AI FUNGHI
Fillets of Sole with Mushrooms

For this delicate dish use the freshest fillets of gray sole you can find. In my mother's household, the fish fillets were placed on a dish over a pot of boiling water for 5 minutes or until they had lost their rawness. This method still is a good one, but now I can use the microwave oven successfully. Fresh porcini mushrooms would be ideal, but fresh shitake mushrooms are an excellent substitute.

1 pound fresh porcini or shitake mushrooms
Olive oil
2 cloves garlic, sliced
Salt
Freshly ground white pepper
12 small fillets of sole (2 to 2 1/2 pounds)
1 tablespoon freshly chopped Italian parsley

Remove and discard most of the stems and any parts that look sandy from the mushrooms. Clean mushrooms with a cloth to remove any debris that might be left. Slice to 1/4-inch thickness.

Heat 6 tablespoons of oil in a large skillet. Add mushrooms, garlic, and salt and pepper to taste, and stir fry for 2 or 3 minutes.

Oil a large microwave-proof serving dish and place the fillets into it, in a single layer if possible. Cook in microwave oven 1 to 2 minutes, or until fish has lost its rawness. Drain any liquid that has formed in cooking, and cover with the mushrooms and all the condiment. Sprinkle with parsley and serve. **Serves 6.**

PASTICCIO DI SOGLIOLE E CAVOLFIORI
Baked Sole and Cauliflower

This is a very fine dairy dish. The vegetable to go with the fish can be anything from potatoes to fennel, as long as it is white, but cauliflower is the vegetable traditionally used in our family.

1 1/2 pounds fresh fillets of sole
1/4 cup dry white wine
Unsalted butter
1 small cauliflower
Salt
Ground white pepper
1/2 cup grated Italian Parmesan cheese
1 1/2 cups medium-thick dairy white sauce (page 216)
2 tablespoons fine bread crumbs

Wash and pat fillets dry. Place in a skillet with the wine and cook just until the fish turns white, approximately 2 minutes. Drain and transfer to the center of a 12x9-inch buttered baking dish.

Separate cauliflower florets and either boil in lightly salted water or steam for 3 minutes. Drain and arrange all around the fish. Lightly season fish and florettes with salt and pepper.

Mix half the Parmesan cheese with the white sauce and pour over the fish and cauliflower. Combine the remaining Parmesan and bread crumbs, and sprinkle over the top. Dot with butter and bake in 400 °F oven for 20 minutes or until top begins to brown. **Serves 6.**

TRIGLIE IN AGRO-DOLCE
Red Mullet with Sweet-and-Sour Sauce

1/2 cup olive oil
1 medium onion, thinly sliced
2 cups peeled ripe tomatoes coarsely cut up*
1 teaspoon salt
1/4 teaspoon crushed red pepper
1/4 cup red wine vinegar
1/4 cup raw sugar
1/2 cup dark seedless raisins
1/4 cup pinoli *(pine nuts)*
6 red mullets, gutted and cleaned but with heads left on
1 tablespoon finely chopped parsley

Place oil and onion in a large skillet and saute until onion is soft and translucent. Add tomatoes, salt, and pepper and cook over moderately high heat, uncovered, for 6 or 7 minutes, stirring occasionally. Add vinegar, sugar, raisins and *pinoli* and cook, stirring, another 2 minutes.

Lower the heat to medium and add fish in a single layer, if possible. Baste with sauce and cook, covered, for 7 minutes. Uncover and simmer until liquid is greatly reduced and fish is in a thick, flavorful sauce. Serve hot or at room temperature. **Serves 6.**

* See instructions on page 45.

FILETTI DI MERLUZZO FRITTI
Fried Cod Fillets

2 pounds cod fillets
1 cup unbleached flour
2 teaspoons baking powder
1/2 teaspoon salt
1 cup cold water
Olive oil
1 lemon cut into wedges

Wash and pat dry the fillet. Remove any bones and cut into strips approximately 1 1/2 x 5 inches.

Combine flour, baking powder, salt, water, and 2 tablespoons of oil and beat with a fork until batter is smooth.

Heat 1 cup of oil in a medium-sized pan. Dip the pieces of fish in the batter and fry a few at a time, turning, until lightly golden on all sides.

Serve piping hot with lemon wedges. **Serves 6.**

BUDINO DI PESCE
Fish Pudding

1 pound boneless, skinless fish such as salmon, scrod, or haddock
2 tablespoons olive oil
1/2 teaspoon salt
1/4 teaspoon white pepper
1 clove garlic, sliced
1 tablespoon chopped parsley
1/4 cup cold water
6 tablespoons unbleached flour
Butter
Milk
1/2 cup grated Italian Parmesan cheese
1 cup ricotta
3 eggs, slightly beaten
Dash or two nutmeg
Seasoned bread crumbs

Place the fish in a skillet with oil, salt, pepper, garlic, and parsley. Add 1/4 cup water and cook over low heat, covered, until fish flakes easily — approximately 2 minutes. Drain and reserve the liquid.

In a heavy-bottomed saucepan, place flour and 4 tablespoons butter. Cook, stirring constantly, until mixture is pale tan. Add enough milk to the reserved fish liquid to make 2 cups and pour all at once into the saucepan. Stir vigorously with a wire whisk and cook, stirring frequently, 3 or 4 minutes. Remove from heat, combine with fish and cheeses and after a minute or two add eggs and nutmeg. Mix well.

Pour into a buttered baking dish sprinkled with bread crumbs. Flatten the top with a rubber spatula, sprinkle with bread crumbs, and dot with butter. Bake in 375 °F oven, uncovered, for 20 minutes or until the top begins to brown. **Serves 6.**

NOTE: This is an ideal dish to be made when there is leftover cooked fish . The pudding, covered with plastic wrapping and aluminum foil, can be frozen before baking, and baked unwrapped, without defrosting, only a few minutes longer than indicated above.

CROCCHETTE DI PESCE PER PESACH
Passover Fish Croquettes

Gefilte fish is traditionally served on Passover and other festivities in the home of the Ashkenazim. In Italy we had never heard of gefilte fish, even though fish was very much part of our festive meals. Here is a traditional fish dish for Passover which reminds us of gefilte fish.

1 1/2 pounds boneless raw fish
3/4 cup cold water
1 whole clove garlic
8 sprigs Italian parsley
3 tablespoons olive oil
Salt
Freshly ground white pepper
Dash or two nutmeg
3 tablespoons pinoli *(pine nuts)*
3 tablespoons non-dairy margarine
1/2 cup Passover cake flour
2 small eggs, slightly beaten
1 cup matza meal
Oil for frying

Cook the fish for 6 minutes with water, garlic, parsley stems (chop and reserve the leaves), 3 tablespoons of olive oil, and salt and pepper to taste. Discard parsley stems and garlic, drain well (reserve the liquid and keep it hot), and place in a bowl with chopped parsley leaves, nutmeg and *pinoli*. In a small skillet heat margarine and flour. Add the reserved hot liquid from the fish all at once and stir vigorously with a wire wisk. Cook 3 minutes, then add to the bowl containing the fish. Stir to cool a little, then add the eggs and mix well.

Spread the matza meal on a piece of waxed paper. Form oval croquettes with the fish mixture and roll in matza meal. Fry in hot oil until golden brown. **Serves 6.**

BACCALÁ COLLA CIPOLLA
Baccalá with Onions

Baccalá, salted and dried cod, can be found in fine Italian grocery stores and in some supermarkets. Baccalá is very nutricious and relatively inexpensive. For this reason, it used to be a staple for the poor and the farmers. The latter, who did not have access to fresh fish, often served baccalá accompanied by their other staple, polenta. Today polenta and baccalá is a marriage that often finds its way to the most sophisticated tables.

Soak dry baccalá in cold water for 24 hours, changing the water several times during this period.

Heat the oil in a large saucepan. Add the onion, lightly season with salt and pepper and cook over moderate heat, stirring occasionally, until onion is limp and translucent.

Drain baccalá and cut into 2-inch squares. Add to the pan with onion, sprinkle with flour and stir. Add 1 cup of water, bring to a boil, and cook for 7 or 8 minutes, shaking the pan often. Taste for salt and pepper and adjust if necessary. **Serves 6.**

1 1/2 pounds white baccalá
1/2 cup olive oil
6 medium white onions, sliced
Salt
Freshly ground black pepper
2 teaspoons unbleached flour
1 cup cold water

NOTE: This dish is especially delicious if served with hot slices of polenta (page 126). Also, keep in mind that baccalá, even more so than fresh fish, becomes hard and stringy if overcooked.

PARADISO
Baccalá on Toast

As its name suggests, this baccalá dish was considered heavenly by its inventors. It was the preferred alternative to pork and poultry made by the peasants in our region for holiday dinners. I first became acquainted with it during World War II when I was welcomed to share a festive meal by a family who defied the Nazi-Fascist terror by sheltering two young American parachutists as well as my sister, a Jewish refugee. (I was staying with someone else.) I include it in my collection not only because baccalá was the only kosher animal protein we had in those days, but also because I want to honor, with this modest recognition, those who risked their lives to save ours.

Soak fish in abundant cold water for about 24 hours, without changing the water. Drain, rinse well, and place in a saucepan with cold water to cover. Bring to a boil and, after 2 minutes, remove from heat. Temporarily transfer the fish to a warm dish (reserve the water) and season with abundant oil and salt and pepper to taste.

Toast the bread slices on both sides and rub the garlic cloves all over them. Dip in reserved baccalá water and arrange on a hot serving plate. Season with salt and pepper to taste, vinegar, and lots of extra virgin olive oil. Place baccalá with all its seasoning on top of the toasted bread and serve. **Serves 4 to 6.**

1 pound baccalá fillets
Extra virgin olive oil
Salt
*Coarsely ground black pepper**
6 1-inch slices Tuscan bread (page 224)
2 large cloves garlic
4 tablespoons red wine vinegar

* See instructions on page 43.

FRITTELLE DI BACCALÁ
Baccalá Pancakes

1 pound dry baccalá
*3 slices stale bread, soaked in water and cooked into a pap**
2 tablespoons freshly chopped Italian parsley
1/8 teaspoon freshly ground black pepper
4 eggs, slightly beaten
4 anchovy fillets, chopped
3 tablespoons grated Parmesan cheese
Olive or other vegetable oil for frying
6 small sprigs parsley
1 lemon cut lengthwise in 6 wedges

Soak baccalá in cold water for 24 hours, changing water two or three times during this period. Drain and place in a saucepan with enough cold water to cover. Bring to a boil and cook 1 minute. Drain and chop very fine. Combine with bread pap, chopped parsley, pepper, eggs, anchovy fillets, and Parmesan cheese. Mix well.

Heat 1/2 cup of oil in a large frying pan; drop baccalá mixture into the oil by the rounded tablespoonful and fry, turning, until golden on both sides. Add more oil as necessary. Remove to paper towel to drain.

Mound on a hot serving plate and garnish with parsley sprigs and lemon wedges. **Serves 6.**

*See instructions on page 39.

TONNO IN BARCHETTA
Tuna-stuffed Zucchini

6 medium zucchini
1 small onion, minced
1 small carrot, peeled and diced
1 tablespoon chopped Italian parsley
2 teaspoons shredded basil leaves
1/8 teaspoon dried oregano
Olive oil
1/4 teaspoon salt
1/8 teaspoon black pepper
1/2 garlic clove, minced fine
1 1/2 cups tomato sauce
2 slices stale white bread
1 13-ounce can tuna, drained and chopped
2 tablespoons seasoned bread crumbs

Wash, trim, and cut zucchini down to 5 inches. Cut up the leftover pieces and reserve. Cut the zucchini in half lengthwise and remove pulp, leaving an edge all around to give the shells the shape of little boats.

Place the pulp, the reserved leftover pieces, onion, carrot, parsley, basil, oregano, 2 tablespoons oil, salt, pepper, and garlic in a large saucepan. Stir; then delicately arrange the boats on top. Cover and cook over moderate heat for about 45 minutes.

Select a baking dish large enough to contain all the boats in a single layer. Cover the bottom of it with tomato sauce and line all the boats in it.

Add stale bread to the saucepan with the cooked vegetables and let it soak in the juice the vegetables have formed. Add tuna and mix well. Fill boats with this mixture, top with bread crumbs and a drizzle of oil. Bake in 400 °F oven for 25 minutes. **Serves 6.**

POLPETTONE DI TONNO
Tuna Loaf

Drain the liquid from the tuna into a bowl. Grind or chop the tuna very fine and add to the bowl. Add bread crumbs, eggs, parsley, and nutmeg and mix to combine. Let rest in the refrigerator for at least 20 minutes.

Shape the mixture into an oval loaf and place the four bay leaves on different spots of the surface. Wrap cheesecloth around the loaf and tie both ends with a string.

Bring 3 cups of water to a boil with 1 teaspoon salt; add the loaf and cook over moderate heat, covered, for 30 minutes. Lift from water, and place between two dishes to cool for at least 2 hours or overnight.

Remove cheesecloth and bay leaves and slice. Arrange on an oval plate, and cover with tuna sauce or sprinkle with oil, lemon juice, salt and pepper to taste. Serve surrounded by lemon slices and oil-cured black olives.

Serves 6.

1 13-ounce can white solid tuna packed in water
1 cup coarse bread crumbs
4 eggs, slightly beaten
2 tablespoons freshly chopped Italian parsley
2 dashes nutmeg
4 bay leaves
3 cups water
Salt
1 cup Tuna Sauce (page 214) or the juice of 1 lemon, extra virgin olive oil, freshly ground black pepper, and 1 lemon sliced very thin
1/2 cup oil-cured black olives

CACCIUCCO
Fish Stew

Cacciucco is most successful if you use different kinds of fish. Try mixing red snapper, sole, salmon, scrod, and other fish, some of which may be small and whole.

1 cup olive oil
1/2 teaspoon crushed red pepper
4 cloves garlic, 2 minced, 2 whole
1 heaping tablespoon tomato paste
1/2 cup dry red wine
4 cups diced freshly peeled tomatoes or canned peeled tomatoes*
1 cup warm water
2 teaspoons salt
5 pounds assorted fish, including skin and bones, cleaned and gutted, cut into 2-inch cubes (or left whole if small)
12 diagonal slices fruste *(page 228) or French bread, toasted*

In a large pot, heat the oil with pepper and minced garlic. When the garlic is lightly golden, add the tomato paste and cook, stirring, 2 minutes. Add the wine and raise the heat for 1/2 minute. Add the tomatoes, 1 cup warm water and the salt and cook 3 or 4 minutes. Add the fish, cover the pot tightly, and simmer for 10 minutes or until the fish is done.

Rub the whole cloves of garlic on both sides of the toast and arrange the slices on a large, deep serving plate. Pour the stew over the toast and serve. **Serves 6 to 8.**

* See instructions on page 45.

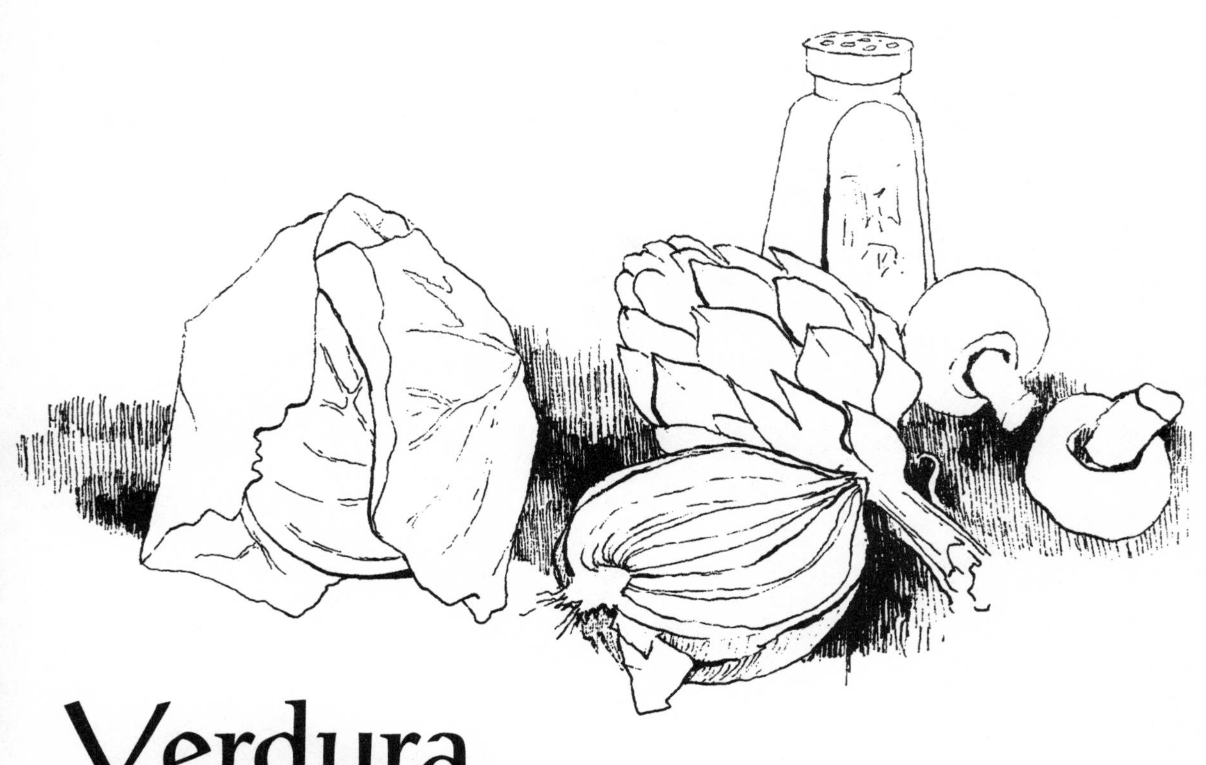

Verdura

VEGETABLES

DON'T BE SURPRISED if vegetarian dishes constitute the bulk of my collection. Historically Jews have been vegetarians whenever kosher animal proteins were inaccessible, and also for ethical and economical reasons. More recently, health considerations have turned many away from fat and cholesterol-laden foods and toward a table on which vegetarian food plays a more prominent role.

On many an occasion, since my first volume was published, I have been asked to make up an all-vegetarian menu for a Bar Mitzvah or a wedding, and innumerable times the suggestion has recurred that I write a totally vegetarian cook book.

Perhaps one day... . In the meantime, whether one is a vegetarian or not, the practice of eating a non-meat meal and 5 or more servings of vegetables a day is recommended both by nutritionists and gourmet experts alike. From the nutritional point of view, we have been told time and again that there are lots of minerals and vitamins and fibers in vegetables which are indispensable for our well being. Any connoisseur, anyone who has an appreciation of good taste, will agree that vegetables add tremendously to the enjoyment of a dish. From a purely aesthetic viewpoint, there would be nothing less appealing, in my opinion, than a piece of meat or fish placed at the center of a dish without any *contorno*, or side dish, to enliven its dullness.

Sauces, sometimes, take the place of vegetables to give life to a dish. The French cuisine makes great use of complicated sauces mostly based on butter. Other cuisines employ sauces laced with all sorts of spices for the same purpose. Also the Italian Jewish cuisine makes use of sauces; however, they are very simple and almost always based on olive oil. Sauces can indeed make an otherwise lackluster dish very exciting. My husband, for one, says that boiled chicken is an excuse to enjoy *salsa verde* (see page 142). However, for all their zest, sauces cannot take the place of vegetables as far as nutrition is concerned.

In compiling this collection, I realized that rosemary is widely used by the Italian Jews. I suspect that the reason is that the Jews who settled in Italy a few thousand years ago made their first home in Sicily where rosemary grows wild.

So, try some of the vegetable dishes in this volume (or in the first one, for that matter) that you are not familiar with, and enjoy an all new world of gourmet experiences.

PEPERONI PICCANTI
Spicy Peppers

3 pounds green, yellow, and red peppers
3/4 cup olive oil
12 anchovy fillets, cut up
2 cloves garlic, minced fine
1/4 teaspoon crushed red pepper
3 tablespoons white wine vinegar
Salt

Wash peppers and place, still wet, on a large baking sheet where they fit in a single layer. Place under the broiler or bake in 550 °F oven until the peel begins to blister and to turn black in some spots.

When peppers look wilted and done, remove from oven and drop into a basin with cold water. As soon as you can handle them, remove and discard peel, stems and core. Cut into strips and rinse in cold water to get rid of all the seeds. Drain thoroughly.

Heat the oil in a skillet. Add anchovies, garlic and crushed red pepper. Stir until anchovies are melted. Add peppers and vinegar and stir until moisture has evaporated. Taste for salt and add if necessary. Serve hot or at room temperature. Or, if you wish to preserve them, place in a tightly closed jar with all the sauce in the refrigerator and leave at room temperature before serving.

Serves 6.

CROCCHETTE DI PATATE
Potato Croquettes

3 pounds boiling potaotes
Unsalted butter
4 tablespoons freshly grated Italian Parmesan cheese
1 egg
1 egg yolk
Salt
Freshly ground white pepper
2 dashes nutmeg
1/2 cup unbleached flour
Vegetable oil for frying

Boil the potatoes in lightly salted water until very tender. Peel and mash, or pass through a vegetable mill. Do not use blender or processor.

Melt 4 tablespoons butter in a skillet; add the mashed potatoes and stir over low heat until potatoes are dry and thick. Remove from heat and let cool 5 minutes. Add Parmesan cheese and mix well. Add egg, egg yolk, salt and pepper to taste, and nutmeg, and mix very well to prevent bursting during frying.

Spread the flour on a working surface. Pour the potato mixture over the flour and quickly knead to incorporate some of the flour. Divide into 3 parts and shape each part into a rope about 1 inch thick. Cut into 2 1/2-inch pieces and give each an elongated egg shape.

Heat butter or oil or a mixture of the two in a skillet to 1-inch thickness and fry the croquettes over moderately high heat, a few at a time, turning delicately, until golden on all sides. **Serves 6.**

PATATE FRITTE A TOCCHETTI
Cubed Fried Potatoes

Once in a while everyone is entitled to indulge in "junk food". Fried potatoes, when eaten in fast-food joints, could be termed just that because we don't know what kind of fat is used, and above all we don't know how many times it is reused. The only fried potatoes we ate during my childhood and we eat now are the ones we prepare ourselves. This makes a world of difference not only in nutritional value, but in taste as well.

2 pounds all-purpose potatoes
1 teaspoon minced garlic
Peppercorns in a mill
2 teaspoons rosemary leaves
1 1/2 cups olive oil
Salt

Peel the potatoes, cut into 1/2-inch cubes and place in a bowl with cold water to cover so that they get rid of some of the starch. Drain and pat dry, then season with garlic, a few turns of the mill with black pepper, 1 teaspoon rosemary leaves, and 1 tablespoon olive oil. Toss to distribute the seasoning evenly and set aside in a cool place for about 1 hour.

Heat the oil in a medium saucepan. Add the potato cubes, making sure that any liquid that has formed remains in the bowl. Fry for 5 minutes stirring occasionally, then turn the heat off.

With a slotted spoon, transfer the potatoes to a colander, and let the oil cool to room temperature.

Fifteen minutes before serving, reheat the oil, add the potato cubes, and fry for another 10 minutes, or until they are golden and make a dry sound when stirred. Transfer to a serving dish lined with paper toweling.

Discard most of the oil, add the remaining rosemary leaves and small amount of salt and pepper to the saucepan, and heat for a few seconds. Distribute over potatoes and serve. **Serves 4.**

PATATE ARROSTO
Baked potatoes

3 pounds best quality baking potatoes
Coarse kosher salt
*Coarsely ground black pepper**
3 tablespoons chopped chives
Extra virgin olive oil

Wash and scrub the potatoes with a vegetable brush. With the tip of a sharp knife, remove every black spot remaining. Place unwrapped in a 500 °F oven and bake for 45 minutes, or until tender when poked in depth with a fork (the peel should be crusty and hard).

Remove from oven, and as soon as they can be handled, cut the potatoes lengthwise. Make a few deep crisscross incisions and season with salt and pepper to taste. Sprinkle with chives and an abundance of extra virgin olive oil. Serve immediately. **Serves 6.**

*See instructions on page 43.

ROLLATA DI PATATE E SPINACI
Potato and Spinach Roll

2 pounds boiling potatoes
Salt
1 cup unbleached flour
2 eggs, slightly beaten
1 pound small-leaved bulk spinach
2 tablespoons olive oil
1 small onion, minced
1/8 teaspoon white pepper
2 quarts water
6 tablespoons unsalted butter, melted
1/2 cup freshly grated Italian Parmesan cheese

Cook the potatoes in lightly salted water until very soft. Peel, mash (do not use blender or processor), and let cool for a while. Add 1 teaspoon salt, flour, and eggs and mix well until a smooth paste is formed. Spread over a piece of cheesecloth making a 15x12-inch rectangle.

Wash and cook spinach*. Drain well and chop fine. Heat the oil in a skillet; add the onion and saute for 2 minutes. Add spinach, pepper, and 1/4 teaspoon salt, and cook, stirring, for 5 minutes or until most moisture has evaporated. Spread over the potato paste, leaving a 1/2-inch margin all around.

Roll the short way as you would a jelly roll. Wrap the cheesecloth around the roll and fasten the two ends with a string.

Bring 2 quarts of water and 1 tablespoon salt to a boil in a fish poacher or a pot; add the roll. As soon as boiling resumes, lower the heat and simmer, covered, for 45 minutes to 1 hour.

Transfer the roll to a warm dish and let it rest for 10 minutes. Remove wrap, cut into 12 slices and dress with all the melted butter and half the cheese. Serve immediately with the remaining Parmesan in a separate dish.

Serves 4 to 6.

*See instructions on page 44..

SPINACI ALL'EBRAICA
Spinach Jewish Style

3 pounds small-leaved bulk spinach
Salt
1/2 cup dark seedless raisins
1 cup lukewarm water
6 tablespoons olive oil
1/2 small onion, minced
1/4 cup pinoli *(pine nuts)*
Freshly ground black pepper
Dash nutmeg

Remove stems and roots from spinach. Rinse in many changes of cold water until any trace of sand is removed. Place in a large pot with a pinch of salt and no water other than that retained from washing. Cook over moderately high heat, covered, for 5 minutes. Drain.*

Soak raisins in 1 cup of lukewarm water for a couple of minutes, then drain.

Meanwhile, heat the oil in a large skillet, add the onion and saute until onion is soft and translucent; add raisins, pinoli, and small amounts of salt and pepper. Saute, stirring, 1 minute. Add spinach and nutmeg and saute, stirring frequently, until spinach looks dry and crisp.

Serves 6.

* See instructions on page 44.

SPINACI ALL'AGRO
Lemon Spinach

3 pounds small-leaved bulk spinach
1/2 teaspoon salt
4 tablespoons olive oil
Juice of 1 lemon

Remove stems and roots from spinach. Rinse in cold water many times until any trace of sand is removed. Place in a large pot with 1/4 teaspoon salt and no water other than that which clings to the spinach from washing. Cook over moderately high heat, covered, until desired tenderness. Transfer to a colander* to cool.

Turn onto a cutting board and chop very fine. Do not use a food processor.

Place in a serving dish and flatten with a spatula. Sprinkle with the remaining salt and the oil. Just before serving, sprinkle with lemon juice. **Serves 6.**

* See instructions on page 44..

BIETOLE ALL'AGRO
Boiled Swiss Chard

Not always is the marriage of a leafy vegetable and garlic a felicitous one. Garlic goes very well with and actually enhances the flavor of spinach and most of the vegetables in the *Brassica oleracea* family, such as cauliflower, broccoli, cabbage, kale. However, garlic would ruin the flavor of escarole and other leafy vegetables generally used raw for salads (but also often cooked), which instead combine well with onion. Likewise, lemon and vinegar are not always interchangeable. Both lemon and vinegar go very well with steamed cauliflower, for instance; however, for *spinaci all'agro* lemon is ideal, and for *bietole all'agro* vinegar is the preferred *agro,* or sour touch. Also, for spinach, which has a strong flavor, we should use a mild olive oil; for mild bietole, extra virgin olive oil is better.

3 pounds Swiss chard
Salt
Freshly ground black pepper
White wine vinegar
Extra virgin olive oil

Remove the tips from the stems and cut the chard into 2 or 3-inch pieces. Rinse very well in cold water and place in a large pot with no water other than what is retained in washing. Add a small pinch of salt and cook on moderately high heat, covered, for 5 to 10 minutes, or until a test piece of stem feels done.

Lift from the water with a slotted spoon and place in a warmed serving plate. Season with salt and pepper to taste, and a generous sprinkling of both vinegar and oil. Serve immediately while still hot. **Serves 6.**

SFORMATO DI BIETOLA

Swiss Chard Pudding

4 pounds Swiss chard
2 ounces dry porcini mushrooms
Olive oil
1 clove garlic, minced
2 tablespoons freshly chopped Italian parsley
1 medium onion, minced
Salt
Freshly ground black pepper
Dash nutmeg
3 eggs, slightly beaten
1/2 cup seasoned bread crumbs

Remove stems from Swiss chard and reserve for later use. Rinse the leaves in cold water a couple of times, then place in a large pot with a pinch of salt and no water other than that retained from washing. Bring to a boil and cook, covered, for 7 minutes. Drain thoroughly and chop fine.

Soak the mushrooms in a cup of warm water for 5 to 10 minutes. Drain* (reserve the water) and chop fine. Place in a small saucepan with 2 tablespoons oil, garlic, parsley, and the reserved water from their bath. Cook uncovered 10 minutes, stirring occasionally.

In a large skillet, heat 6 tablespoons of oil with onion and saute until onion is slightly golden. Add the chopped Swiss chard and the cooked mushrooms and saute, stirring, until most liquid has evaporated. Remove from heat and cool for a while.

Add small amount of salt and pepper, the nutmeg, and the eggs and stir to combine. Place in an oiled baking dish sprinkled with bread crumbs. Flatten with a rubber spatula. Top with bread crumbs and a drizzle of oil. Bake in a 350 °F oven for 30 to 45 minutes. Delicious hot or at room temperature.

Serves 6.

* See instructions on page 43.

COSTE DI BIETOLE ALLA VENEZIANA

Swiss Chard Stems Venetian Style

For this dish you need to buy the type of Swiss chard with large, white stems. The green leafy part is not used here, but you needn't worry about wastefulness since with it you can prepare another delectable dish (see preceding recipe).

4 pounds Swiss chard
1/2 cup olive oil
1 clove garlic, minced
1 tablespoon finely chopped Italian parsley
Salt
2 tablespoons white wine vinegar

Cut the stems from the leaves. Wash the stems and dice them. Place in a pot with cold water to cover and bring to a boil. Cook approximately 5 minutes, then ladle most of the water out and add oil, garlic, parsley and a small amount of salt.

Cook over moderate heat, covered, until quite tender. Uncover and let most of the moisture evaporate. Add vinegar and keep uncovered until the vinegar also has evaporated and the stems are in a flavorful oil sauce.

Serves 4 to 6.

FINOCCHI ALLA GIUDIA
Fennel Jewish Style

12 medium round fennel knobs
2 garlic cloves
1/2 cup olive oil
Salt
Freshly ground white pepper
3/4 cup water

Remove and discard all the bruised and tough parts of the fennel and cut into 4 or 6 wedges each. Wash thoroughly and blot dry.

Place garlic and oil in a large skillet and saute until the garlic is browned. Discard the garlic and add the fennel. Season with small amounts of salt and pepper and saute for approximately 10 minutes, stirring frequently.

Add water and cook over moderate heat, tightly covered, for 10 to 15 minutes or until tender. Uncover the skillet and let the liquid evaporate and the fennel acquire a nice golden tone. Serve hot or at room temperature.

Serves 6.

SFORMATO DI FAGIOLINI
Green Bean Pudding

2 pounds green beans
Olive oil
Salt
Freshly ground black pepper
3 sage leaves or 1 teaspoon crushed sage
1 teaspoon dried rosemary leaves
2 cloves garlic
2 tablespoons coarsely chopped Italian parsley
1 cup cold water
1/2 cup bread crumbs
3 eggs, slightly beaten

Trim the beans at both ends, wash and drain.

Heat 3 tablespoons of oil in a large saucepan. Add 1 teaspoon salt, 1/4 teaspoon pepper, and the sage and rosemary leaves. Saute on high heat for 1 or 2 minutes, stirring frequently, then remove and discard sage and rosemary, making sure that salt and pepper remain in the pan.

Add garlic, beans, and 1 cup water to the aromatic oil; bring to a boil. Cover and cook on moderately high heat for about 10 minutes. Remove from heat and let cool for a while.

Drain liquid into a bowl. Chop beans fine and add to the bowl. Add 2 tablespoons bread crumbs and the eggs and stir to combine. Pour into an oiled baking dish sprinkled with bread crumbs. Spread flat with a rubber spatula. Top with bread crumbs, sprinkle with oil, and bake in 450 °F oven for 20 to 30 minutes, or until the top is lightly browned.

Serves 6 to 8.

FAGIOLINI IN TEGAME
Stewed Green Beans

Trim the beans at both ends, wash, and cut into 1 1/2-inch pieces. Place in a saucepan with all the other ingredients, including 1 cup of cold water, and cook covered for 3/4 hour or until desired tenderness. Uncover and boil rapidly another 5 or 6 minutes or until excess liquid has evaporated and beans are in a thick and flavorful sauce. **Serves 6.**

* See instructions on page 45.

- *2 pounds green beans*
- *1 medium onion, sliced thin*
- *2 cups peeled tomatoes (fresh* or canned) with juice*
- *1 tablespoon shredded basil leaves*
- *6 tablespoons olive oil*
- *1/2 teaspoon salt*
- *2 dashes freshly ground black pepper*
- *1 cup cold water*

FAGIOLI ALL'UCCELLETTO
Beans Bird Style (Stewed Beans)

In a large skillet, place the oil, garlic and sage, and saute for 1 1/2 minutes, or until the garlic turns lightly golden. Add the beans and small amounts of salt and pepper, and saute 2 more minutes, shaking the skillet a couple of times.

Add the diluted tomato paste and cook over moderate heat, uncovered, until moisture is greatly reduced — about 10 minutes — and beans are in a thick, flavorful sauce. Taste for salt and pepper and correct if necessary. Stir and serve. **Serves 6.**

- *1/2 cup olive oil*
- *2 cloves garlic*
- *5 sage leaves*
- *5 cups cooked white beans, drained (page 40)*
- *Salt*
- *Ground red pepper*
- *2 tablespoons tomato paste, diluted in 3/4 cup water*

FAGIOLI CON LA LATTUGA
Beans and Romaine Lettuce

Very often we find that the Roman Jews, who knew about nutrition more than we recognize, combined highly caloric vegetables such as beans and artichokes, with a lighter vegetable, almost always lettuce. (See also *Carciofi colla Lattuga* on page 187, and *Piselli colla Lattuga* on page 192.)

1 1/2 cups dry beans such as Great Northern beans or navy peas
2 quarts hot water
Salt
1 clove garlic, husk on
2 large sage leaves
3 large heads Romaine lettuce
1/2 cup olive oil
2 cloves garlic, sliced
Freshly ground black pepper
1 tablespoon freshly chopped Italian parsley
1 tablespoon tomato paste

Remove stones and any debris from beans. Rinse 2 or 3 times in warm water, then place in a large pot with 2 quarts of hot water and 1 teaspoon salt and bring to a rapid boil. Lower the heat to minimum, and after 15 minutes add the garlic with husk on and the sage. Continue to simmer, covered, 30 minutes, or until beans are cooked but still slightly underdone.

Wash lettuce thoroughly. With a sharp knife, shred into thin stripes. Heat the oil in a large saucepan, add the garlic, and saute until garlic is slightly golden. Add lettuce, small amounts of salt and pepper, and all the parsley, and saute for 10 minutes.

Add tomato paste and saute, stirring, 5 more minutes. Drain the beans and add to the saucepan with lettuce. Cover and simmer, shaking the pan from time to time, for 15 minutes. Beans and lettuce should cook in a thick, flavorful sauce. However, if it becomes necessary, add a few tablespoons of water during the cooking period.

Serves 6 to 8.

COPPE DI ZUCCHINI
Zucchini Cups

In Italy *coppe* are made with the ball-shaped, pale-green variety of zucchini which taste best if picked when they are no larger than a medium orange. I have not been able to locate these zucchini, nor have I found the seeds to grow them in my garden. Since this is one of my favorite dishes, however, I make it quite successfully with the long zucchini that are available in any vegetable store and supermarket.

Wash, trim, and cut zucchini into 2 1/2-inch segments. Select 18 of the wider segments and reserve the rest.

With a melon scoop, carefully remove the pulp from the selected segments, leaving less than 1/4-inch thickness in the wall and at the bottom, thus forming little cups. Reserve the pulp.

Chop the reserved segments and pulp together (you should have 8 to 9 cups), and place in a large saucepan with onion, basil, parsley, salt, pepper, and 3 tablespoons oil. Stir, flatten down, then place the zucchini cups over the pulp mixture. Cover the pan and cook over moderate heat for 15 to 20 minutes, shaking the pan occasionally.

Delicately transfer the zucchini cups to an oiled baking dish, leaving the cups standing snugly close to one another.

Cook the zucchini puree, uncovered, stirring frequently, until the moisture is greatly reduced. (There should be about 4 1/2 cups of cooked puree left.)

Remove the pan from heat and let cool for at least 5 minutes. Add Parmesan cheese, if desired, reserving 2 tablespoons. Add eggs and stir to combine.

Fill all the cups with this mixture. If you have opted for using the cheese, combine the reserved cheese with the bread crumbs and top the cups with this mixture. Sprinkle with oil and bake in preheated 350 °F oven for 30 minutes, or until the tops are browned. Serve hot or at room temperature.

Serves 6.

8 medium to large green zucchini (6 or 7 pounds)
1/2 cup chopped onion
1 tablespoon shredded fresh basil leaves
2 tablespoons freshly chopped Italian parsley
1 teaspoon salt
1/8 teaspoon freshly ground black pepper
Olive oil
1/2 cup freshly grated Italian Parmesan cheese (optional)
3 eggs, slightly beaten
1/2 cup coarse bread crumbs

ZUCCHINI TRIFOLATI

Zucchini Truffle Style

Trim zucchini at both ends and wash thoroughly. Slice very thin and place in a large skillet with the oil. Quickly fry over moderately high heat for 2 or 3 minutes, stirring frequently. Sprinkle with small amounts of salt and pepper, add the lemon juice, and stir-fry an additional 2 minutes. Taste for seasoning and tenderness, but keep in mind that zucchini trifolati should remain crisp.

Serves 6.

2 1/2 pounds small green zucchini
5 tablespoons olive oil
Salt
Freshly ground black pepper
2 tablespoons lemon juice

ZUCCA GIALLA IN TEGAME
Stewed Butternut Squash

Zucca gialla is the name given to any large squash, be it acorn, butternut, or any of the winter type. I use butternut squash because of its unique sweet taste and pleasant texture, but any other variety of squash can be prepared this way.

- *1 large butternut squash (3 to 4 pounds)*
- *1 cup water*
- *1/2 cup finely chopped fresh onion or 2 tablespoons dehydrated minced onion*
- *4 tablespoons olive oil*
- *1 teaspoon salt*
- *1/8 teaspoon freshly ground black pepper*
- *1 tablespoon shredded basil*

Trim and pare the squash. Cut in half lengthwise and remove the seeds and the fibers around them. Slice into 1/4-inch slices, then cut each slice into diamonds or squares. Place in a large skillet with all the other ingredients and cook over high heat, covered, for 5 minutes, shaking the pan frequently. Do not stir, since butternut is very delicate and it would turn into a puree. Lower the heat and cook 5 minutes longer. **Serves 6.**

NOTE: Do not overcook butternut squash because unless you serve it immediately, it continues to cook while it is hot in the pan, even though the heat has been turned off. If it does happen to overcook and the pieces lose their shape, stir vigorously and serve as a puree. The texture will be different, but the taste just as good.

ZUCCA SFRANTA IN FORNO
Baked Mashed Squash

- *1 large butternut or any winter squash you like (3 to 4 pounds)*
- *Water*
- *1/2 cup finely chopped fresh onion or 2 tablespoons dehydrated minced onion*
- *1 tablespoon coarsely chopped Italian parsley*
- *1 tablespoon shredded basil*
- *1 small garlic clove, minced*
- *Olive oil*
- *3 eggs, slightly beaten*
- *Bread crumbs*

Trim and pare the squash. Cut in half and remove the seeds and most of the fibers around them. Cut coarsely (approximately 3/4-inch cubes), and place in a pan with 1 cup water, onion, parsley, basil, garlic, and 4 tablespoons oil. Cook over moderately high heat, covered, for 10 minutes, stirring frequently. Add a few tablespoons of water if necessary, but keep the squash rather dry.

Remove from heat and coarsely mash. (Do not puree.) After it cools a little, add eggs and mix well.

Oil a baking dish and sprinkle abundantly with bread crumbs. Pour the mashed squash into it; flatten with a rubber spatula, sprinkle the top with bread crumbs and drizzle with oil. Bake in preheated 350 °F oven for 45 minutes or until well puffed and the top begins to brown.

Serves 12.

CARCIOFI RITTI
Standing Artichokes

18 small to medium artichokes
Olive oil
1 cup water
2 cloves garlic, minced
2 tablespoons finely chopped parsley
Salt
Freshly ground black pepper
1 cup seasoned bread crumbs

Discard outer leaves and lop off the tips from artichokes using the kitchen scissors. Cut the stems so that the bottoms are flat. Peel and chop the stems fine and set aside.

Place the artichokes in a pan with 1/2 cup of oil and all the water, and cook covered for 5 minutes. Remove to a dish, reserving the liquid.

When the parboiled artichokes are cool enough to handle, take one at a time, gently open the leaves, and season with small amounts of garlic, parsley, salt and pepper.

Mix together bread crumbs and the reserved chopped stems. Place in a small skillet with 2 tablespoons of oil, and quickly stir-fry for a couple of minutes. Place 1 tablespoon of this mixture between the leaves of each artichoke.

Arrange the artichokes, standing, in an oiled oven-proof pan, where they can fit snugly. Pour over them all the reserved liquid and bake in a 350 °F oven for 30 to 45 minutes, or until the water has evaporated and the artichoke tops are browned. **Serves 6 to 8.**

CARCIOFI IN SALSA D'UOVO
Artichokes with Egg Sauce

12 small to medium artichokes
2 lemons, juice and rinds
1 small celery stalk
3 or 4 parsley stems
1 carrot stick
4 tablespoons olive oil
2 teaspoons unbleached flour
1 1/2 cups water
1 1/2 teaspoons salt
1/8 teaspoon freshly ground black pepper
2 egg yolks
Juice of 1 lemon

Trim and clean artichokes.* Cut lengthwise in 1/4-inch slices and drop into the bowl with lemon water until you're ready to cook.

With a piece of white string, tie together celery stalk, parsley stems, and carrot. Place in a large skillet with oil and lightly saute for 1 minute. Dissolve the flour in 1 1/2 cups of water and add to skillet. Simmer, covered, for 5 minutes.

Drain artichokes and add to skillet. Add salt and pepper, and cook over moderately high heat for 10 to 20 minutes, depending on size and freshness of artichokes. Remove and discard bouquet of herbs.

Mix egg yolks with lemon juice. Pour mixture over artichokes and immediately turn the heat off. Shake the skillet or stir gently to combine. **Serves 6.**

* See instructions on page 36.

CARCIOFI FRITTI
Fried Artichokes

12 medium artichokes
2 lemons, juice and rinds
3/4 cup unbleached flour
1/2 teaspoon salt
1/8 teaspoon freshly ground white pepper
1/2 cup cold water
1 egg
2 egg yolks
Olive oil for frying
1 lemon, cut into 6 wedges

Trim and prepare artichokes*. Cut in half lengthwise and remove any choke. Slice each half into 3 or 4 wedges and drop into the bowl with acidulated water until you are ready to fry.

Combine flour, salt, and pepper with 1/2 cup of cold water in a bowl and beat with a fork. Add egg, egg yolks, and 2 tablespoons of oil and beat some more until the batter is smooth.

Drain the artichoke pieces and pat dry with a paper towel.

Heat 1 cup of oil in a small frying pan. Dip the artichokes in batter and fry a few pieces at a time in the hot oil until lightly golden. Serve hot garnished with lemon wedges. **Serves 6.**

* See instructions on page 36.

CARCIOFI AL BURRO
Buttered Artichokes

12 medium artichokes
2 lemons, juice and rinds
3/4 cup water
6 tablespoons sweet butter
Salt
Freshly ground white pepper

Clean and trim artichokes.* Cut in half lengthwise and drop into the bowl with lemon water until ready to cook.

Bring 1 cup of water to a boil in a large skillet. Cut artichokes into very thin slivers and add to boiling water. Cook rapidly, stirring occasionally, for 5 minutes or until all the moisture has evaporated. Add butter and salt and pepper to taste and saute until lightly golden.

Serves 6.

*See instructions on page 36

CARCIOFI STUFATI
Stewed Artichokes

Clean and trim artichokes* and keep in the acidulated water until ready to cook.

Cut into 6 wedges each, remove any choke and place in a saucepan with all the other ingredients, including small amounts of salt and pepper.

Cook over moderate heat, covered, for 30 minutes, or until the bottom parts feel tender. Add a few tablespoons of water if necessary, but at the end uncover the pan and let the moisture evaporate so that the artichokes are left in a flavorful oil sauce. Taste for salt and pepper and correct. **Serves 6.**

12 medium artichokes
2 lemons, juice and rind
1 cup water
2 cloves garlic, sliced
2 tablespoons coarsely chopped Italian parsley
6 tablespoons olive oil
Salt
Freshly ground black pepper

* See instructions on page 36.

CARCIOFI COLLA LATTUGA
Artichokes and Romaine Lettuce

Clean and trim artichokes.* Cut into wedges, remove any choke, and drop into the bowl with acidulated water for a few minutes. Drain and toss into a large skillet. Add 6 tablespoons of oil, garlic, onion, and small amounts of salt and pepper and saute for approximately 10 minutes, stirring frequently.

Separate lettuce leaves and wash thoroughly. Shred fine with a sharp knife and add to the skillet with artichokes. Add small amounts of salt and pepper and a sprinkle of oil, and cook over moderate heat, covered, 10 more minutes, or until lettuce and artichokes are done. Uncover and raise the heat to evaporate any remaining water since this dish is delicious in a flavorful oil sauce.
Serves 6.

12 small to medium artichokes
1 large lemon, juice and rind
Olive oil
2 large cloves garlic, sliced
1 small onion, minced
2 pounds Romaine lettuce
Salt
Freshly ground black pepper
1 tablespoon freshly chopped Italian parsley

* See instructions on page 36.

RADICCHIO ROSSO BRASATO
Brazed Red Radicchio

6 large heads of red radicchio
2 large carrots, peeled and sliced
1 large onion, thinly sliced
6 tablespoons olive oil
1 tablespoon freshly chopped Italian parsley
Salt
Freshly ground black pepper
1 1/2 cups water

Discard outer, bruised leaves from radicchio; cut into wedges and wash thoroughly.

In a large pot place carrot slices, then onion slices, then radicchio wedges, and pour the oil over all of it. Sprinkle with parsley and small amounts of salt and pepper, then add all the water. Cook over moderate heat, covered, for 20 to 30 minutes. Uncover, raise the heat, and cook until excess liquid is gone and radicchio is lightly browned. **Serves 6.**

FUNGHI IN TEGAME
Stewed Mushrooms

2 1/2 pounds firm white mushrooms
1/2 ounce dried porcini mushrooms
1/2 cup warm water
6 tablespoons olive oil
2 tablespoons coarsely chopped Italian parsley
1/4 teaspoon dried savory
3 large cloves garlic
Salt
Freshly ground black pepper

Trim, wash, and drain mushrooms. Cut the larger ones into halves or into four pieces and leave the smaller ones whole.

Soak the dried mushrooms in 1/2 cup of warm water for 5 to 10 minutes. Lift them from their bath with a fork, reserving the water. Remove and discard any parts that still have some dirt attached to them. Place in a non-metallic saucepan with the fresh mushrooms; add the oil, parsley, savory, garlic, and small amounts of salt and pepper.

Carefully pour in the reserved water from the soaked mushrooms, making sure that any sand remains at the bottom of the cup.* Cook uncovered over low heat for 20 to 30 minutes, or until the liquid is reduced to a few tablespoons. Discard the three garlic cloves and serve.

Serves 6.

*See instructions on page 43.

FUNGHI PICCANTI
Spicy Mushrooms

Trim, wash and drain mushrooms. Slice very thin. Place in a non-metallic saucepan with oil, garlic, and onion and cook uncovered, over moderately high heat, for 5 minutes, stirring occasionally.

Wash and cube the tomatoes and add to the saucepan. Add basil, parsley, salt, and pepper, and cook, uncovered, 10 to 15 minutes longer. Add vinegar and capers, stir, and remove from heat. Let cool. Serve at room temperature as an appetizer or reheat in a saucepan to serve as a side dish. **Serves 6.**

2 pounds firm, small white mushrooms
4 tablespoons olive oil
1 clove garlic, minced
1 medium onion, sliced thin
3 large ripe, firm tomatoes
1 tablespoon shredded basil leaves
1 tablespoon freshly chopped Italian parsley
2 teaspoons salt
1/4 teaspoon ground red pepper
1/4 cup white wine vinegar
2 tablespoons tiny capers, drained

BROCCOLI STUFATI
Stewed Broccoli

Make sure to choose broccoli that are tight and of a bluish dark-green color.

Rinse broccoli in cold water, holding by the stems. (Broccoli do not need much washing, but once in a while you will find a green worm clinging to one of the smaller stems and cold water will compel the intruder to let go.)

Remove and discard large stems. Separate the big flowers into many florets and place in a saucepan with the oil, salt, pepper, and garlic. Add 1/2 cup cold water and bring to a rapid boil. Cook, covered, for 5 minutes. Uncover and cook another 2 minutes or until broccoli are tender but still crisp and most liquid is gone. Serve immediately while still bright green. **Serves 6 to 8.**

2 bunches fresh broccoli
4 tablespoons olive oil
1 teaspoon salt
1/4 teaspoon freshly ground black pepper
2 large cloves garlic, sliced
1/2 cup cold water

CAROTE STUFATE
Stewed Carrots

1 1/2 pounds carrots, peeled and sliced (about 5 cups)
3 tablespoons olive oil
1 tablespoon dehydrated minced onion
1 teaspoon salt
1/8 teaspoon freshly ground black pepper
3/4 cup water
1 tablespoon freshly chopped Italian parsley

Place sliced carrots in a skillet with oil, onion, salt, and pepper. Add 3/4 cup of water and bring to a boil. Lower heat and simmer, covered, for 15 minutes.

Uncover and cook over high heat, stirring, 2 minutes longer or until most liquid is gone. Add parsley, stir and remove from heat. **Serves 6.**

CAVOLFIORE IN SALSA PICCANTE
Cauliflower with a Piquant Sauce

1 large, white cauliflower
1/2 cup olive oil
8 anchovy fillets, cut up
2 cloves garlic, minced
2 tablespoons capers, drained and chopped fine
Salt
Freshly ground white pepper
1/4 cup white wine vinegar

Remove and discard outer leaves of cauliflower. With a sharp knife separate florets and cut the larger ones into halves or quarters. Boil or steam for 10 minutes or until fork tender, but not mushy. Drain and transfer to a warmed deep dish.

Meanwhile, lightly heat the oil in a saucepan; add the anchovies and garlic and stir until anchovies are almost melted. Add capers, small amounts of salt and pepper, and the vinegar, and remove from heat. Pour over the cauliflower and serve immediately. **Serves 6.**

CAVOLETTI DI BRUXELLES
Brussels Sprouts

2 pints Brussels sprouts
4 tablespoons olive oil
1/2 teaspoon salt
1/8 teaspoon freshly ground black pepper
1 large clove garlic, minced
1 tablespoon freshly chopped Italian parsley
1/2 cup cold water

Discard outer leaves from sprouts and cut the bottoms flat. Wash thoroughly and place in a saucepan with oil, salt, pepper, garlic, and parsley. Add 1/2 cup of cold water and bring to a rapid boil. Loosely cover pan and cook for 15 minutes or until sprouts are tender and excess moisture has evaporated. **Serves 6.**

CAVOLO RICCIO IN PADELLA
Sauted Kale

2 1/2 pounds fresh young kale
1 cup cold water
Salt
2 cloves garlic, minced
6 tablespoons olive oil
Freshly ground black pepper

Discard all large stems and yellowed leaves, if there are any. Rinse kale in cold water several times. Place in a large pot with 1 cup of cold water and a pinch of salt. Cook over moderately high heat, covered, for 5 to 15 minutes or until tender. (Cooking time depends on freshness of kale.) Drain.

In a large skillet or iron frying pan, place garlic, oil, and small amounts of salt and pepper. Saute over moderate heat until garlic is lightly golden. Add kale and cook, stirring frequently, until kale has lost much of its moisture and it is crisp and tasty. **Serves 6.**

CAVOLO CAPPUCCIO
Savoy Cabbage

2 pounds Savoy cabbage
2 cloves garlic, sliced
Salt
Ground red pepper
2 tablespoons olive oil
2 medium ripe tomatoes, peeled, or 1 cup canned peeled tomatoes*
1/2 cup water

Remove and discard outer, tough leaves from cabbage. Cut into 4 wedges and remove and discard the core and some of the larger ribs. Cut each wedge into three segments and wash thoroughly. Place in a cassarole with small amounts of salt and pepper and the remaining ingredients.

Cook over moderately high heat, covered, for 15 to 20 minutes (cooking time depends on freshness of cabbage). Uncover and let some of the liquid evaporate. Taste for salt and pepper and correct if necessary. **Serves 6.**

* See instructions on page 45.

PISELLI IN TEGAME
Stewed Peas

4 tablespoons olive oil
*1 tablespoon dehydrated minced onion**
1 tablespoon freshly chopped Italian parsley
1/2 teaspoon salt
2 dashes black pepper
1 cup water
3 pounds small fresh peas (about 2 cups after shelling) or 2 10-ounce packages frozen tiny peas

Place oil, onion, parsley, salt, and pepper in a skillet. Add 1 cup of water and bring to a boil. Cook for 3 or 4 minutes.

Add shelled peas, loosely cover pan, and cook over moderately high heat for approximately 8 minutes or until most liquid has evaporated and peas are tender but not overcooked. **Serves 6.**

* Dehydrated onion is preferred to the fresh one, since it adds sweetness to the already sweet peas.

PISELLI COLLA LATTUGA
Peas with Lettuce

1/2 large head Romaine lettuce
2 10-ounce packages frozen tiny peas
2 young scallions, sliced
6 tablespoons olive oil
1/2 teaspoon salt
1/8 teaspoon freshly ground black pepper

With a sharp knife, shred the lettuce and rinse in cold water. Place in a saucepan with no water other than what the lettuce retains in washing, cover tightly, and cook 5 minutes. Add frozen peas, scallions, oil, salt, and pepper; cover the pan again and cook over moderate heat for 10 minutes. Stir and cook, uncovered, another 10 minutes, or until most of the moisture has evaporated and peas and lettuce remain in a flavorful oil sauce.

Serves 6.

POMODORI AL FORNO
Baked Tomatoes

12 ripe round medium tomatoes
Olive oil
1 1/2 teaspoons salt
1/4 teaspoon freshly ground black pepper
1 clove garlic, minced
2 tablespoons freshly chopped Italian parsley
2 large fresh basil leaves, shredded, or 1 teaspoon dried basil
1/2 teaspoon ground dried savory
1/2 cup seasoned bread crumbs

Wash tomatoes and dry with paper toweling. Cut in half and place in an oiled baking dish with the cut side up. Sprinkle with salt and pepper and set aside for a few minutes.

Combine garlic, parsley, basil, and savory. Spread approximately 1/2 teaspoon of this mixture over each tomato half. Drizzle with oil, top with bread crumbs and sprinkle abundantly with oil. Bake uncovered in 375 °F oven for 45 minutes. Serve hot or at room temperature.

Serves 6

POMODORI RIPIENI DI RISO
Tomatoes Stuffed with Rice

8 round ripe tomatoes (about 3 pounds)
3/4 cup Italian rice
1 large clove garlic, minced
6 tablespoons olive oil
Salt
Freshly ground black pepper
1/2 teaspoon oregano
1 tablespoon freshly chopped Italian parsley
1 tablespoon shredded basil leaves

Wash tomatoes, pat dry, and line on a working surface with stem side down. Slice the upper part almost through, but not quite, since you will use this as a lid.

With the help of a teaspoon, gently remove pulp, juice, and seeds out of the tomatoes into a bowl. Arrange the tomato shells, standing with lids open, in an oiled baking dish.

Add rice, 3 tablespoons oil, 2 teaspoons salt, 1/8 teaspoon pepper, parsley, and basil to the bowl with tomato pulp and juice and mix well to combine.

Sprinkle the inside of the tomato shells with small amounts of salt, pepper and oil, then fill with the rice mixture and close the lids as best you can.

Loosely cover with aluminum foil and bake in 375 °F oven for 1 hour. Delicious hot or at room temperature.

Serves 4.

MELANZANE ALLA GIUDIA
Eggplant Jewish Style

4 pounds medium-sized, firm eggplant
Salt
1 cup olive oil
2 large cloves garlic
1/4 teaspoon freshly ground black pepper
2 tablespoons freshly chopped Italian parsley

Wash and trim eggplant, but leave the peel on. Cut in half lengthwise, then cut each half into 3 or 4 wedges. With a sharp knife remove part of the pulp from each wedge (reserve this pulp for the recipe that follows) leaving the wedges 1/2-inch thick. Cut into 1-inch sections and place in a large bowl. Add 3 to 4 teaspoons salt, toss to distribute the salt evenly, then cover with an inverted dish slightly smaller than the bowl and leave in the refrigerator for at least 1 hour.

Rinse eggplant in cold water, squeeze the liquid out, and blot-dry with paper toweling.

Place the oil and garlic in a large frying pan over high heat. When the garlic is slightly golden, add the eggplant and stir-fry for 2 minutes.

Lower the heat and cook, covered, 5 or 6 minutes. Uncover, add pepper and parsley, and cook another 7 to 10 minutes, stirring occasionally.

With a slotted spoon lift the eggplant and let most of the oil drain through before transferring the eggplant to a serving dish. Serve hot, cold, or at room temperature.

Serves 6.

CROCCHETTE DI MELANZANE
Eggplant Croquettes

I always make these croquettes at the same time I make eggplant Jewish style, so that I can use the pulp from the preceding recipe. However, you can make this recipe by itself using whole eggplant, but make sure to remove and discard the peel.

3 cups diced pulp from eggplant
Salt
2 eggs, slightly beaten
Unseasoned bread crumbs
1/2 cup grated Italian Parmesan cheese (optional)
2 tablespoons freshly chopped Italian parsley
2 cloves garlic passed through a garlic press
Freshly ground black pepper
Olive oil for frying

Place eggplant pulp in a saucepan with 1 teaspoon salt and cold water to cover. Bring to a boil and cook 5 minutes. Drain, let cool, then place in a piece of cheesecloth and squeeze the liquid out.

Place in a food processor with eggs, 1/2 cup bread crumbs, Parmesan cheese (if you opt for it), parsley, garlic, and salt and pepper to taste. Process a few seconds, or just until everything is mixed. Let rest for a while.

Have a dish or a piece of wax paper with a thick layer of bread crumbs at hand.

Heat 1 cup of oil in a medium frying pan. Drop eggplant mixture by the rounded tablespoonful over the bread crumbs and roll to coat. Fry a few croquettes at a time in the hot oil until golden brown on all sides. Serve hot. **Serves 6.**

CICORIA CATALOGNA BRASATA
Brazed Catalonian Chicory

2 bunches Catalonian chicory (approximately 3 pounds)
1/2 cup cold water
1 medium onion, thinly sliced
4 tablespoons olive oil
3/4 teaspoon salt
1/8 teaspoon freshly ground black pepper

Trim the bunches at the bottom and discard the outer, bruised leaves of chicory. Cut each bunch into half lengthwise, then each half into 4 wedges. Cut each wedge into 3 sections and rinse in fresh water several times. Drain and pat dry with a paper towel.

Place in a pot with all the other ingredients and bring to a boil. Lower the heat and simmer for 10 to 15 minutes (cooking time for leafy vegetables depends on their freshness and stage of growth). Uncover, raise the heat, and cook until excess liquid is gone. **Serves 6.**

CICORIA CATALOGNA ALL'AGRO

Boiled Catalonian Chicory

I always make this vegetable at the same time I make *Puntarelle* (page 208), so there is no waste. However, if puntarelle is not your primary object, you only need to buy 1 or 2 bunches of this vegetable and steam the whole bunch, including the core and the whitest leaves.

Leftover from puntarelle *or 3 pounds Catalonian chicory*
1/2 cup cold water
Salt
Extra virgin olive oil
Red wine vinegar

If using the leftover from puntarelle, steam only the green parts. Otherwise steam the entire bunch. Trim at the bottom and remove and discard any bruised leaves. Cut into 2-inch sections and wash thoroughly in cold water.

Place in a pot with 1/2 cup water and a pinch of salt and boil over moderately high heat, covered, for approximately 10 minutes.

Drain* and place in a warmed deep serving dish. Season with salt, oil, and vinegar to taste and toss. Serve warm. **Serves 6.**

*See directions on page 44.

Insalate

SALADS

ARANCE CONDITE
Orange Salad

Toward the end of World War II, after retaking possession of our home which had been occupied by fascists while we were in hiding, we heard a knock at our door early one morning. Before us stood a British officer, who politely introduced himself. He explained that he was in charge of buying wine for his company and needed to leave the money with a trustworthy family who knew English, and our family had been mentioned to him. After this flattering introduction, we let him in and without hesitation he emptied his knapsack into a cupboard, filling it with a mountain of 1000-lire bills. Then he disappeared and we didn't see him until late that afternoon, quite loaded, in the company of the farmer who had sold him the wine. He begged my father to pay the man, pocketed the remaining bills, thanked us, and left. After that he came back once a month, and as a result we became close friends. To amuse us (as a civilian he had been a schoolteacher) he would recite the alphabet from A to Z and then in reverse in one breath. Often he would arrive when we were still in bed and, after my father had let him in, he would walk directly to the bedroom where my sister and I were still asleep and shout from the door, "Get up, lazies, it's almost 7 o'clock!" Then he would empty his sack and go about his business.

One afternoon he came back as we were about to eat our orange salad (in Italy salad is served at the end of the meal, not at the beginning), and my father offered him some. He looked puzzled and, frankly, quite revolted at the idea of coupling oranges with olive oil, but out of courtesy he tried the salad. He truly liked it, and it became his favorite snack when he came around. He swore he would introduce it in England, where his family ran a small restaurant business.

I never found out whether the British officer did introduce the orange salad in England, but I have introduced it in America quite successfully.

9 large, seedless oranges
1 citron or 1 large lemon (optional), peeled and diced
Coarse salt
*Coarsely crushed black pepper**
Extra virgin olive oil

Peel the oranges with a sharp knife, leaving some of the white part of the peel attached to the fruit. Cut into 1/4-inch slices and arrange them on a serving platter. Sprinkle with salt, pepper, and oil to taste. Serve with a crust of Tuscan or fruste bread. **Serves 6.**

NOTE: We served our orange salad just as I have described it. However, some prefer to cut the sweetness of the oranges by adding a few pieces of citron or lemon to it.

* See instructions on page 43.

INSALATA DI RISO NATURALE
Brown Rice and Lentil Salad

1 cup brown rice
3 cups cold water
Salt
1 cup dried lentils, rinsed in cold water
Freshly ground black pepper
1 clove garlic, husk on
1 sprig fresh rosemary or 1 teaspoon dry rosemary leaves wrapped in cheese cloth
3 tablespoons chopped chives
1 tablespoon coarsely chopped Italian parsley
1 small sweet red pepper, cored and diced
Extra virgin olive oil

Place the rice in a saucepan with 3 cups of cold water and 1 teaspoon salt. Bring to a rapid boil, then reduce the heat to minimum, cover, and simmer for 20 to 25 minutes.

At the same time, place the lentils in another saucepan with hot water to cover, 1 teaspoon salt, dash pepper, garlic and rosemary. Bring to a boil, then lower the heat and simmer, covered, for 20 to 25 minutes. (If the lentils are of a good quality, they should be ready at the same time as the rice is.)

Discard garlic and rosemary. Drain any liquid that might be left from rice and lentils, then combine the two in a salad bowl. Add chives, parsley, and red pepper. Season with salt and pepper to taste, sprinkle abundantly with olive oil and toss. Serve hot or at room temperature.

Serves 6.

CECI CONDITI
Chickpeas Salad

1 pound dried chickpeas
4 quarts warm water
Salt
1 small branch fresh rosemary or 1 teaspoon dried rosemary leaves, wrapped in a piece of cheese cloth
1 clove garlic, husk on
*Coarsely ground black pepper**
2 tablespoons chives or scallion greens, chopped
Extra virgin olive oil

Distribute chick peas on a flat surface. Pick and remove stones and any debris. Rinse 2 or 3 times in warm water and place in a large pot. Add 4 quarts of warm water and 1 tablespoon salt, and bring to a boil. Lower the heat to minimum, add rosemary and garlic, and simmer, covered, for 1 hour or until tender.

Remove and discard rosemary and garlic.

With a slotted spoon, transfer to a bowl; add chives or scallion greens, and season with salt and pepper to taste. Sprinkle with extra virgin olive oil and toss. Serve hot.

Serves 6 to 10.

* See instructions on page 43.

INSALATA DI CUSCUSSU
Couscous Salad

This salad can be served as a refreshing alternative to potato salad in summer dinners, or as an excellent hors d'oeuvre in any season. Couscous, pre-cooked and raw, can be found in most health food and specialty stores. I prefer to use the raw type.

1 cup raw couscous
6 tablespoons extra virgin olive oil
Salt
3 1/2 cups cold water
3/4 cup oil-cured black olives, pitted and cut up
1/2 large red pepper, cored and diced
1/2 yellow pepper, cored and diced
1/4 cup freshly minced onion
2 tablespoons Italian parsley leaves
Freshly ground black pepper

Place the couscous in a large pan with 2 tablespoons of oil and mix until all the grains are coated. Add 1 teaspoon salt and all the water and stir. Bring to a boil over high heat, stirring occasionally. Lower the heat and simmer, stirring frequently, 1/2 hour or until couscous feels tender to the bite.

Let cool to room temperature, stirring from time to time to fluff it up, then add the chopped olives, peppers, onion, and parsley. Add salt and pepper to taste and the remaining oil. Mix to combine. **Serves 6 to 8.**

POMODORI CONDITI
Tomato Salad

What's so Italian Jewish about a tomato salad? I'll tell you: the fuss and care in preparing it. I was present once when two Italians, one a journalist from Bologna and the other a professor from Sicily, argued for hours over the relative merits of their respective ways of preparing a tomato salad. Each was convinced that his own method was the best. One insisted on lots of garlic, the other on oregano. Finally, the oregano party won. We were at the mountain lodge of the Bolognese in the Appenines, with no oregano in the pantry. So the loser had to drive a half-hour each way to the nearest village to buy a box of dried oregano! In my opinion each of their ways was good, but not as good as the way my mother prepared it. Here is her recipe for this simple, rustic, delightful delicacy.

12 leaves Boston, Bibb, or Salad Bowl lettuce
6 large round tomatoes, ripe but firm
1 large clove garlic
1/2 cup extra virgin olive oil
2 teaspoons salt
Black peppercorns in a mill
1/2 teaspoon dried oregano
1 tablespoon shredded fresh basil leaves
1 tablespoon freshly chopped Italian parsley

Rinse the lettuce leaves and pat dry with paper toweling. Arrange on a large serving plate or, better, place 2 leaves on each of six individual salad dishes.

Wash and dry the tomatoes and place on a cutting board with the round side up. Rub the garlic on both sides of the sharp blade of a pairing knife and slice the tomatoes without cutting through. The slices should open like an accordion, remaining attached to one another at the bottom. Rub the garlic again on the blade of the knife for each tomato. Arrange all the accordions on the serving plate with lettuce leaves, or place 1 over each individual salad dish.

Season in between the slices with half the oil, and with salt, pepper, and oregano. Sprinkle the top with the remaining oil, and finally with basil and parsley.

Serves 6.

POMODORI E MOZZARELLA
Tomato and Mozzarella Salad

6 medium-to-large ripe tomatoes
1 1/2 pounds bocconcini *(fresh, bite-size mozzarella cheese)*
A handful Italian parsley leaves, coarsely chopped
2 tablespoons shredded basil leaves
2 cloves garlic, minced
Salt
Freshly ground black pepper
Extra virgin olive oil
Balsamic vinegar (optional)*

Remove some of the peel — that which comes off easily — from the tomatoes and dice them into a bowl. Add bocconcini (the larger ones may be cut in half). Add parsley, basil, garlic, and salt and pepper to taste. Gently toss. Sprinkle abundantly with olive oil and a small drizzle of vinegar if so desired. **Serves 6.**

NOTE. If you serve this salad as an appetizer, you may want to present it differently. Slice the tomatoes and place on a large plate, possibly on a single layer. Season with salt and pepper, and sprinkle abundantly with oil, but only a hint of vinegar if so desired. Top with bocconcini, then sprinkle with herbs.

* See instructions on page 46.

UOVA SODE COLL'INSALATA
Hard-Boiled Eggs with Lettuce

1 small head Romaine lettuce
2 large heads Boston lettuce
*9 hard-boiled eggs, shelled**
Extra virgin olive oil
1 1/2 teaspoons salt
Dash or two freshly ground black pepper
2 teaspoons wine vinegar
4 small scallions, chopped

Discard the tough, outer leaves from lettuce. Rinse many times in cold water, then drain, and pat dry with paper toweling.** Shred by hand into a large salad bowl.

Cut the eggs into six wedges each. Reserve half and add the rest to the bowl with the lettuce. Add the oil and toss gently. Sprinkle with salt, pepper, and vinegar and toss again very lightly. Top with chopped scallions and garnish with the reserved egg wedges. Serve immediately.

Serves 6.

*See instructions on page 38.

** Even though you may spin some salad greens such as chicory and escarole to rid them of excess water, do not spin such delicate lettuce as Boston, because it would wrinkle and wilt.

PATATE NOVELLE E ZUCCHINE CONDITE
New Potato and Zucchini Salad

This salad excels when both potatoes and zucchini are picked not fully grown. In Italy zucchini are sold by the number and not by the weight, so that one pays the same amount for an overgrown *zucchino* weighing a kilo as for a baby one, barely 3/4" diameter by 6" long, weighing much less than one tenth of a kilo. I say this to give the reader an idea of how the Italians value baby vegetables.

2 pounds very small white or red new potatoes
2 pounds very small zucchini
2 scallions finely chopped
Salt
*Coarsely ground black pepper**
*2 tablespoons balsamic vinegar***
Extra virgin olive oil

Wash and scrub potatoes with a vegetable brush. Trim zucchini at both ends and wash. Steam potatoes until almost tender, then add zucchini until both are done. Peel the potatoes, if you wish, or leave the peel on. Slice the potatoes and place in center of a serving plate. Cut zucchini into two sections and cut each lengthwise into four wedges. Arrange around potatoes. Sprinkle with scallions, salt and pepper to taste, vinegar, and abundantly with olive oil. Serve hot or at room temperature. **Serves 6.**

*See instructions on page 43.
** See instructions on page 46.

PATATE ARROSTO A INSALATA
Baked Potato Salad

3 pounds best quality baking potatoes
Coarse table salt
*Coarsely ground black pepper**
Extra virgin olive oil

Wash and scrub potatoes with a vegetable brush. With the tip of a sharp knife, remove every black spot that might remain. Place unwrapped in a 500 °F oven and bake for 3/4 of an hour, or until potatoes feel tender when poked in depth with a fork (the peel should be crusty and hard).

Remove to a working surface. Cover with a clean kitchen towel and press one by one with the palm of your hand. This way most of the burnt peel will crack and easily come off. Cut the potatoes with the remaining peel into chunks and place into a bowl. Season with salt and pepper to taste and an abundance of the best extra virgin olive oil you can find and afford. Serve immediately. **Serves 6.**

* See instructions on page 43.

INSALATA DI TONNO E PATATE
Tuna and Potato Salad

6 large all-purpose potatoes
3 6 1/2-oz cans tuna packed in olive oil
3 tablespoons chopped scallions with greens
Freshly ground black pepper
Salt
Extra virgin olive oil

Steam the potatoes until tender but not mushy. Peel, cut in chunks and place in a bowl. Let cool a little. Drain the tuna and shred into the bowl with potatoes.

Add scallions, salt and pepper to taste, and a generous sprinkling of extra virgin olive oil. Toss gently and serve. **Serves 6.**

INSALATA DI TONNO E FAGIOLI SGRANATI
Tuna and Fresh Beans Salad

"*Sgranati*," when we talk about beans, means that you buy the beans fresh in their shell, and you do the shelling yourself just before cooking them. If you are unable to find fresh beans, you may want to try this salad with the dried ones. Both the texture and flavor will be different, but then, it is better than no tuna and beans salad at all.

2 1/2 pounds fresh white beans in their shells or 1 cup dried white beans
Salt
2 sage leaves
3 6 1/2-oz cans tuna, packed in olive oil
1/4 cup thinly sliced white onion
Freshly ground black pepper
Extra virgin olive oil

Shell the beans if you have fresh ones. You should obtain 2 to 2 1/2 cups. Place in a saucepan with cold water to cover. Add 1/2 teaspoon salt and the sage and bring to a boil. Lower the heat and cook until tender, 20 to 25 minutes. Discard the sage. Meanwhile, drain and discard the oil from tuna, and shred the latter into a bowl. When beans are done, drain and add them to the bowl with tuna. Add onion and season with salt, pepper, and extra virgin olive oil to taste. Toss and serve. **Serves 6.**

NOTE: If you use dry beans, see cooking directions in the following recipe.

INSALATA DI FAGIOLI CALDA
Warm Bean Salad

This is a refreshing alternative to the multi-beans cold salad most people are familiar with. In its simplicity this warm beans salad is very tasty and a favorite at my dinner table. I prefer to use white beans, such as cannellini, navy peas, and others, but kidney, black, or pinto beans are also good prepared this way.

1 pound white, black or other dry beans
2 to 3 quarts hot water
Coarse table salt
1 large clove garlic, husk on
2 sage leaves
2 small scallions, cut up, including the green
*Coarsely ground black pepper**
Extra virgin olive oil

Pick and discard stones and any unhealthy-looking beans. Rinse 2 or 3 times in warm water, and place in a large pot with 2 to 3 quarts of hot water. Add 1 tablespoon salt and bring to a boil.

Lower the heat to minimum, add garlic and sage, and simmer, covered, for 1/2 hour to 1 hour or until beans are soft but not mushy. Discard garlic and sage.

With a slotted spoon, transfer the beans to a warmed serving bowl. Add scallions and salt and pepper to taste, and toss very gently to mix. Add an abundance of extra virgin olive oil and let it seep through before serving.

Serves 6 to 10.

* See instructions page 43.

INSALATA DI CARCIOFI, FINOCCHIO E ASPARAGI
Artichoke, Fennel, and Asparagus Salad

6 small, fresh artichokes
1 lemon, juice and rind
2 medium knobs fennel
1 1/2 pounds small asparagus
1 scallion, cut up, with some green
Salt
Freshly ground black pepper
4 tablespoons extra virgin olive oil
*2 tablespoons balsamic vinegar***
1 clove garlic
1 medium head red radicchio

Trim artichokes* and keep in acidulated water until ready to use. Remove outer leaves from fennels; cut off and discard the long stems and most of the greens. Wash under running water and pat dry. Cut into small cubes (1/3 inch) and toss into a bowl.

Cut the tips of asparagus to be 2 inches long (discard the rest) and cut again in half. Add to the bowl with fennel.

Drain and pat artichokes dry, cut in half, then into thin wedges, and place in the bowl. Add scallion, and season with salt, pepper, oil, and vinegar. Gently toss.

Separate the radicchio leaves, wash, and pat dry. Rub the garlic on the inside of a serving plate, then discard. Line the plate with radicchio leaves, pour the salad over it and serve. **Serves 6**.

* See instructions on page 36.
** See instructions on page 46.

INSALATA RICCIOLINA
Chicory Salad

The chicory for this salad should be the short and very curly type. If you find it, you don't need anything else to make a delightful salad out of it. If, on the other hand, color is important to you, mix it with a few leaves of watercress, bits of radicchio, and orange or tangerine sections.

2 round heads of chicory (1 to 1 1/2 pounds)
2 sprigs watercress (optional)
1 small head of radicchio (optional)
1/2 cup orange or tangerine sections, sliced (optional)
1/3 cup extra virgin olive oil
*Balsamic vinegar**
Salt
Freshly ground black pepper

Discard some of the outer leaves and part of the greens from the chicory. Wash and pat dry with paper toweling the remaining leaves, and shred by hand into a salad bowl.

If you opt for watercress and radicchio, wash them and pat dry. Use only the leaves of watercress, shred the radicchio fine with a sharp knife, and add both to the bowl.

Add the orange or tangerine, if so desired, pour in all the oil, and sprinkle with vinegar and salt and pepper to taste. Toss and serve. **Serves 6.**

* See instructions on page 46.

INSALATA MISTA
Mixed Salad

In autumn and winter you can prepare a beautiful mixed salad using red cabbage, broccoli, sliced mushrooms, spinach leaves, iceberg lettuce, and other vegetables that grow in cold weather.

In spring and summer, your choice is quite wide. Look for red and green loose leaf lettuce, salad bowl, bib lettuce, *cicoria romanesca* (Roman chicory), *rughetta* (arrugula), *erba stella*, also called *barba dei cappuccini* (a very flavorful grass-like green), *cicoria rossa* (red chicory), *radicchio rosso*, watercress, and Belgian endive.

1 to 2 pounds various lettuces
2 scallions, cut up
Extra virgin olive oil
Salt
Freshly ground black pepper
*Balsamic vinegar**

Separate all the leaves and choose only the healthiest ones. Rinse in many changes of cold water and place in a large strainer or colander. Gently pat the leaves dry as you transfer them into a salad bowl. (Do not spin these delicate salads lest they lose their crispness.) Add scallions.

Sprinkle with oil and toss gently until the leaves are coated. Add small amounts of salt and pepper and a drizzle of vinegar. Toss gently and serve. **Serves 6.**

* See instructions on page 46.

MISTICANZA
Salad Mixture

The difference between this salad mixture and the mixed salad of the preceeding recipe is not only in the name but also in the "age" of the salads. The salad leaves for the *misticanza* are picked at an immature stage; at the stage, that is, when the young plants are thinned out in the fields before they become full-grown bunches. You will find these salad leaves, already mixed, only in spring, for the reason described above. Salads made with these young leaves are simply outstanding.

3/4 to 1 pound mixed young salad leaves
1 tablespoon freshly chopped chives
Extra virgin olive oil
Salt
Freshly ground black pepper
*Balsamic vinegar**

Rinse the salad leaves in many changes of cold water, then place in a large strainer or colander. Gently pat dry before transfering to a large bowl. (Remember not to spin any delicate salad, but especially NOT *misticanza.*) Add chives.

Sprinkle with oil and gently toss until leaves are coated. Add small amounts of salt and pepper and only a drizzle of vinegar. Toss gently and serve. **Serves 6.**

* See instructions on page 46.

PUNTARELLE
Catalonian Chicory Salad

This is an ancient Roman Jewish recipe for an unusual and most delectable salad. It is made with the core and the few inner whitish leaves of *cicoria catalogna*, Catalonian chicory. All the remaining green leaves of the bunches are then steamed for *Cicoria Catalogna all'Agro.*

3 large bunches Catalonian chicory
Salt
Freshly ground black pepper
Extra virgin olive oil
Balsamic vinegar (optional)*

Trim off the bottom of the bunches, and remove most of the outer leaves (reserve for later use). Use only the core of the bunches, the whitest part of them.

With a sharp knife, cut lengthwise into very thin wedges. Rinse in cold water, then place in ice water for 1 hour or until the little wedges have curled up.

Drain, place in a salad bowl, and season with salt, pepper, and oil to taste, and a small sprinkle of vinegar, if so desired. Toss gently and serve. **Serves 6 to 8**.

* See instructions on page 46.

Salse
SAUCES

SALSA DI POMODORO E BASILICO
Tomato and Basil Sauce

This sauce used to be a summer favorite in my family. Now that we can find basil on the market throughout the year, we do not have to wait until summer to enjoy it.

1/2 cup extra virgin olive oil
2 large cloves garlic, crushed
2 pounds ripe, firm tomatoes, peeled and drained or 1 1-lb.12-oz. can peeled plum tomatoes, drained*
1 1/2 teaspoons salt
Dash or two ground red pepper
1/4 cup firmly packed whole tiny or shredded large basil leaves

Heat half the oil in a large saucepan. Add the garlic and saute until golden, then discard.

Add tomatoes, salt, and pepper and cook over moderately high heat, stirring frequently, 5 to 10 minutes.

Add basil and cook 1 minute longer. Remove from heat and add remaining oil.

Yields approximately 2 1/2 cups; serves 6 to 8.

*See directions on page 45.

SALSA MARINARA
Marinara Sauce

1/4 cup olive oil
3 large cloves garlic
2 1/2 cups canned or fresh peeled tomatoes, drained and chopped*
1/2 teaspoon crushed red pepper
1/2 teaspoon salt
1 tablespoon freshly chopped Italian parsley
1/4 cup extra virgin olive oil

Heat 1/4 cup oil in a saucepan with 1 clove of garlic and saute until garlic is golden brown. Discard garlic, add tomatoes, pepper, salt, and oregano and cook over low heat, uncovered, for 3/4 to 1 hour, stirring occasionally.

A moment before removing from heat, add parsley, extra virgin olive oil, and the remaining 2 cloves of garlic passed through a garlic press and stir. **Serves 6.**

*See how to on page 45.

SALSA MARINARA BIANCA
White Marinara Sauce

This sauce is anything but white. Anchovies, herbs, and especially black olives stain it quite a bit. However, it is called "white" as opposed to the "red" marinara sauce, which is made with tomatoes. It is a quick sauce to prepare and a very tasty one.

1/2 cup olive oil
2 cloves garlic, minced
12 anchovy fillets
1/3 cup finely chopped pitted oil-cured olives
1/4 teaspoon dried oregano
2 tablespoons tiny capers, drained
1 tablespoon freshly chopped Italian parsley
1 tablespoon shredded basil leaves
1/4 teaspoon white pepper

Heat the oil in a saucepan, add garlic and saute until lightly golden. Add anchovies, olives, oregano, and capers and saute 1 minute longer. Add parsley, basil, and pepper and stir before removing from heat. Serve on poached eggs or on pasta. **Serves 6.**

NOTE: Since this sauce is salty as is, little salt, if any, is needed to cook the pasta.

SALSA ARRABBIATA
Angry Sauce

Angry in this case means hot and spicy. In fact this sauce is so "angry" that it bites your tongue.

1/2 cup olive oil
1 to 2 teaspoons crushed red pepper
1/2 teaspoon salt
1/4 teaspoon oregano
1/8 teaspoon powdered sage
1/8 teaspoon crushed rosemary leaves
1/4 teaspoon dried basil leaves
1 tablespoon salted capers, washed, drained, and chopped
2 large cloves garlic, minced
6 anchovy fillets
1/2 cup extra dry red wine
2 cups fresh or canned peeled tomatoes, drained and coarsely chopped*

In a saucepan over moderate heat, place the oil with pepper, salt, oregano, sage, rosemary, basil leaves, capers, anchovies, and garlic, and stir a little. When anchovies are almost melted, add wine and raise the heat to let the alcohol evaporate.

Add tomatoes and cook over medium heat for 10 to 15 minutes, stirring occasionally.

Use immediately, or cool before storing in a tightly closed jar in the refrigerator where the sauce keeps fresh for several weeks without need of freezing.

Yields approximately 2 cups.

*See instructions on page 45.

PESTO COL FRULLATORE
Processor or Blender Pesto

1 cup firmly packed fresh basil leaves
6 large sprigs Italian parsley, stems removed
2 cloves garlic, coarsely cut up
1/2 cup pinoli *(pine nuts) or walnut meats*
3/4 cup extra virgin olive oil
1/2 cup grated Italian Parmesan cheese
1/4 cup grated Sardo or Romano cheese
Salt
Freshly ground black pepper

If you must, wash basil leaves and pat them dry with paper toweling. However, if basil is clean, do without washing, since water will cause it to darken.

Place the basil in the processor together with parsley and garlic. Process just until all is chopped fine. Add nuts and chop a few seconds longer.

Transfer to a sauce bowl. Add the oil and the two cheeses and stir to combine. Add salt and pepper to taste and store in refrigerator, where it will keep fresh up to 2 weeks. Let it stand at room temperature for at least 1 hour before using. **Yields approximately 1 1/2 cups.**

NOTE: If you don't own a food processor but have a blender, you might have to add 1/2 cup of water to the bowl before processing. The parsley will help preserve the bright green. In any case, use as soon as possible.

SALSA MAIONESE COL FRULLATORE
Blender or Processor Mayonnaise

2 eggs
2 tablespoons lemon juice
2 teaspoons wine vinegar
1 teaspoon salt
1/4 teaspoon dry mustard
1/8 teaspoon white pepper
1 1/2 to 2 cups olive oil

Place eggs, lemon juice, vinegar, salt, mustard, and pepper in the bowl of a blender or a processor. Start the motor and process for 30 seconds. Without stopping the motor, begin to add the oil in a thin steady stream. Before you use up all the oil, check the consistency of the sauce. For a thinner sauce add a few drops of vinegar or lemon; for a thicker sauce add oil. Process after each addition. **Yield about 2 cups.**

SALSA DI TONNO
Tuna Sauce

1 egg
1 egg yolk
Juice of 1 lemon
2 tablespoons capers packed in vinegar, drained
1 3 1/2-ounce can chunk tuna packed in olive oil
4 anchovy fillets
1 cup olive oil

Place the tuna with its oil in the bowl of a blender or processor; add all the other ingredients except for the olive oil, and begin to process at medium speed.

With the motor still on, add all the oil in a thin steady stream until a sauce the consistency of mayonnaise is formed. Use with poached fish or on cold slices of boiled chicken or meat. **Yields about 1 1/2 cups; serves 6.**

SALSA DI FORMAGGIO COL FRULLATORE
Blender Cheese Sauce

2 cups hot milk
3 tablespoons butter
1/3 cup unbleached flour
8 ounces mozzarella or Muenster cheese, shredded
2 tablespoons grated Italian Parmesan cheese

Place milk, butter, and flour in the bowl of a blender and process at high speed for 5 seconds. Pour into a saucepan and cook over moderate heat for 4 minutes, stirring frequently. Add the shredded cheese and cook, stirring, until cheese is melted. Turn the heat off, add Parmesan and stir to combine.

Yields about 2 cups; serves 6.

SALSA DI RICOTTA
Ricotta Sauce

This is a simple sauce you can prepare at the very last moment, provided you have all the ingredients at hand. It is mostly used to dress a pasta dish, but it is equally good on poached fish, steamed vegetables, or baked potatoes.

If you make this sauce to dress pasta, heat the serving bowl while the pasta is cooking by letting a cup of boiling water swash in it.

Discard the water and place the powdered instant soup in the bowl. Add 1/2 cup boiling water all at once, then add butter, pepper, and ricotta and stir with a fork to combine. Add parsley and chives just a moment before using the sauce on pasta or on vegetables.

Yields 2 1/2 cups; serves 6.

Boiling water
1 envelope instant vegetable soup
3 tablespoons butter at room temperature
1/4 teaspoon white pepper
1 pound whole milk ricotta at room temperature
2 tablespoons finely chopped Italian parsley
1 tablespoon freshly chopped chives

SALSA DI FUNGHI
Mushroom Sauce

Soak dried mushrooms in 1 cup of warm water for 10 minutes. Lift them with a fork, reserving the water. Remove and discard any parts which still have sand attached and coarsely chop.

Wash, drain, and thinly slice the fresh mushrooms.

Place oil, onion, garlic, parsley, savory, salt, and pepper in a saucepan, and saute for 1/2 minute. Add the two mushrooms and cook over moderately high heat for 5 minutes, stirring frequently. Add tomato paste and wine and cook over high heat, stirring, until the alcohol has evaporated—about 2 minutes.

Add the reserved water from the soaked mushrooms, taking care not to include any sand that might remain at the bottom of the cup.* Cook over high heat 5 minutes longer or until liquid is greatly reduced.

Yields about 3 cups; serves 6 to 8.

1/2 ounce imported dried porcini mushrooms
1 cup warm water
2 pounds small, firm white mushrooms
6 tablespoons olive oil
2 tablespoons finely chopped onion
1 clove garlic, minced
1 tablespoon freshly chopped Italian parsley
1/4 teaspoon dried savory
1 teaspoon salt
1/4 teaspoon freshly ground black pepper
2 tablespoons tomato paste
1/2 cup dry white wine

*See instructions on page 43.

SALSA BESCIAMELLA COL FRULLATORE
Blender White Sauce

2 cups hot milk
4 tablespoons butter
1/4 cup unbleached flour
Dash nutmeg

Place milk, butter, and flour in the cup of a blender and process at high speed for 5 seconds.

Pour into a saucepan and cook over moderate heat for 6 minutes, stirring frequently. Add nutmeg and cook 1 minute longer.

Yields about 2 cups; serves 6.

SALSA BESCIAMELLA SENZA LATTE
Non-Dairy White Sauce

2 cups hot clear chicken or vegetable broth
4 tablespoons bone marrow or non-dairy margarine
1/4 cup unbleached flour
Dash freshly ground white pepper

Place liquid, fat, and flour in the cup of a blender and process at high speed for 5 seconds.

Pour into a saucepan and cook over moderate heat for 6 minutes, stirring occasionally. Add pepper and cook 1 minute longer. **Yields about 2 cups; serves 6.**

SALSA DI NOCI
Walnut Sauce

This sauce is a delightful complement to any pasta dish, but it is especially suited for *Panzotti di Spinaci.*

2 cups healthy walnut meats
Boiling-hot water
1/2 cup milk
3/4 cup cold water
1/4 cup granulated sugar
1/4 teaspoon cinnamon
1/4 teaspoon salt
1/3 cup freshly grated Italian Parmesan cheese

Soak walnut meats in boiling-hot water to cover for 1 hour or longer. Drain and rinse in cold water. Place in the work bowl of a blender or processor and start the motor. With the motor still on, add milk, 3/4 cup cold water, sugar, cinnamon, and salt, and process until you have a cream. Add Parmesan cheese and process just to mix. **Yields about 2 cups; serves 6.**

SALSA VERDE PER BOLLITI
Green Sauce for Boiled Meats

Wash parsley, pat dry, and place in the workbowl of the processor. Start the motor and while processing the parsley add onion pieces, carrot pieces, capers and garlic. When all is well chopped transfer to a sauce dish.

Place anchovies, tuna, egg, egg yolk, and vinegar in a blender or processor and turn the motor on. Gradually add the oil and process until all is well blended and has the consistency of a mayonnaise.

Add to the bowl with chopped parsley, add salt and pepper to taste, and mix to combine. Use on boiled meats.

Yields approximately 1 cup.

1 cup firmly packed parsley leaves
1 small onion, quartered
1 small carrot, peeled and cut up
1 tablespoon tiny capers, drained
1 small clove garlic
3 anchovy fillets
1 3 1/4-oz can white tuna fish, drained
1 hard-boiled egg
1 hard-boiled egg yolk
2 tablespoons wine vinegar
1/2 cup olive oil
Salt
Freshly ground black pepper

SALSA AGRO-DOLCE SVELTA
Quick Sweet and Sour Sauce

Combine the first three ingredients in a saucepan. Bring to a boil and cook, stirring, for 1 minute. Add the diluted starch and cook an additional minute stirring frequently.

Yields 2 1/2 cups.

1 cup orange marmalade (page 250)
1 cup Classic Tomato Sauce (page 218)
2 tablespoons red wine vinegar
1/2 teaspoon potato starch diluted in 1/2 cup water

CHAROSET CON MANDORLE
Fruit and Almond Paste for Passover

Chop dates and apples fine. Add orange juice, wine, chopped almonds, lemon peel, and raisins. Mix well to combine. Add matza meal as needed for a mortar-like paste. Serve during the Passover Seder.

Serves 12.

1 pound pitted dates
3 apples, cored and peeled
1 cup orange juice
1/4 cup sweet red wine
1 1/2 cups chopped almonds
Grated peel of 1 lemon
1/2 cup seedless raisins
Matza meal as needed

RAGU DI MANZO
Beef Ragù

Olive oil
1 small onion, minced
1 medium carrot, peeled and diced
1 celery stalk, chopped
3/4 pound lean ground beef
1/2 pound lean ground veal
Salt
Freshly ground black pepper
1 whole clove
1 heaping tablespoon tomato paste
1/2 cup dry white wine
1 cup clear beef broth
1 clove garlic, minced
1 tablespoon freshly chopped Italian parsley

In a medium saucepan, place 6 tablespoons of oil, onion, carrot, celery, and the two meats and brown on moderately high heat, stirring frequently, until all is quite dark.

Add salt and pepper to taste, 1 whole clove, and the tomato paste and stir thoroughly. Add the wine and raise the heat to let the wine evaporate completely. Add the broth, lower the heat, and simmer, covered, for 1/2 hour, or until the sauce is thick and flavorful. Add garlic and parsley, 2 tablespoons of fresh oil, and stir.

Yields approximately 3 cups; serves 6 to 8.

SALSA DI POMODORO CLASSICA
Classic Tomato Sauce

1/2 cup extra virgin olive oil
1 large clove garlic, minced
1/2 medium onion, chopped fine
1 small carrot, peeled and chopped
1 small celery stalk with leaves, chopped fine
1 1/2 teaspoons salt
1/4 teaspoon freshly ground black pepper
1/4 teaspoon dried oregano
3 cups fresh or canned peeled tomatoes, drained and chopped*
1 tablespoon finely chopped Italian parsley

Heat 1/4 cup of oil in a large saucepan. Add garlic, onion, carrot, celery, salt, pepper, and oregano, and saute over moderately high heat, stirring, until the herbs have acquired a golden color.

Add peeled tomatoes, lower the heat, and cook uncovered, stirring from time to time, 1/2 hour or until the sauce is thick and flavorful.

Remove from heat, add parsley and the remaining oil and stir. **Yields approximately 3 cups; serves 6 to 8.**

*See instructions on page 45.

Pane, Grissini, Pizze, Ciambelle

BREAD, BREAD STICKS, PIZZAS, BAGELS

THE WORDS "FRENCH BREAD" immediately summon up the image of a man rushing through a narrow street of Paris holding tight under his arm a long, unwrapped bread baguette, munching on morsels pulled from one extremity of the deliciously fragrant stick.

"Italian bread," on the other hand, does not evoke similarly strong imagery, because there is not such a thing as a "national" bread in Italy. Bread in Milan, for example, is quite different from bread in Florence or in Rome. It follows that the bread sold in America as "Italian bread" is misnamed. In fact the variety of breads from region to region and from city to city that are sold in bakeries is quite impressive, and the habit of baking bread at home has long been abandoned by the average household. For the same reason, breads are seldom, if ever, listed in Italian cookbooks.

However, the Jews, to comply with the laws of kashruth and with tradition (Challa bread for Shabbat, *Maritucci* for Sukkot, to cite two examples), have maintained the habit of bread-baking at home. I have offered in my first volume, as in this one, many types of breads, none of which could particularly be termed "Italian bread" in the American context. Nevertheless, they are indeed breads that are made in Italy, some only by Jews (*bollo*), others by bakeries and Jews alike.

CHALLA DI ROSH HASHANA
Rosh Hashana Challa Bread

2 envelopes active dry yeast
2 tablespoons sugar
1/4 cup honey
1 tablespoon salt
1 1/2 cups warm water
7 cups unbleached flour
1/4 cup warm olive oil
3 eggs, slightly beaten
1 egg yolk, beaten with 1 teaspoon of water

Place yeast, sugar, honey, salt, and water in the large bowl of a mixer and beat for 1 minute. Add 2 cups of flour and beat for another minute. Cover with a clean towel and set aside in a draft-free place for 1 hour or until the batter begins to bubble.

Replace the beaters with the dough hook. Add oil, beaten eggs, and enough flour to make a rather stiff dough. Knead until the dough is satiny and easily parts from the sides of the bowl. Shape into a ball and place in a lightly oiled bowl; turn it once, cover with a towel, and set aside until it has more than tripled in bulk.

Turn onto a lightly floured working table, punch down and divide into 2 parts. Shape each part into a long rope and roll the rope in a spiral, first flat on the table, then over itself, until you have a pyramid-like loaf. Repeat with the second rope. Place the loaves over a lightly oiled and floured baking sheet, well apart. Cover loosely with a towel and set aside for 1 hour or until more than doubled in bulk.

Brush the tops with the egg-yolk-and-water mixture and bake in a 400 °F oven for 30 minutes or until the crust is deep brown. Remove to cooling rack. **Yields 2 1 1/2 pound loaves.**

PANE DEL SABATO CON LIEVITO CASALINGO
Sourdough Challa Bread

*1 cup sourdough starter**
1 1/2 cups warm water
7 cups unbleached flour
3 tablespoons sugar
1/4 cup warm olive oil
1 tablespoon salt
3 eggs, slightly beaten
1 egg yolk, mixed with 1teaspoon water

Have all the ingredients at room temperature. (In winter you might have to take the starter out of the refrigerator the night before baking.) Place the sourdough starter in the large bowl of a mixer. Add 1/2 cup of warm water and 1 cup of flour and beat very well. Cover the bowl with plastic wrap and let rest in a draft-free place for several hours until doubled in bulk. Add sugar, oil, salt, eggs, and 1 cup warm water, and beat to homogeneity. Replace the beaters with the dough hook. Gradually add 5 1/2 cups of flour and beat until the dough easily leaves the sides of the bowl. Spread the remaining flour on a working surface and turn the dough onto it. Knead while incorporating enough flour to make a rather stiff dough. Shape into a ball and place in an oiled bowl, turning once. Cover with plastic wrap and set aside for 2 hours, or until more than tripled in bulk.

Turn on the working surface and punch down. Divide into two equal

* See next recipe

parts. Divide each part into three equal parts and roll each into a 13-inch rope bulging at the center and tapering at the ends. Fasten 3 ropes at one end and make a braid; fasten the other end. Repeat with the remaining 3 ropes.

Place on a lightly oiled and generously floured baking sheet and set aside for 1 more hour, or until doubled.

Brush the tops with the egg-yolk-and-water mixture and bake in preheated 400 °F oven for 15 minutes. Lower the temperature to 350 °F and bake for another 30 minutes, or until the crust is deep brown.

Yields 2 1 1/2-pound loaves.

IL LIEVITO CASALINGO
Sourdough Starter

To start this starter, simply mix 1 1/2 cups of unbleached flour and 1 teaspoon of active dry yeast with 1 1/2 cups of warm water in a glass, ceramic, or plastic container. Cover with a plastic wrap and leave at room temperature until the batter grows and bubbles (this may take several hours to happen, especially in winter). Place in the refrigerator until you are ready to use it.

The day you wish to make bread, take the container out of the refrigerator and leave it at room temperature for a few hours. Use 1 cup of batter, and replenish the starter by adding 1 1/4 cups of unbleached flour and 1 cup of warm water to the container. Mix just a little (lumps will dissolve by themselves) and leave at room temperature a few hours, then return to the refrigerator until next time.

If a long time elapses between bread makings, you may find that your sourdough starter looks different. There might be either a dry crust or a greyish liquid at the top, and even some mould. Do not use as it is, of course, but do not throw it away either. Remove the crust or the liquid and any parts that look spoiled. Transfer the remaining yeast into a clean container, add 1 1/4 cups of unbleached flour and 1 cup of warm water, mix a little, and let stand at room temperature for a couple of hours; your starter will be fresh and ready to use again.

NOTE: In winter you may want to use sourdough in conjunction with a teaspoon of active dry yeast to speed up the rising process.

PANE TOSCANO COL LIEVITO CASALINGO
Sourdough Tuscan Bread

This bread is a staple among the Tuscan Jews, who use it to soak up the gravy from stews, to complement a dish of bean salad and to make the heartiest of garlic breads, as well as several bread soups and salads. It is the simplest of all breads, using only yeast, flour, and water. To be authentic, in fact, Tuscan bread must be salt free.

1 cup sourdough starter at room temperature (page 223)
8 cups unbleached flour
2 1/4 cups warm water

Place the sourdough starter in the large bowl of an electric mixer. Add 1 cup of warm water and 1 cup of flour and beat well. Cover with a plastic wrap and set aside in a draft-free place to rise for 2 to 3 hours.

Replace the beaters with the dough hook. Add the remaining water and enough flour to make a rather stiff dough. Turn onto a floured surface and knead for 5 minutes. Divide into two equal parts; knead each a couple of minutes, then shape each piece of dough into an oval loaf and place on a lightly oiled and generously floured baking sheet as far apart as possible.

With a sharp knife cut 3 slashes widthwise, 1/2 inch deep, on top of each loaf. Cover with a towel and let rise in a warm, draft-free place for 2 to 3 hours, or until more than doubled in bulk. If when you're ready to bake you see that the loaves don't seem to have expanded quite enough, put the baking sheet on the middle rack of a cold oven. Place a shallow pan with cold water on the rack below it; set the thermometer at 400 °F and the timer at 15 minutes. When the timer goes off, lower the temperature to 375 °F and bake 30 minutes longer or until the crust is uniformly light brown. While the oven warms up the bread has a chance to leaven some more.

If, on the other hand, the loaves are well expanded (it takes a bit of practice to recognize the ideal leavening point), it is better to bake them in a preheated 450 °F oven for 10 minutes, omitting the water whose steam facilitates leavening, then lower the heat to 375 °F and proceed as above. This way the already leavened bread gets cooked quickly and does not become overleavened.

Remove to a wire rack for at least 1 hour before serving.

Yields 2 1 1/2-pound loaves.

NOTE: You may freeze this bread, as any other bread, after wrapping it in aluminum foil and plastic wrap. However, while you use the bread, don't keep it inside a plastic bag or in the refrigerator, where it will become soggy. For a crusty and fresh texture, wrap in a towel and leave at room temperature.

PANE TOSCANO COL LIEVITO DI BIRRA
Tuscan Bread with Commercial Yeast

This version of Tuscan Bread is even simpler than the one in the preceding recipe. It is not the authentic sourdough bread of my childhood, but it's easier to make and almost as tasty.

1 envelope active dry yeast
2 1/2 cups warm water
8 cups unbleached flour

In a large bowl dissolve the yeast in 1/2 cup warm water. Add enough flour to form a soft dough. Cover the bowl with a clean kitchen towel or plastic wrap and set aside in a draft-free place for about 2 hours.

Add 2 cups warm water and manipulate with your hand, or the dough hook of an electric mixer, until leavened dough is almost completely dissolved. Gradually add enough flour to make a rather stiff dough. Pour onto a floured surface, divide into 2 equal parts, and knead each a couple of minutes. Cover with a towel and let rest for 5 minutes.

Shape each piece of dough into an oval loaf and place on a lightly oiled and generously floured baking sheet, as far apart as possible. With a sharp knife cut 3 slashes widthwise, about 1/2 inch deep, on top of each loaf. Cover with a towel and let rest in a draft-free place for 1 hour or until doubled in bulk.

Place on the middle rack of a preheated 450 °F oven. After 10 minutes lower the temperature to 375 °F and bake 30 minutes longer or until the crust is uniformly light brown. Remove to a wire rack for at least 1 hour before serving. (See note in preceding recipe on how to keep this bread.)

Yields 2 1 1/2-pound loaves.

PAN DI RAMERINO
Rosemary Bread

2 envelopes active dry yeast
2 cups warm water
7 cups unbleached flour
1 tablespoon salt
1/3 cup warm olive oil
1/2 cup Malaga or Muscatel raisins

Dissolve the yeast in 1/2 cup of warm water and let rest for 10 minutes. Add 1 1/2 cups of water, salt, oil, and enough flour to make a not-too-stiff dough. Manipulate with your hand or dough hook of an electric beater until the dough easily leaves the sides of the bowl. Turn onto an unfloured working table and knead 2 minutes. Spread the raisins over the table and knead until the dough has incorporated all of them. Divide into 6 parts, knead each 2 minutes, then cover with a towel and let rest for 10 minutes.

Shape into oval little loaves and place on a well-floured baking sheet.

1 tablespoon rosemary leaves
1 egg yolk, beaten with 1 teaspoon water

Gash the tops diagonally in both directions forming a criss-cross pattern. Sprinkle with rosemary and press down with your fingers to anchor the rosemary leaves into the dough. Cover with a towel and set aside for 1 to 2 hours, or until doubled in bulk.

Brush the tops with the egg-yolk-and-water mixture, taking care of not disturbing the rosemary, and bake in preheated 350 °F oven for 30 minutes, or until crusts are nicely browned. **Yields 6 1/3-pound loaves.**

PANE TOSCANO INTEGRALE
Whole Wheat Tuscan Bread

Whole wheat flour is highly perishable because of its fat content; therefore, you should keep it in the refrigerator or even in the freezer. However, since it is a good practice to have all the ingredients at room temperature for baking, you should take the flour from the freezer several hours before starting. There are various types of wholewheat flour; for this bread I prefer the stone-ground, unsifted type.

Unbleached flour
1 envelope active dry yeast
2 teaspoons salt (optional)
2 1/2 cups warm water
4 cups unsifted whole wheat flour

Combine 1/2 cup unbleached flour with dry yeast and salt in a large bowl. Gradually add 1/4 cup warm water and mix to form a soft dough. Cover with a towel and leave in a warm place for 1 hour.

Add 2 1/4 cups lukewarm water and manipulate with your hand, or the dough hook of your electric mixer, until yeast mixture is almost completely dissolved. Add the whole wheat flour, mixing until a smooth and satiny dough is formed. Turn out on a working surface sprinkled with unbleached flour, and knead 2 minutes. Divide into 2 parts, knead each 2 minutes, and let rest 5 minutes, covered.

Shape each piece of dough into a ball and place on a well-floured baking sheet, at least 4 inches apart. Cover with a towel and put aside in a warm, draft-free place to rise for about 1 hour, or until doubled in bulk. Bake in preheated 400 °F oven for 30 to 35 minutes.

Yields 2 1-pound loaves.

PANE COLLA FARINA GIALLA

Cornmeal Bread

Mix 1 cup unbleached flour with corn meal, salt, sugar and dry yeast in a large bowl. Add warm water and sourdough starter and mix thoroughly. Cover with a kitchen towel and let stand in a warm place for 30 minutes.

Spread the remaining 2 cups of flour on a working surface. Pour the mixture over it and work with your hands until you have incorporated enough flour to make a very stiff dough.

Knead for another 5 minutes. Shape into a ball and place on a baking sheet previously sprinkled with cornmeal. Cover with a kitchen towel and leave in a warm, draft-free place for 1 hour or until more than doubled in bulk.

Bake in preheated 425 °F oven for 30 minutes or until a nice dark crust is formed. Transfer to a rack until thoroughly cooled, then wrap in a kitchen towel. Reheat in a 425 °F oven for 15 minutes before serving.

Yields 1 2-pound loaf.

3 cups unbleached flour
1 cup whole grain cornmeal
1 1/2 teaspoons salt
2 tablespoons sugar
1 teaspoon active dry yeast
1 1/2 cups warm water
1 cup sourdough starter

CROSTELLO

Crusty Corn Pie

Combine cornmeal, sugar, and salt in a bowl. Add 1 1/2 cups boiling water and mix until dry ingredients are thoroughly moistened. Add raisins and nuts and mix well.

Oil a 10-inch pie pan; spread the mixture evenly in the pan, and flatten with a rubber spatula. Coat the top with oil and sprinkle with rosemary leaves. Bake in 375 °F oven for 1/2 hour. Good hot or at room temperature. Serve as a side dish, as a bread, as a snack, or as an appetizer. **Serves 6.**

1 1/2 cups cornmeal
1 1/2 tablespoons sugar
1/2 teaspoon salt
1 1/2 cups boiling water
1/2 cup dark, seedless raisins
1/4 cup pinoli *(pine nuts)*
3 tablespoons extra virgin olive oil
1 teaspoon dried rosemary leaves

PANE AI QUATTRO GRANI CON LIEVITO CASALINGO
Four-grain Sourdough Bread

1 cup sourdough starter at room temperature
1 tablespoon honey
1 tablespoon salt
2 1/4 cups warm water
7 cups unbleached flour
1/4 cup oat bran
1/4 cup buckwheat or rye flour
1/4 cup raw wheat germ or cracked wheat
1/4 cup whole grain corn meal

In a large bowl place sourdough starter, honey, salt, water, 1 cup unbleached flour, and all the other flours and grains. Stir and let stand uncovered for 20 to 30 minutes or until mixture begins to bubble.*

Add enough unbleached flour to make a rather stiff dough, knead 10 minutes, then make a ball, place in an oiled large bowl and turn it once. Cover with a kitchen towel and let rise in a warm, draft-free place for 1 hour or until more than doubled in bulk.

Turn onto a floured work surface, punch down, divide into four parts and shape each part into an elongated oval, tapering the ends. Place on a floured baking sheet, gash the tops diagonally, cover loosely with a kitchen towel, and let rise until doubled—1/2 to 1 hour.

Bake in preheated 400 °F oven for 25 minutes or until tops are browned. Remove to cooling rack for 1 hour before serving or wrap and freeze. Reheat for 15 minutes, unwrapped, in a 400 °F oven and texture will be even better. **Yields 4 loaves; serves 12 or more.**

NOTE: Buckwheat and rye will cause the bread to come out dark. For a lighter look, use barley flour instead. The taste will be delicious in any case.

*In winter add 1 teaspoon commercial yeast to boost the leavening process.

FRUSTE
Whips

1 envelope active dry yeast
2 cups warm water
6 cups bread flour
2 tablespoons olive oil
1 teaspoon salt

Dissolve the yeast with 1/4 cup warm water in a large bowl. Add enough flour (approximately 1/2 cup) to make a soft dough. Cover the bowl with a clean kitchen towel and leave in a warm place for about 1 1/2 hours.

Add 1 3/4 cups warm water and work with your hand, or the dough hook of an electric mixer, to dissolve the leavened dough. Add oil, salt, and enough flour to make a rather stiff dough. Turn onto a floured working surface and knead 2 minutes. Divide into 6 equal parts; knead a couple of minutes each, then cover and let rest for 5 minutes.

Roll each piece of dough into a long stick about 1 inch in diameter.

Dredge with flour and place on a well-floured baking sheet. Loosely cover with a towel and let rise in a warm place for 1 hour or until doubled in bulk.

Bake in preheated 375 °F oven for 20 minutes or until *fruste* have acquired a lovely hazel nut color. Eat the same day, or freeze well wrapped in aluminum foil and plastic wrap and eat as soon as defrosted.

Yields 6 5-ounce whips.

CIAMBELLE
Bagels

1 envelope active dry yeast
Sugar
1 1/4 cups warm water
4 cups unbleached flour
1 1/2 teaspoons salt
1 1/2 tablespoons dehydrated minced onion
2 tablespoons olive oil
4 quarts water

Dissolve the yeast and 1/2 teaspoon sugar in 1 1/4 cups of warm water and let rest for 5 minutes.

Combine 3 1/2 cups of flour with the salt and half the onion in a bowl. Add the yeast mixture and the oil, and mix while gathering enough flour to make a rather stiff dough. Place the remaining flour on a working surface; turn the dough onto the flour and knead for 3 minutes. Cover with a towel and let rest for 10 minutes.

Divide into 24 equal parts. Take one piece of dough at a time and shape into a ball. With thumbs and forefingers punch a hole in the center of each ball and set aside on a floured board.

Starting from the first, gently lift each bagel and stretch it to make the hole larger. Cover with a towel and set aside to rise in a warm, draft-free place for 20 minutes.

Bring 4 quarts of water with 2 tablespoons of sugar to a boil in a large pot. Lower the heat to a gentle simmer. Drop 4 bagels at a time into the simmering water and cook 3 minutes on each side, turning only once.

Place on an ungreased baking sheet and sprinkle with the remaining minced onion. Bake in preheated 375 °F oven for 30 minutes. **Yields 12.**

NOTE. For garlic, sesame, or other flavorings, substitute the ones you like for onion. For plain bagels omit the onion.

PASTA PER PIZZE
Basic Pizza Dough

3 cups unbleached or bread flour
1 cup warm water
1 envelope active dry yeast
1 teaspoon salt
1 cup warm water
Vegetable oil

Combine 2 1/2 cups of flour with dry yeast and 1 teaspoon salt in a large bowl. Gradually add 1 cup warm water and 1 1/2 tablespoons oil and mix into a soft dough.

Spread the remaining flour over a working surface. Turn the dough onto it and knead until dough is smooth and elastic. Shape into a ball, place in an oiled bowl and turn it once. Cover with a clean kitchen towel and leave to rise in a warm place for 2 hours or until it has more than doubled in bulk.

Punch down and let rest for 1 hour longer or until ready to use.

Yields enough dough to make 2 12-inch round pizzas or 1 10x16-inch rectangular one. **Serves 4 to 6.**

PIZZA COLLA CIPOLLA E ACCIUGHE
Onion and Anchovy Pizza

2 large white onions, sliced
4 tablespoons olive oil
Salt
*Coarsely ground black pepper**
1 recipe pizza dough (page 230)
8 anchovy fillets, cut up

Place onion and oil in a skillet and saute until onion is translucent. Season with salt and pepper to taste and set aside.

Roll pizza dough into a 10x16-inch rectangle, leaving a higher ridge all around. Place on a baking sheet and spread the onion over it. Top with anchovy fillets and bake in preheated 450 °F oven for 15 to 20 minutes or until edges and onion begin to burn.

Yields 1 10x16-inch pizza; serves 6.

*See instructions on page 42.

CALZONE EBRAICO
Calzone Jewish Style

Originally this calzone was conceived with *bottarga* (the roe of fine fish salted and dried in its own sack) grated over the mozzarella. Here *bottarga* is still a rarity, and I have used anchovies which make calzone even tastier, if less delicate.

1 envelope active dry yeast
1 teaspoon salt
1 1/2 cups warm water
3 1/2 cups bread flour
12 oz. mozzarella, shredded
12 anchovy fillets
*6 rounded tablespoons ricotta, drained**
Peppercorns in a mill
6 tablespoons unsalted butter, melted

Place yeast and salt in a bowl with the warm water, stir, and let rest for 5 minutes. Add enough flour and mix to make a rather stiff dough. Turn out onto a floured working surface and knead for 1 minute. Cover with a clean kitchen towel and let rest in a warm, draft-free place for 1 hour, or until more than doubled in bulk.

Divide into 6 parts, shape each into a ball, and flatten each ball into a disk approximately 6 inches in diameter.

Spread 2 ounces of mozzarella over each disk, and place two anchovy fillets over the cheese. Cover anchovies with one tablespoon of ricotta, sprinkle with pepper, and drizzle with butter. Fold the disks and close edges tightly. Cut slots on the top of calzones to let the expanding hot air out. Brush with the remaining butter and bake in preheated 450 °F oven for 15 minutes or until edges are quite browned. **Serves 6.**

* See instructions on page 43.

PIZZA SVELTA

Quick Pizza

This pizza might not be as authentic as the ones made with a yeast dough; it has the advantage, however, of requiring a very short time for its preparation and it is always a big hit, especially with children.

2 cups self-rising flour
1/4 cup olive or any other vegetable oil
1 cup milk
1 1/2 cups tomato sauce (page 218)
3/4 pound mozzarella cheese, shredded
2 teaspoons dried oregano
Freshly ground black pepper
2 tablespoons olive oil

Combine flour and vegetable oil in a bowl and mix until you have a coarse meal. Gradually add the milk, stirring, until a soft dough is formed.

Turn out on a floured working surface and gently knead for 1/2 minute. Roll out into a very thin disc, leaving 1/4-inch ridge all around.

Place on an ungreased baking sheet. Cover with half the tomato sauce, spread all the cheese over it, then drizzle with the remaining sauce.

Sprinkle with oregano, with pepper to taste, and with olive oil. Bake in a preheated 450 °F oven for 12 minutes or until the cheese bubbles and the edges begin to brown.

Yields 1 15-to-16-inch pizza; serves 4 to 6.

ROSCHETTE SALATE
Salty Rings

I am always skeptical when I try a recipe for something I haven't tasted since childhood, partly because my tastes have changed from the time when everything tasted delicious to my new, unsophisticated buds, and partly because I tend to associate those foods with the happy memories of those times. But when I made *roschette* recently, they tasted every bit as good as the ones my Aunt Letizia used to bring from Leghorn to our Jewish summer camp on the shores of Caletta di Castiglioncello on visiting day.

1 teaspoon active dry yeast
2 cups unbleached flour
1 teaspoon salt
1/2 teaspoon sugar
1/4 cup lukewarm olive oil
2/3 cup warm water

Combine the dry ingredients in a small bowl. Gradually add the oil and 2/3 cups warm water, mixing until you have a rather stiff dough. Turn onto a smooth, unfloured surface and knead 5 minutes.

Divide the dough into 3 equal parts. Divide each in half and each new part into 4. Cover the 24 little pieces of dough with a slightly damp towel. Take one little piece of dough at a time and roll between the palms of your hands into a thin rope about 7 inches long. Fasten the two ends to make a ring and place on an ungreased baking sheet 1 inch apart.

When all rings are made, cover with a towel and leave in a warm place to rise for 40 minutes to 1 hour.

Bake in preheated 375 °F oven for 15 to 20 minutes or until *roschette* are crisp and light brown. **Yields 24.**

CIAMBELLINE
Breakfast Rings

1 1/2 cups unbleached flour
1/2 cup whole wheat flour
1 teaspoon salt
1 teaspoon baking powder
2 teaspoons anise seeds
3/4 cup milk
1/4 cup olive or any other vegetable oil

Sift together the two flours, salt, and baking powder into a large bowl. Add anise seeds and stir to combine. Gradually add milk and oil and mix to form a soft ball. Turn out on a floured working surface and knead 1/2 minute. Divide into 12 equal parts and shape each into a ball.

With your thumbs and forefingers, make a hole through the center of each ball shaping it into a ring, approximately 3 1/2-inches in diameter.

Place on a lightly oiled and well-floured baking sheet and bake in preheated 425 °F oven for 20 to 25 minutes. **Yields 12.**

GRISSINI TORINESI ALL'OLIO
Turin Bread Sticks

1 teaspoon dry active yeast
1 teaspoon salt
1/4 cup olive oil
1/2 cup warm water
2 cups unbleached or bread flour

In a small bowl place yeast, salt, oil and water. Stir a little, then add enough flour to make a rather stiff dough. Knead 2 or 3 minutes, then form into a ball. Cover the bowl with a damp towel and set aside in a warm place to rise until doubled in bulk.

Turn out onto a working surface, punch down, and divide into 32 small pieces. Roll the pieces of dough into sticks, as thin as you can make them (they should measure about 10 inches in length), and arrange on an ungreased baking sheet 1 inch apart. Cover and set aside to rest for 1/2 hour.

Place baking sheet in a peheated 400 °F oven, place a shallow pan with cold water on the lower rack,* and bake 10 minutes or until bread sticks are lightly browned. **Yields 32.**

* If you have a gas stove, you don't need the addition of water in the oven.

GRISSINI AL SESAMO
Sesame Seed Bread Sticks

1 teaspoon active dry yeast
1 teaspoon salt
1/4 cup olive oil
1/2 cup warm water
2 cups unbleached or bread flour
Toasted sesame seeds

In a small bowl place yeast, salt, oil and water. Stir a little, then add enough flour to make a rather stiff dough. After the dough has doubled in bulk, punch down, turn on a working surface and divide into 24 pieces. Roll the pieces to 5 to 6 inches length. Roll in sesame seeds and arrange on an ungreased baking sheet, 1 1/2 inches apart. Let rest for 1/2 hour, then bake in preheated 400 °F oven for 15 minutes. **Yields 24**.

GRISSINI AL BURRO
Butter Bread Sticks

5 tablespoons soft butter
1/2 teaspoon salt
2 tablespoons milk
1 cup bread flour

Place butter, salt, and milk into a bowl. Add enough flour to make a rather stiff dough. Cover with a towel and let rest 1/2 hour at room temperature.

Divide into 24 pieces. Shape pieces of dough into sticks about 6 inches long. Arrange on a buttered and lightly floured baking sheet 1 inch apart. Bake in 375 °F oven for 15 minutes or until lightly browned. **Yields 24.**

GALLETTE COL LIEVITO CASALINGO
Sourdough Crackers

4 cups unbleached flour
2 teaspoons salt
1 teaspoon poultry seasoning
1/2 teaspoon black pepper
1 cup sourdough starter at room temperature
1/2 cup warm olive oil
1/2 cup warm water
Oil
Coarse corn meal

Sift together all the dry ingredients except for corn meal. Add sourdough starter, warm oil, and enough warm water to make a rather stiff dough. Knead for a few minutes, then set aside to rest for 20 minutes.

Oil a baking sheet and sprinkle it with coarse corn meal. With a heavy rolling pin, roll 1/4 of the dough at a time very thin, and spread it over the prepared baking sheet. Score it with a pizza or pastry cutter into small squares or rectangles, brush with oil and sprinkle with corn meal.

Bake in preheated 450 °F oven for 10 minutes. Break into crackers, let cool thoroughly, then store in a jar.

Makes several dozen crackers.

GALLETTE PER PESACH

Passover Crackers

For these crackers to be used on Passover, you must buy Passover flour, and all the other ingredients should be, of course, Kosher l' Pesach. On the other hand, since they are so tasty and always a big success, you may want to serve these crackers all year round substituting unbleached flour for Passover flour.

1 cup cold water
1/2 cup olive oil
1 tablespoon salt
1 tablespoon freshly minced garlic
1/4 teaspoon powdered red pepper
*5 cups Passover flour**

Mix together the first 5 ingredients. Add enough flour to form a rather stiff dough. Knead a few minutes on a lightly floured working surface. Roll thin with a heavy rolling pin or, better, with a metal, hand-operated pasta machine, with the rollers at the next-to-the-thinnest notch. Spread over a lightly oiled baking sheet and score with a dented pastry cutter into 2"x6" rectangles.

With a metal comb,** prick all over in a crisscross pattern to prevent swelling and blistering during baking, and bake in 550 °F for 5 or 6 minutes. Break into crackers and cool thoroughly before storing inside a clean white cotton sack. (A new, washed pillow case used only for the purpose would be perfect.) Do not store in refrigerator.

Makes approximately 6 dozen crackers.

* See page 42.

** This gadget can be found in any reputable kitchen supply store.

Dolci

DESSERTS

STORE-BOUGHT DESSERTS, like breads, are so delicious in Italy that no home-prepared ones can favorably compare with the former. Whether it is the dainty pastry that is freshly prepared every day by the single pastry shops, or the mass-produced packaged desserts that are distributed through *pasticcerie,* bars, *latterie, alimentari,* and even supermarkets, Italian desserts are superior, and homemakers wouldn't dare try to imitate them.

However, because of the dietary laws, the traditions, and the symbolism that play so great a part in the conservation of their religion, the Jews have had a far greater need to make their own desserts at home. (There are no kosher bakeries in Italy.) In the course of centuries, they have developed skills that almost match those of the mass producers.

Each holiday has one or more desserts attached to it, and each holiday is preceded by the preparation of the various traditional sweets, with Passover and Purim holding the lion's share.

Passover celebrates the most important event in Jewish history — the deliverance of all the Jews from bondage in the land of Egypt — and it is, perhaps, the most important holiday. Because we are reminded of the haste with which the Jews fled Egypt without waiting for their bread to be leavened, the desserts we prepare, like anything we eat during the eight days of Passover, are characterized by the lack of leavening agents (*Torta di Noci, Torta al Cioccolato, Moscardini,* others).

Purim, on the other hand, is considered a minor holiday (perhaps because of the silliness associated with its celebration). However, it is the most joyous of holidays, because it reminds us of the only time in our history when wisdom has prevailed over tyranny. Mordechai, the good uncle of Queen Esther, the Jewish bride of the Syrian King Ahasuerus, had the upper hand over the wicked Haman, who wanted to destroy all the Jews and was himself destroyed instead. Children relate to this one better than to other more solemn holidays, and therefore Purim is also known as the children's holiday. Sweets abound. *Orecchi di Haman* of the Italkim, the counterpart of *Homentashen* of the Ashkenazim, are the most typical, but the number of Purim sweets in Italy is countless.

TORTA TUNISINA
Tunisian Ice Cream Cake

This cake was brought to Italy by the Tunisian Jews. I remember that it suddenly became popular in the late 1940s when many Tunisian Jews fled to Italy after the establishment of Israel and the subsequent persecution of the Jews in the Arab countries. The recipe was given to me by my cousin Eugenia. It is a simple-to-prepare and yet delicious summer dessert.

3 eggs
1 cup fine granulated sugar
12 ounces unsalted butter at room temperature
1 1/2 teaspoons vanilla extract
70 or 80 tea biscuits
1 1/4 cups strong espresso, laced with 3 tablespoons brandy

Cream together eggs and sugar until thick and lemon-colored. Add butter, one third at a time, beating until the cream is light and fluffy. Add vanilla extract and beat to mix.

Line the bottom and walls of a glass bowl with biscuits quickly dipped in the coffee mixture. Cover with cream and keep on making alternate layers of biscuits dipped in the coffee mixture and cream until all the ingredients are used up. Cover the bowl with plastic wrap and aluminum foil, and place it in the freezer for at least a few hours before serving.

With the warmed blade of a knife separate the ice cream from the walls of the bowl, and after a few minutes unmold over a cake dish.

Serves 12 or more.

TORTA DI NOCI PER PESACH
Passover Walnut Cake

2 tablespoons non-dairy margarine
3 tablespoons matza meal
2 1/2 cups (10 ounces) choice walnut meats
6 eggs, separated
1/8 teaspoon salt
1 1/2 cups granulated sugar

Grease a 10-inch springform pan with margarine, sprinkle with matza meal, and invert to remove excess. Place the walnut meats into the working bowl of a processor with the metal blade on, and process until chopped fine—10 to 15 seconds.

Beat the egg white with salt until stiff and dry, and set aside.

In a large bowl, beat the egg yolks with sugar until the mixture is thick and pale-lemon colored. Gradually add the finely ground walnut meats and one fourth of the beaten egg white. Add grated orange rind, honey, vanilla extract, and cinnamon and beat only to combine.

Delicately fold in the remaining egg white by hand,** then spoon into the prepared cake pan. Place in the center of the middle rack in preheated 325 °F oven and bake for 1 hour without opening the oven door.

Test with a skewer; if it comes out dry, the cake is done; otherwise bake another 10 to 15 minutes. Turn the heat off and leave the door ajar for 15 minutes. Remove to a wire rack for a few minutes, then invert over the rack and let cool thoroughly before unmolding upside down over a cake dish. Lightly sprinkle with vanilla-flavored sugar. **Serves 12 or more.**

Grated rind of 1 orange
1 teaspoon clove honey
1/2 teaspoon vanilla extract
1/2 teaspoon cinnamon
*Vanilla-flavored sugar**

* See instructions on page 45.

** See instructions on page 41.

TORTA DI CIOCCOLATA PER PESACH
Passover Chocolate Cake

5 tablespoons non-dairy unsalted margarine
2 tablespoons fine matza meal
4 ounces unsweetened chocolate
1 tablespoon soluble dark coffee
5 eggs, separated
Pinch of salt
1 cup sugar
*1 1/4 cups finely ground toasted almonds**
1 teaspoon almond extract
1 teaspoon vanilla extract
1 tablespoon freshly grated orange peel
3/4 cup toasted hazel nuts, coarsely chopped
4 ounces semi-sweet chocolate, coarsely chopped
*3 tablespoons unsweetened cocoa or milk-chocolate shavings***

Grease a 9-inch springform cake pan with 1 tablespoon margarine, sprinkle with fine matza meal, and invert to remove excess.

Melt the unsweetened chocolate with the remaining margarine in a heavy saucepan over very low heat. Add dry soluble coffee and stir until all is well amalgamated.

Beat the egg whites in the small bowl of an electric mixer with a pinch of salt until stiff and dry. Set aside.

Beat the egg yolks in the larger bowl with the sugar until lemon-colored and thick. With the beaters going, gradually add the chocolate/coffee mixture, the almonds, almond extract, vanilla extract, orange peel, and one third the egg whites. Lower the speed and add the hazel nuts and the chocolate pieces.

Stop beaters and fold in*** the remaining egg white by hand.

Pour into the prepared cake pan and bake in preheated 325 °F oven for 40 minutes. Turn the heat off, open the oven door ajar and allow the cake to cool off a bit inside for 10 minutes. Remove from oven and let cool thoroughly on rack. Invert over a cake dish, brush off loose matza meal and sprinkle with cocoa or, if milk is no object, with chocolate shavings. **Serves 12.**

* See instructions on page 36.

** See instructions on page 39.

***See instructions on page 41.

MOSCARDINI DI PESACH
Passover Moscardini

1 1/2 cups coarsely ground toasted almonds*
1 cup sugar
Small pinch salt
1/4 cup unsweetened cocoa
1/4 cup matza meal
Grated rind of 1 orange
1/2 teaspoon almond extract
1 egg, slightly beaten
1 egg yolk
Oil and matza meal for the baking sheet

Combine all the ingredients in a small bowl. Drop the mixture by the rounded teaspoonful on an oiled and dusted baking sheet 1 1/2-inch apart. Shape each cookie into an oval and flatten with the back of a fork.

Bake in preheated 350 °F oven for 10 minutes, then transfer to a cooling rack.

Yields approximately 2 1/2 dozen 3x1 1/2-inch cookies.

* See instructions on page 36.

TORTA DI INES
Ines's Cake

A slice of this simple and delicious cake, a dollop of homemade vanilla ice cream, and a small glass of sweet vermouth were the only refreshments served on the day of my Bat Mitzvah — June 5, 1938 (Shavuoth 5698).

3/4 cup granulated sugar
6 tablespoons soft butter
3 eggs
1/2 teaspoon vanilla extract
Grated rind of 1 lemon
1 1/2 cups cake flour
1 teaspoon baking soda
3 teaspoons cream of tartar
1/2 cup milk
*Vanilla-flavored sugar**

Cream granulated sugar and butter together. Add the eggs, one at a time, beating after each addition. While beating, add vanilla extract and lemon rind. Gradually add the flour and beat only until a smooth batter is formed.

Place the baking soda and the cream of tartar in a cup and stir to combine. Add the milk while stirring. The mixture will foam and expand. When about to overflow from the cup, pour the mixture into the bowl with the batter. Quickly stir just until the batter is smooth again.

Pour into a buttered and lightly floured 9-inch cake pan and bake in preheated 350 °F oven for 35 to 40 minutes, or until a straw inserted at the center of the cake comes out dry. Remove from oven and let cool on a wire rack for 1/2 hour. Transfer to a cake dish upside down and sprinkle with vanilla-flavored sugar.

Serves 8 or more.

*See instructions on page 45.

CREMA INGLESE
English Custard

In olden times in Italy all that was delicate and elegant was referred to as "English." (My mother used to call my older daughter *Inglesina*, little Englishwoman, because of her refined manners.) This custard is called "English" as opposed to any other custard that uses flour or other thickeners.

6 egg yolks
3/4 cup sugar
2 cups hot milk
1 teaspoon vanilla extract
Savoiardi *(recipe follows)*

Beat egg yolks and sugar together until frothy and lemon-colored. Add the hot milk a little at a time, beating constantly.

Pour into a heavy-bottomed saucepan and place over moderate heat. Cook, stirring constantly, until the cream coats the spoon evenly. (Be careful not to allow the cream to reach the boiling point.) Add vanilla extract and stir. Remove from heat.

Cool to room temperature, stirring from time to time. Pour into individual custard cups and refrigerate. Serve with lady fingers. **Serves 6.**

SAVOIARDI
Lady Fingers

2 eggs, separated
1/4 teaspoon cream of tartar
Dash salt
1/2 cup sugar
3/4 cup cake flour
1/2 teaspoon baking powder
1/4 teaspoon lemon extract
1/4 teaspoon vanilla extract
2 tablespoons butter (or non-dairy margarine)

In a small bowl beat the egg whites with cream of tartar and salt until very dry.

In another small bowl beat the yolks with sugar until frothy and lemon-colored.

Sift together flour and baking powder and gradually add to the beaten egg yolks while mixing. Add lemon and vanilla extracts and mix well. Fold in the egg whites.*

Grease a large baking sheet with butter (or margarine) and sprinkle with flour. Pour all the batter into a pastry bag with a 1/2-inch aperture. Squeeze the bag, while twisting the top closed, over the baking sheet to form 3-inch strips. Place in preheated 325 °F oven for 13 minutes or until fingers are pale golden. Remove from oven and transfer to a wire rack to cool. **Yields approximately 3 dozen.**

* See instructions on page 41.

TIRAMISU

Tirami su means, literally, pull me up. And in fact this rich, delicious, yet delicate dessert was once used to give convalescent people new strength. I recall that many, many years ago (I was a child of seven), when my mother was recovering from an illness, our maid made *tiramisu* almost every day and that's when I learned to love it.

In recent years *tiramisu* has made a triumphal comeback and has become a household name both in Italy and in this country, and a favorite at fine Italian restaurants.

- *1 pound mascarpone cheese*
- *1/4 cup vanilla-flavored sugar**
- *1 recipe* Crema Inglese
- *1 recipe* Savoiardi
- *1/4 cup rum or other liqueur you favor*
- *1/4 cup espresso*
- *4 ounces milk chocolate, melted**
- *2/3 cup milk-chocolate shavings* or 1/3 cup unsweetened cocoa*

Have all the ingredients at room temperature. Gently mix mascarpone and sugar with a rubber spatula. Add *Crema Inglese* a little at a time and keep on stirring by hand until all is amalgamated.

Place 1/3 of the *savoiardi* at the bottom of a square or rectangular oven-to-table dish. Mix liqueur and espresso and drizzle the cookies with 1/3 the mixture, cover with 1/3 the mascarpone mixture, and sprinkle with 1/2 the melted chocolate.

Repeat layering in the same order, covering the top layer with chocolate shavings or unsweetened cocoa. Place in refrigerator until ready to serve.

Serves 8 or more.

*See instructions on page 39.

LATTE ALLA PORTOGHESE
Caramel Custard

- *2 cups sugar*
- *1 egg*
- *7 egg yolks*
- *1 quart milk*
- *2 1/2x2-inch strips lemon peel*
- *1 teaspoon grated lemon rind*
- *1 teaspoon vanilla extract*

Cook 1 cup sugar with a few drops of water until melted and honey-colored. Pour into an oval oven-resistant 1 1/2-quart container or into 10 individual ramekins. Tilt the container or the ramekins to completely coat the bottom and part of the sides.

Beat egg and egg yolks with 1 cup of sugar until fluffy and lemon-colored.

Bring milk with lemon peel to a gentle boil and cook for 10 minutes, stirring often to make sure that it does not burn at the bottom. Strain and add grated lemon rind and vanilla extract. Cool for a while.

Pour milk, a bit at a time, into beaten eggs, stirring to mix. Pour this mixture into the oval container or the individual ramekins, then place in a shallow pan with 1/2 inch of hot water.

Bake in 350 °F oven for 30 to 45 minutes, or until tops are browned and a straw inserted into the custard comes out clean. Let cool to room temperature, then refrigerate, loosely covered with waxed paper, until ready to serve.

With a thin blade separate custard from container wall, then invert over an oval serving plate or individual desert dishes. **Serves 6 to 8.**

GRANITA DI CAFFE` CON PANNA
Coffee Ice with Whipped Cream

4 cups freshly made espresso
4 tablespoons sugar
1/2 cup brandy or anisette
1 pint heavy cream
1/2 cup vanilla-flavored sugar (optional)*
6 fluted glasses, chilled

Sweeten the coffee with sugar while it is still hot. Place into 2 ice-cube containers, and place the containers in the freezer for several hours or overnight.

Whip the cream until soft peaks form; add vanilla-flavored sugar, if so desired, and beat a few seconds longer, but be careful not to overbeat and end up with butter.

Crush the iced-coffee cubes in an electric crusher and distribute evenly among the chilled glasses. Add 1 tablespoon liqueur to each glass and top with whipped cream. Serve immediately. **Serves 6.**

NOTE: If you don't have an electric ice crusher, place a few cubes at a time into a clean cloth and crush with a hammer, the good old way. Don't attempt to do the crushing with a food processor or the granita (hail-like pieces of ice) will become snow and the texture will be lost.

* See instructions on page 45.

CIAMBELLINE DELLA ZIA DELIA PER PURIM
Aunt Delia's Purim Doughnuts

Aunt Delia, like most housewives in Italy fifty years ago, did not have an oven in her kitchen in Pisa, where she lived, nor did she have easy access to a public one, as we did in Pitigliano. Because of this, most of her specialties were fried. I have successfully converted many of her fried dishes into baked ones. For these delicious doughnuts, however, I give the authentic recipe as it was passed on to me.

2 1/2 cups unbleached flour
1 cup sugar
1/2 cup unsweetened cocoa
1 teaspoon baking soda
1/2 teaspoon salt
1/3 cup olive oil
4 eggs
1/2 cup toasted almonds, chopped
1 teaspoon vanilla extract
Oil for frying
*Vanilla-flavored sugar**

Sift 1 1/2 cups of flour with sugar, cocoa, baking soda, and salt into a large bowl. Add olive oil and eggs and beat at medium speed just until you have a homogeneous batter. Add almonds and vanilla extract and mix to combine. Add enough of the remaining flour to make a soft dough. Turn out onto an oiled working surface and quickly knead for a minute or so.

Divide into 24 or 30 equal pieces and shape each piece into a ball. With your thumbs and forefingers, make a hole through the center of each ball shaping it into a ring.

Heat enough oil in a small saucepan to be 3 inches deep. Fry one doughnut at a time for 1 minute on each side, turning only once. Transfer to a plate with paper toweling. When all the doughnuts are done, roll them in vanilla-flavored sugar. Let cool thoroughly before serving.

Yields 2 to 2 1/2 dozen.

*See instructions on page 45.

ROSELLINE DI PURIM
Purim Rosettes

Purim is the holiday when Jewish housewives most display their artistry and patience in preparing a varied number of sweets to make this joyous holiday especially festive. Rosettes should be watched while being prepared by the expert, since the actual preparation is not as complicated as its description. My friend Wanda Caro has kindly done the demonstration for me and I'll try to pass it along as best I can.

2 eggs
1/8 teaspoon salt
1 1/2 cups unbleached flour
1 1/2 cups olive or other vegetable oil for frying
1 1/2 cups honey

Lightly beat eggs and salt together. Gradually add 1 1/4 to 1 1/2 cups of flour and mix until a rather soft dough is formed. Knead for 1 minute, then roll as thin as you can. With a pizza cutter or a very sharp knife, make 2x9-inch strips. Fold lengthwise in half. Pinch the open side of the strips close at 1 1/2-inch intervals. Loosely roll each strip in a spiral and pinch here and there. Fasten the outer end so it will not open while frying.

Heat the oil in a small frying pan until a piece of dough dropped into it sizzles immediately. Fry 1 rosette at a time until golden on both sides, turning once. Hold a few seconds above the pan to drip, then gently place on a paper towel.

When all the rosettes are done, heat half the honey in a small saucepan. As honey starts to bubble dip 2 or 3 rosettes in it to coat. Remove to a serving plate, pinched side up. Lower the heat and continue to dip the rosettes in the hot honey until all are coated, gradually adding more honey as necessary. **Yields about 24.**

"TORZETTI DELL' ABBREI"
Hard Cookies of the Jews

Torzetti and *Marroncini* were two Pitigliano specialties made for both holidays and family celebrations. When I went to Pitigliano some time ago to learn from my old aunt how to make them, she regretfully told me that she didn't remember because she had not made them for decades. No written recipe had ever existed; both were handed from generation to generation by word of mouth and observation. I almost never had seen them made, because my mother preferred to have her sisters-in-law make the Pitigliano specialties for her and reciprocate the courtesy with her Roman specialties. However, my aunt told me that one of the public bakeries was making them much like the originals. I went to interview the baker — an intelligent young Christian woman — and I found out to my amusement that she had bestowed on them the attribute *dell'abbrei*, the way of saying "of the Jews" in Pitiglianese dialect.

I asked her how she knew about *torzetti* and she told me this interesting story: she had learned to make them from *La Bafifa*, the old woman who had been our baker for over half a century. The old woman was so jealous of the treasured recipes she had learned from the Jews that she was very reluctant to share them with anyone. Only after a lot of pressure from the young baker had she finally agreed to show her how to make them. However, she withheld one detail. When the moment came to show how to test the sugar, the old woman held her large apron high, as a screen to block the other's view. It took a lot of begging to win the old woman's heart, but at last the young baker gained the skill that would otherwise have been lost forever. (None of my cousins remembered exactly how to make *Torzetti* or *Marroncini*, although I stirred up a world of beautiful memories when I mentioned them.)

The young baker kindly invited us to watch her while she made them. So, while I paid strict attention, and my husband stood ready with paper and pen, we recorded two of the oldest Italian-Jewish recipes. Typical of the generosity of the Pitiglianesi and of their long-standing friendship with the Jews, after the cookies were baked, the young woman insisted that we take all of them as a gift. She bakes them for her customers only around Christmas, she told me, and these were made — in the middle of the summer — expressly for me and my family!

3 cups unbleached flour
*1/2 teaspoon ammonium bicarbonate or 1 teaspoon baking powder**
1 teaspoon ground cloves
Grated rind of 1 orange
Grated rind of 1 lemon
1 cup cold water
1 1/4 cups sugar

Combine flour, baking powder, cloves, and rinds. Mound on a working surface and make a well in the center.

Place 1 cup of cold water and the sugar in a saucepan and bring to a boil. When the solution begins to reach full boil, start stirring with a wooden spoon. After 3 minutes, begin to test for the ideal cooking point of the syrup, which comes when a drop held between thumb and forefinger, in an opening and closing motion, forms a thread at the fourth opening.

Pour all the hot syrup in the center of the well. Quickly mix in the flour mixture and knead while the dough that forms is still hot. With a rolling pin, roll down to 1/2-inch thickness. Cut into 2-inch-tall diamonds with a sharp knife; then coat the diamonds all over with the flour mixture left on the working surface.

Place on a well-floured baking sheet and bake in preheated 400 °F oven for 10 to 12 minutes. If everything went well, including the right temperature, *torzetti* should be slightly less white and each should have formed a bubble of air at the center. **Yields about 50 cookies.**

*Ammonium bicarbonate can be purchased from pharmacies. It is not the same as sodium bicarbonate (baking soda) available in supermarkets.

MARRONCINI
Purim Nut Cookies

The name *marroncini* derives from the Hebrew *maror,* bitter. These cookies are given their name because the Jews in Pitigliano used the almond of peach pits to make them, and peach pits are bitter indeed! I recall that, after drying them in the sun, peach pits were saved in old pillow cases throughout the entire peach season. We were aware that they contained prussic acid, which is a poison, but we also knew that our ancestors, who had been eating *marroncini* for centuries, had enjoyed good health and many had reached ripe old ages. (The aunt I went to visit to learn this recipe recently died at the age of 94, not looking or behaving, until the very last minute, one day older than 50!) At any rate, we can now afford to use other kinds of nuts, and I have seen these cookies made (and make them myself) with hazel nuts or almonds and they are delicious.

3 cups unbleached flour
*1 1/2 cups coarsely chopped hazel nuts or almonds, toasted**
*1/2 teaspoon ammonium bicarbonate or 1 teaspoon baking powder***
Grated rind of 1 lemon
1 1/2 cups sugar
2 cups cold water
1 1/2 teaspoons almond extract

Combine flour, nuts, baking powder, and lemon rind and mix well. Mound on a flat working surface and make a well in the center.

Place the sugar and 2 cups of cold water in a saucepan and bring to a boil, When the solution reaches full boil, begin to stir with a wooden spoon. After 3 minutes start to test for the right cooking point. (See preceeding recipe for this test.)

Add almond extract, stir, and pour into the center of the well. Quickly mix in the dry ingredients and, also quickly, knead for a minute or two.

Divide the dough into 4 parts and roll each part into a cylinder 1 1/2 inches in diameter. Cut each cylinder into 1-inch-thick disks. With your thumb, make a depression at the center of each disk. Coat with the flour mixture that has remained on the working surface.

Place on a well-floured baking sheet and bake in preheated 400 °F oven for 15 to 20 minutes. Cookies are done when the bottom is golden brown. **Yields about 50 cookies.**

* See instructions on page 36.

**See footnote on preceding recipe

CROSTATA CON PASTA DI MANDORLE
Almond Torte

1 cup peeled almonds
1 cup sugar
1 cup unbleached flour
1 teaspoon ground cinnamon
1/4 pound butter or non-dairy margarine, chilled
1 egg
2 egg yolks
1 1/2 cups orange preserve plus a few large pieces (recipe follows)

Place almonds in a food processor and process 10 seconds. Add sugar, flour, cinnamon and butter and process just enough to obtain a coarse meal. (Do not overprocess.)

Add egg and egg yolks and mix with a fork until all is moist. Take 2/3 of the mixture and line a 10-inch pie plate with it. Spread the preserve over the crust.

With the remaining crust mixture, make strips and form a lattice over the preserve. Garnish with the orange pieces, and bake in preheated 350 °F oven for 45 minutes or until the crust is golden brown. **Serves 12.**

MARMELLATA DI ARANCI
Orange Marmalade

Orange marmalade is one of my sister Marcella's many specialties. She made large quantities of it not only for her family's consumption, but also for the pleasure of supplying my family with it, since she knew that homemade marmalade is our favorite preserve. When Marcella and her family made aliya to Israel, she passed her incredibly simple recipe to me and I have made orange marmalade successfully ever since.

3 pounds oranges
Water
Sugar
1 1/2 teaspoons vanilla extract

Keep the oranges in fresh water for a few hours, changing the water often. Place in a large pot with water to cover and bring to a boil. Lower the heat and simmer until soft (30 to 45 minutes). Drain and let cool for a while.

With a sharp knife, cut a few oranges in half lengthwise, then cut in wedges approximately 1/3-inch wide at the largest point. Cut the rest of the oranges in chunks and process in a blender a few at the time until chopped fine.

Weigh wedges and chopped oranges with all their juice and place in a heavy pot with equal weight of sugar. Bring to a boil, then simmer, uncovered, until the sugar is thickened. Stir frequently with a wooden spoon. When the spoon comes out coated with a dense syrup, the marmalade is done. Add the vanilla extract and stir. Wait until thoroughly cooled before storing in air-tight glass jars. **Yields approximately 2 pints.**

PANFORTE
Festive Fruit Cake

3/4 cup sugar
1/3 cup honey
1/2 teaspoon cinnamon
1/2 teaspoon clove
1 teaspoon vanilla extract
1 cup almonds
1/2 cup candied citron peel
2/3 cup flour
*Vanilla-flavored sugar**

In a large skillet, place sugar, honey, cinnamon, clove, and vanilla extract. Bring to a boil and cook 3 minutes, stirring occasionally. Add almonds, citron peel and flour. Remove from heat and mix for 1 minute.

Lightly oil and flour an 8-inch springform cake pan. Pour the mixture into it and flatten with a spatula. Bake in a preheated 325 °F oven for 5 minutes. Let cool to room temperature, then transfer to a serving dish and sprinkle abundantly with vanilla-flavored sugar. **Serves 6.**

*See instructions on page 45.

PIZZA ROMANA
Jewish Fruit Pie

Don't let the name "pizza" deceive you. This is not one of the many varieties of pizza you might be familiar with, nor is it a version of any of the many pies found in kosher bakeries throughout the world. Pizza Romana is an ancient Roman dessert created and used by Jews for family celebrations such as B'nei Mitzvah, Brith Milot, etc. Commercially it can still be found only in the Jewish bakery in the Roman Ghetto, where people from every part of the capital, and even from other cities in Italy, go to buy it. The bakery is the last vestige of what was once the greatest conglomeration of Jewish specialty food shops in Italy. My frequent visits to Italy wouldn't seem complete if I didn't go to the Portico d'Ottavia (called by the Jews of Rome "piazza") to buy pizza for the entire family. In the old days, it was cut into large diamonds (6 or 7 inches tall) and at the end of the festivities it was distributed among special members of the family (grandparents, great aunts and uncles, and so on) to bring home. Nowadays it is cut into small rectangles and I am not sure that the generous custom of giving it away still exists.

6 cups unbleached flour
1 1/2 cups sugar
1 teaspoon salt
1 1/2 cups unblanched almonds, coarsely cut up
3/4 cup pinoli *(pine nuts)*
1 cup dark, seedless raisins
3/4 cup diced candied citron peel or mixed candied fruit peel
1 1/4 cups olive oil
1 cup dry white wine with 1 teaspoon vanilla extract

Sift together flour, sugar and salt into a large bowl. Add nuts and fruits and mix well. Add the oil and mix just until the ingredients are moistened. Add enough wine-and-vanilla mixture to make a solid pastry dough.

Spread over an ungreased 12"x18" baking sheet with low borders, and flatten down to an even thickness. With a long sharp knife, make cuts in the pastry — 6 lengthwise and 6 widthwise — to obtain 49 rectangles.

Bake in preheated 400 °F oven for 30 minutes or until borders begin to brown. Remove the baking sheet from the oven and let it cool for a while before transfering the pieces to a cooling rack (pizza romana is very brittle when hot). When thoroughly cool, store in a cookie jar where it will keep for several weeks. **Yields 49 pieces.**

CASSATA SICILIANA
Ricotta Cake

1 pint whole milk ricotta
1 cup sugar
1/2 cup semi-sweet chocolate chips
Lady fingers (page 243)
1/4 cup cherry brandy
3 egg whites
*3/4 cup vanilla-flavored sugar**
1 tablespoon lemon juice
1/2 cup mixed candied fruit

Beat together ricotta and sugar until creamy and light. Add chocolate chips and stir to mix.

Line the bottom of a 9-inch shallow souffle dish with lady fingers and sprinkle all the brandy over them. Add the ricotta mixture, then cover with lady fingers.

Beat the egg white with vanilla-flavored sugar and lemon juice. Cook in a double-boiler, stirring constantly, for 3 or 4 minutes, or until the mixture begins to thicken. Pour over the cake and spread evenly with a spatula. Garnish with candied fruit arranged to look like flowers, and place in the refrigerator until ready to serve. **Serves 6.**

* See instructions on page 45.

NOTE: If you can buy large pieces of candied fruit, you can cut them into strips, disks and diamonds for a striking-looking floral arrangement.

DOLCE DI MIELE
Honey Cake

In Italy we call this cake *dolce*, sweet, instead of *torta*, cake, because the word *torta* presumes something roundly shaped and somewhat fancy. Honey cake can be baked in a ring or in a loaf pan, and it never looks very elegant. Conversely, in spite of its appearance, it is a favorite among food connoisseurs.

1/2 cup olive oil
1/2 teaspoon salt
1/4 cup sugar
4 eggs
1 cup honey
1/2 cup espresso
3 tablespoons rum
3 cups unbleached flour
2 teaspoons baking powder
1 teaspoon baking soda
1 teaspoon cinnamon
1/4 teaspoon black pepper
1/4 teaspoon cloves
1 teaspoon grated orange rind
1/2 cup walnut meats, coarsely chopped

Cream together oil, salt, and sugar. Add the eggs, one at a time, beating constantly. Meanwhile, mix honey, coffee and brandy in a container with a spout, and sift together flour, baking powder, baking soda, cinnamon, pepper, and cloves on a piece of waxed paper.

Alternatively add honey and flour mixture to the bowl. Stir in orange rind, chopped walnut meats, raisins, dates, citron peel, and pinoli.

Pour into a greased loose-bottom tube pan. Top with the walnut or pecan halves, and bake in 375 °F oven for 45 minutes, or until a testing straw inserted into the highest part of the cake comes out dry.

Remove to a wire rack for 15 minutes. Invert over a piece of aluminum foil and let cool thoroughly before unmolding and placing on a cake dish.

Serves 8 or more.

1/2 cup dark seedless raisins
1/2 cup diced dates
1/4 cup diced citron peel
1/4 cup pinoli *(pine nuts)*
10 or 12 walnut halves

CASTAGNE
Chestnuts

Some thirty years ago, chestnuts were rather a rarity in this part of the country. Now they are more popular and practically every supermarket carries them during their short season. Raw chestnuts can be bought fresh, dried, and in powdered form.

Nature must have thought of chestnut trees as a very precious species, since she very ingeniously protected their seeds (the actual chestnut) from predators in a prickly burr. In mid-autumn — the season for reproducing — the burrs open and three shiny chestnuts fall to the ground from each one. But two more skins, both very hard to remove, protect the edible flesh of the seeds.

There are three basic ways of cooking chestnuts which change their Italian names to: *ballotte,* when boiled with both skins on; *bruciate,* when roasted; and *mondine,* when peeled before cooking. Their uses are varied, ranging from the sophisticated *marrons glaces* of the French, to a more basic, but nevertheless outstanding, poultry stuffing.

Chestnuts are a highly perishable fruit; therefore, the fresh ones can be used only in season. However, dried chestnuts are available in most Italian grocery stores throughout the year. They have the disadvantage, of course, of having lost some of their original aroma and texture, but they have the definite advantage of being almost entirely peeled, and of being there at any time of the year when you need them.

Powdered chestnuts, or chestnut flour, can be found in late fall in some Italian grocery stores. It is not an item widely known, but if you tell your grocers that you want it, they will provide it for you. Keep chestnut flour in a tightly closed tin or glass jar in the refrigerator or even in the freezer, and use it as soon as possible. Since it tends to get lumpy, sift it before each use.

When buying fresh chestnuts, be sure to choose the large, healthy ones without bruises or holes, since these are sure signs that they are already rotten or beginning to rot. Another way of deciding whether they are healthy, is to sniff them. Your nose should be able to determine their freshness and edibility, since a rotten chestnut has a definite acrid, unpleasant odour.

BALLOTTE
Boiled Chestnuts

This is the simplest way of cooking chestnuts. They are fun to eat as they are, and they are also used to prepare sophisticated desserts.

2 pounds fresh chestnuts (4 to 6 dozen)
1 tablespoon salt

Place the chestnuts in a saucepan with the salt and with water to cover. Bring to a boil, then lower the heat and simmer, covered, for 40 to 50 minutes. Drain.

With a sharp knife cut each chestnut in half, not quite going through the bottom, so that the two halves remain attached to one another. Serve them immediately and let each person scoop out the pulp with a little spoon or a dull knife. **Serves 6.**

BRUCIATE
Roasted Chestnuts

These are by far the most fun of all the cooked chestnuts. When we were little children and walked 1 or 2 miles to school, autumn mornings could be really nasty, and frostbite was a common ailment among schoolchildren. One way our mother tried to overcome this problem was to fill our coat pockets with *bruciate* just as we were about to leave the house. We would keep our mittened hands next to the hot chestnuts and arrive at school safe and warm. Later we would eat the chestnuts as a midmorning snack. Now I make *bruciate* because I haven't yet found anyone who doesn't like them.

2 pounds fresh chestnuts (4 to 6 dozen)
1 long-handled chestnut pan or a baking sheet*

With a sharp knife make a gash on each chestnut deep enough to reach the meat, but not so deep that it splits the chestnut. This will prevent an explosion from air expansion while roasting.

If you have a fireplace, place the chestnuts in the pan in a single layer; wait until the coals are bright, then place the pan directly over the embers. Roast the chestnuts until their shells become charred, shaking the pan frequently to turn them.

If you don't have a fireplace, roast the chestnuts on a baking sheet under the broiler for 15 to 20 minutes, shaking the baking sheet occasionally.

Transfer the *bruciate* to a basket lined with a piece of quilted cloth or a kitchen towel folded many times, cover with another folded towel, and serve immediately. **Serves 6.**

* A chestnut pan is a tin pan the bottom of which has been pierced all over with holes, much like a cheese grater.

MONDINE
Peeled Boiled Chestnuts

2 pounds fresh chestnuts (4 to 6 dozen)
1 teaspoon fennel seeds
2 teaspoons salt

Remove the outer, dark-brown shell from chestnuts this way: pare the little hairy tip of each chestnut, then insert the tip of a small sharp and pointy knife into the shell, without touching the meat, and cut down until the shell can be easily removed. The chestnuts are now left with their inner light-brown skin, which should not be removed at this point. Place them in a saucepan with fennel and salt and enough water to cover. Bring to a boil, then simmer, covered, for 20 minutes or until chestnuts are tender, but still firm.

Serve hot and let each person peel his or her own chestnuts, since this is part of the fun of eating them. **Serves 6.**

NOTE: If you use *mondine* for poultry stuffing, peel off the inner skin as soon as you can handle them, because after they get cool it will be almost impossible to peel them successfully.

CASTAGNE SECCHE
Dried Chestnuts

Dried chestnuts are an acceptable substitute for fresh ones in poultry stuffing. Since, inevitably, among the dried chestnuts you buy there will be many that are spoiled, you must inspect each chestnut very carefully before cooking. If even one or two rotten chestnuts remain in the bunch, all will take on a bad taste.

1 1/2 pound dried chestnuts
1/2 teaspoon salt
1/2 teaspoon fennel seeds
6 cups hot water

Discard any chestnuts that are obviously spoiled. Rinse the remaining ones in warm water, then place in a saucepan with salt and fennel and 6 cups of hot water. Bring to a boil, then reduce the heat and simmer, covered, 3/4 hour. Remove from heat. If you find that bits of peel are floating, or still attached to the chestnuts, it is easy to remove them at this point.

Transfer the chestnuts to another saucepan and strain the liquid over them. Boil, uncovered, to reduce the liquid to a few tablespoons. Use in place of *mondine*. **Yields approximately 3 1/2 cups.**

MARMELLATA DI CASTAGNE
Chestnut Cream

2 pounds fresh chestnuts
1/2 teaspoon salt
2 1/2 cups granulated sugar
1 1/2 cups water
1 teaspoon vanilla extract

Remove outer dark-brown shell from chestnuts.* Place in a saucepan with salt and enough water to cover. Bring to a boil, then simmer, covered, until tender (20 to 30 minutes). Drain.

Peel off the inner skin and pass through a vegetable sieve. Place in a saucepan with the sugar and 1 cup water and bring to a slow boil. Cook on low heat, stirring almost constantly, for approximately 30 minutes. Add a few tablespoons of water if it becomes necessary to prevent cream from becoming too thick.

Remove from heat, add vanilla extract, and stir. Let cool, stirring occasionally, then pour into glass jars. Let cool thoroughly, then cover with lids and store at room temperature. **Yields approximately 3 cups.**

* See *Mondine* recipe for easy method

LA PATTONA
Chestnut-flour Polenta

Pattona and *ditalini* (little thimbles) were the fun food of our childhood. *Ditalini* were made this ingenious way: we filled Mamma's sewing thimbles with chestnut flour, pressed the flour firmly, and left the thimbles on the red ambers for a minute or so. We removed them with tongs, let them cool for a while, then unmolded them and feasted on them. Of course, after this treatment Mamma's thimbles were no longer shiny and sometimes they became unusable. But Mamma didn't mind buying a few new ones for the pleasure that she derived from our creativity. *La Pattona* was made for us and here is how to do it.

3 cups water
1 teaspoon salt
3 cups chestnut flour
1 pint ricotta (optional)

Bring 3 cups of water with 1 teaspoon salt to a boil in a saucepan. Sift chestnut flour and add to the boiling water all at once, stirring vigorously with a wooden spoon. As soon as the mass gathers into a single lump, remove from heat and pour onto a board or a dish. Cover with a clean kitchen towel for a couple of minutes, then serve with ricotta or alone.

Serves 6.

PIZZARELLE DI FARINA DOLCE

Chestnut-flour Latkes

Serve these pancakes as a dessert, as a snack, as an unusual addition to a luncheon, and, omitting the cream, as a side dish to roasted or broiled chicken.

3 cups chestnut flour
1/2 teaspoon salt
1/3 cup pinoli *(pine nuts)*
1/2 cup dark seedless raisins
1 cup cold water
3 eggs, slightly beaten
Vegetable oil for frying
1 cup heavy cream, whipped (optional)

Sift chestnut flour and salt together. Add pinoli, raisins and water and stir until you have a rather thick batter. Add eggs and mix well.

Heat 1/3 cup oil in a medium skillet. Drop the mixture by the tablespoonful into the skillet and fry until browned on both sides. Transfer to paper toweling to drain. Continue to make pancakes, adding a tablespoon or two of fresh oil if necessary. Serve when slightly cooled with or without whipped cream.

Yields about 24 pancakes.

General Index

Q

R

S

T

U

V

Index of Dairy Recipes

Index of Meat Recipes

Index of Pareve Recipes

T

U

V

W

Z